Torturous Etiquettes

THE SUNY SERIES
HORIZONS OF CINEMA
MURRAY POMERANCE | EDITOR

RECENT TITLES

Jonah Corne and Monika Vrečar, *Yiddish Cinema*

Jason Jacobs, *Reluctant Sleuths, True Detectives*

Lucy J. Miller, *Distancing Representations in Transgender Film*

Tomoyuki Sasaki, *Cinema of Discontent*

Mary Ann McDonald Carolan, *Orienting Italy*

Matthew Rukgaber, *Nietzsche in Hollywood*

David Venditto, *Whiteness at the End of the World*

Fareed Ben-Youssef, *No Jurisdiction*

Tony Tracy, *White Cottage, White House*

Tom Conley, *Action, Action, Action*

Lindsay Coleman and Roberto Schaefer, editors, *The Cinematographer's Voice*

Nolwenn Mingant, *Hollywood Films in North Africa and the Middle East*

†Charles Warren, edited by William Rothman and Joshua Schulze, *Writ on Water*

Jason Sperb, *The Hard Sell of Paradise*

William Rothman, *The Holiday in His Eye*

Brendan Hennessey, *Luchino Visconti and the Alchemy of Adaptation*

Alexander Sergeant, *Encountering the Impossible*

Erica Stein, *Seeing Symphonically*

George Toles, *Curtains of Light*

Neil Badmington, *Perpetual Movement*

A complete listing of books in this series can be found online at www.sunypress.edu

Torturous Etiquettes

Film Performance and Social Form

Daniel Varndell

Cover image: Brad Pitt and Christoph Waltz in *Inglourious Basterds* (Quentin Tarantino, 2009). Universal Studios/Photofest

Published by State University of New York Press, Albany

© 2023 State University of New York

All rights reserved

Printed in the United States of America

No part of this book may be used or reproduced in any manner whatsoever without written permission. No part of this book may be stored in a retrieval system or transmitted in any form or by any means including electronic, electrostatic, magnetic tape, mechanical, photocopying, recording, or otherwise without the prior permission in writing of the publisher.

For information, contact State University of New York Press, Albany, NY
www.sunypress.edu

Library of Congress Cataloging-in-Publication Data

Name: Varndell, Daniel, 1983– author.
Title: Torturous etiquettes : film performance and social form / Daniel Varndell.
Description: Albany : State University of New York Press, 2023. | Series: SUNY series, horizons of cinema | Includes bibliographical references and index.
Identifiers: LCCN 2022044572 | ISBN 9781438493510 (hardcover : alk. paper) | ISBN 9781438493497 (ebook) | ISBN 9781438493503 (pbk. : alk. paper)
Subjects: LCSH: Etiquette in motion pictures. | Motion pictures—United States. | Motion pictures—Europe.
Classification: LCC PN1995.9.E86 V37 2023 | DDC 791.43/655—dc23/eng/20221128
LC record available at https://lccn.loc.gov/2022044572

10 9 8 7 6 5 4 3 2 1

For Robert and Andie Varndell
Thank you for raising me right

Contents

List of Illustrations   ix

Acknowledgments   xi

Introduction: Minding Manners   1

Part I: Initiation

1   Close Encounters: Greetings   13

2   Home Invasions: Hospitality   43

3   Crossing the Line: Embarrassment   69

Part II: Exchange

4   No Joke: Humor   89

5   The Butler Did It: Service   111

6   Racist Etiquette: Disservice   137

Part III: Dissolution

7   Garments of the Mind: Clothes   155

8	Tabular Outrages: Dinner	181
9	Tresses and Distresses: Intimacy	207
Conclusion: As Time Goes By		219
Notes		225
Bibliography		235
Index		243

Illustrations

1.1	Liam Neeson in *Schindler's List*.	19
1.2	Robert De Niro in *Cape Fear*.	21
1.3	Touching distance in *Philadelphia*.	36
2.1	Communion in *The Beguiled*.	52
2.2	Testing thresholds in *Funny Games*.	57
2.3	Ralph Fiennes in *A Bigger Splash*.	66
3.1	Anya Taylor-Joy in *Emma*.	84
4.1	Morgan Freeman in *Seven*.	92
4.2	Jack Nicholson in *Chinatown*.	101
4.3	Joe Pesci in *Goodfellas*.	107
4.4	Joe Pesci in *Goodfellas*.	107
5.1	Punctuating the point in *Jezebel*.	121
5.2	Forest Whitaker in *The Butler*.	132
6.1	The slap heard around the world: *In the Heat of the Night*.	142
7.1	Alec Guinness in *Our Man in Havana*.	158
7.2	Leonardo DiCaprio in *Titanic*.	162
7.3	Will Smith in *Six Degrees of Separation*.	167

7.4	Michelle Pfeiffer in *The Age of Innocence*.	172
7.5	Bette Davis and Henry Fonda in *Jezebel*.	176
8.1	Scoffing in *Tom Jones*.	183
8.2	Scoffing in *Tom Jones*.	183
8.3	Marlon Brando in *A Streetcar Named Desire*.	185
8.4	Lording it in *American Beauty*.	188
8.5	Tabular desecration in *Hannibal*.	195
8.6	Edward Norton in *American History X*.	201
8.7	Edward Norton in *American History X*.	201
9.1	Audrey Hepburn in *Roman Holiday*.	211
9.2	Emmanuelle Riva in *Amour*.	216

Acknowledgments

Without the generosity and insights, the encouragement and support—indeed the friendship—of the following people, this book would be infinitely poorer. To William Brown, Alex Clayton, Richard Cuming, Jude Davies, Gary Farnell, Ruth Gilbert, Leighton Grist, Laura Hubner, Mick Jardine, Penny Phillips, Robert Johnson, Matt Leggatt, Dan Levene, Sarah Lightman, Elliott Logan, Bill Marshall, Fran Mason, Chris Mounsey, Barton Palmer, Nick Rowe, Steven Rybin, Lewis Simpson, Carol Smith, Tony Smith, George Toles, Christina Wilkins, and Linda Ruth Williams: all of you have, in some large or small way, inspired me. Thank you.

I'd also like to thank everyone at SUNY Press for their wonderful patience and unfailing support throughout, especially James Peltz, Rafael Chaiken, Ryan Morris, and Eric Schramm (thank you), but also the peer reviewers—whose generous feedback and considered insights (I hope they agree) have hugely improved the scope and rigor of this work.

A special thanks is due to Murray Pomerance: without your inspiration, guidance, encouragement, and friendship there would be no book.

To my family—especially my children, Dylan and Emily, and my rock, Naomi—I hope the finished book makes you proud and goes some way to justifying the torture its writing inflicted upon you.

And a final thanks to my colleague and friend Professor Neil McCaw (December 1969–March 2020), whom I dearly miss.

Introduction

Minding Manners

I dare to assert that torture is the most horrible event a human being can retain within himself.

—Jean Améry, *At the Mind's Limits*

Etiquette is knowing how to yawn with your mouth closed.

—Noted toastmaster, quoted in Rees

∼

"Manners are of more importance than laws," wrote Edmund Burke at the turn of the eighteenth century, "upon them, in a great measure, the laws depend." While the law "touches us but here and there, and now and then," continued Burke, "manners are what vex or soothe, corrupt or purify, exalt or debase, barbarize or refine us, by a constant, steady, uniform, insensible operation, like that of the air we breathe in. [They] give their whole form and colour to our lives, [yet] according to their quality, they aid morals, they supply them, or they totally destroy them" (qtd. in Hazlitt, n.p.). Manners, wrote C. Dallett Hemphill, serve three social functions. First, they have a regulatory function as a system of social control. Second, they have a creative function in helping people assume their social roles. And third, they have a communicative function in telling us about our place in the social order. She offers the example of an inferior bowing to their superior: the bow initially just acknowledges the existence of a social hierarchy determining social position. But it also helps the inferior to feel deferential before their superior and enables them to express that deference. "The sociological argument," wrote Hemphill,

> is that although the 'big rules' of social life—our systems of law, morality, and religion—are necessary if humans are to live in groups, the 'little rules' of manners are necessary to enact the larger social order in every encounter. Manners also constitute a mediating level of culture between a society's abstract 'ideals' and the varied behaviors of its individual members. These meaning-laden acts and gestures are the signal flags of an encounter, by which we communicate, often nonverbally, who we are and what we expect of each other. (4)

Historically, etiquette was the codification of deference, guidance on grace. Etiquette guides were written for those not born to lofty social positions to teach them the basic rules of high society in a time (the eighteenth and nineteenth centuries) of unprecedented social mobility.

Of course, etiquette has been attacked for doing quite the opposite. "Etiquette is the barrier," began Charles William Day's 1842 book,

> which society draws around itself as a protection against offences the '*law*' cannot touch,—it is the shield against the intrusion of the impertinent, the improper, and the vulgar,—a guard against those obtuse persons who, having neither talent nor delicacy, would be continually thrusting themselves onto the society of men to whom their presence might (from the difference of feeling and habit) be offensive, and even insupportable. (9)

If for vulgar one substitutes the word "common" (both share a root), this statement confirms suspicions that etiquette was about the social exclusion of the lower classes. While good manners might be regarded (by most) as fundamental to keeping good relations and living in a harmonious society, we moderns tend to regard "etiquette" with suspicion: as antiquated, arcane, and arbitrary; rules designed by the upper classes to frustrate and intimidate—indeed "torture" the lower social classes who were pressing on their flanks. "We might quibble over elbows on the table," writes Pen Vogler, "but nobody thinks it acceptable to blow their nose on the tablecloth," so can't we just dispense with guidelines written for the uncivilized times of a bygone era? Don't we now live in a world in which the inscrutable rules of social form have become moot? ("Chivalry is not only dead, it's decomposing," declares John [Rudy Vallee] to Gerry [Claudette Colbert] in *The Palm Beach Story* [1942].)

Cinema is compulsively drawn to etiquette as a theme. It often details the minutiae of social behavior and its impact on human drama, or else dramatizes rules and violations for our pleasure. Apropos of the novels of Henry James, Slavoj Žižek writes that "tragedies occur and whole lives are ruined during what appears to be a polite dinner-table conversation" (*Plague* 197). In film, dining etiquette can be unpredictable. It can be destroyed by the smallest of faux pas—a maid accidentally using her master's familiar name, thus betraying that they are having an affair (*Gosford Park*)—or upheld even after the most devastating exposure—an adult son being quietly ignored after using a speech to publicly accuse his father of having molested him as a child (*Festen*). Sometimes, we fall in love with the blundering parvenu, either because she is adorably ingenuous (Anne Hathaway in *The Princess Diaries*) or because her naivete shows up the boorishness of more savvy dinner companions (Julia Roberts in *Pretty Woman*). At other times, tabular desecration puts our hero beyond the pale—slicing the frontal lobe from the skull of one's guest, sautéing it, then feeding it to him (*Hannibal*). In film, rudeness can be performed to keep safe one's dinner guests from a worse threat—as when Bruce Wayne insults his guests to drive them away before a terrorist attack (*Batman Begins*)—while at other times, violence ends what we might call "hostile etiquette."—as when Al Pacino's character chokes his brother-in-law for insulting him during an excruciating Thanksgiving dinner (*Scent of a Woman*). These are just some of the examples in cinema where table manners become torturous etiquettes.

The "purpose of etiquette," then, is far from singular. "Etiquette is laughably old-fashioned and hidebound," writes Vogler, and belongs not to a modern society "but to seventeenth-century France." Today, we all (broadly) subscribe to the rules of the "social contract." We simply call these rules "manners." This book insists, however, that we are as obsessed by etiquette as our ancestors were. We wring our hands at formal occasions when called to "stand on ceremony." We speak of "biting" and "holding" our tongues in polite society. We "put ourselves out" and "bend over backwards" for others, and we "agonize" over local mores (we blush when we "slip up," and are "mortified" when we slip up badly). We might not regard our behavior as "ceremonial," but at formal occasions we all try to do the "done thing," just as those who don't are quickly censured (if they are lucky), or disinvited in the future (if not). We might not call it "etiquette," but the rules governing behavior run through our lives. "That which we call a rose, / By any other name would smell as sweet" (*Romeo and Juliet*, 2.2.43–44).

Speaking of roses: "The best ingredients for likeableness," wrote the doyenne of decorum, Emily Post, "are a happy expression of countenance, an unaffected manner, and a sympathetic attitude. If she is so fortunate as to possess these attributes her path will have roses enough. But a young woman with an affected pose and bad or conceited manners, will find plenty of thorns" (68). This book asks whether one can ever have the social equivalent of "roses" without "thorns." It asks to what extent one's path in society can be smoothed by manners, and whether some are condemned to thorns simply on account of who they are. Without the correct breeding, must one suffer social torture?

At its best, etiquette is the recognition of another person's humanity. It says, "I see you." At its worst, it is the opposite: "imagine a boot," wrote George Orwell in his dystopic novel *1984* (1949), "stamping on a human face—forever."

Speaking of Torture . . .

I use the word "torture" as a prism through with to think about the degrees of suffering associated with etiquette. One can torture out of punishment or revenge, to extract information or a confession, or for sheer sadistic cruelty. But we also speak colloquially about being "tortured" when in pain. It might be physical pain ("a toothache which tortures"), emotional pain ("grief which tortures"), or psychological pain ("a secret torture"). Torture also means to twist or distort, to put into an unnatural position (torture, from *tortūra*, meaning "to twist"), hence to pervert. My two epigraphs were deliberately intended to provoke. While writing this book I have been confronted by more than one raised eyebrow at the suggestion there is any confluence between etiquette and torture. What could possibly bring the most barbaric and uncivilized abuse of human beings into contact with the system most heavily associated with civility and decorum? Doesn't its very premise pervert both terms? The wires of torture and etiquette nonetheless touch in compelling ways.

First, there is the sense that etiquette involves at least a modicum of discomfort ("Good manners," wrote Emerson, "are made up of petty sacrifices"). This is captured by the former butler Charles MacPherson, who describes etiquette with the analogy of the swan: "She's a vision of poise and beauty as she glides effortlessly across the water's surface. But, in fact, what we don't see when we admire her are her powerful webbed feet pedalling furiously underneath her" (3). Some must pedal harder and more furiously than others to maintain the same image of poise and beauty; some fail to maintain the image (regardless of their efforts); others simply drown. We often say that "manners cost nothing" and remind children to "mind their P's and Q's" (pleases and thank-yous). But equally we are "at pains" to ensure a gracious host doesn't "put herself out" or "go to too much trouble." And if they do, we tell them they "shouldn't have" (seeing them in discomfort on account of our comfort makes us, well, uncomfortable). There are degrees of discomfort in etiquette, too. It requires almost no effort to hold a door open for someone rather than let it crash into them. Somewhat more effort is required to feign interest at a long and tedious speech, however, and considerably more to resist punching an oafish dinner guest who is ruining your long-planned dinner party. The road to good grace is peppered with failings, embarrassments, and, if we cannot sufficiently contain our true feelings, disgrace.

Second, there is a preponderance in the language of etiquette to speak of it in terms of torture. I've already mentioned "biting one's tongue" and "standing on ceremony," but we also "hold a door" and "wait in line." We tell children using bad language to "wash their mouths," and when we get a "slap on the wrist" for a misdemeanor, it means to get off lightly. But historically, beating someone on the wrists or washing a child's mouth with soap for blaspheming and using profanity were not exaggerations or mere figures of speech. That neither practice still occurs has not stopped the currency of the expressions. "Spare the rod," so the saying went, "ruin the child." In Michael Haneke's *The White Ribbon* (2009), a pastor (Burghart Klaussner) reprimands his children (Maria-Victoria Dragus and Leonard Proxauf) for being late to supper and tells them they will be thrashed the following evening as punishment. "I must beat you," he tells them rather solemnly, "and the lashes will cause us [he and their mother] more pain than you." This is a classic variation on the way torturers account for the unjustifiable cognitive dissonance arising from their cruelty. By instrumentalizing the act ("you give me no choice"), they disavow themselves as agents in the torture. As a result, the blame for the cruelty is placed on the "choice" (refusing to talk, or be on time for dinner, etc.) made by the victim, who bears a responsibility both for her original transgression, as well as for her torturer's punishing corrective. She makes her torturer (whence, the pastor's final, perverse, logic that beating his children will hurt him more than them).[1] Since corporal punishment is used less often today, one is more likely to hear beleaguered parents warned by older generations of making a "rod for their own back" by letting bad behavior go unpunished. In any case, the language of manners is shaped by violent hyperbole, and is more violent still in the etiquette guides themselves. Post describes the ballroom as a "torture chamber" for young woman (268), Margaret Visser describes eating dinner as "violence" (*Rituals* 3), and Judith Martin ("Miss Manners") describes her book as a "guide to excruciatingly correct behavior." The language of torture, violence, and the crucifixion, right at the heart of the manuals on manners.

Third, the torturer has his "ways to make men talk" (as the famous line from *The Lives of a Bengal Lancer* puts it [1935]). Torturers use coercion; in addition to physical pain, they demean, embarrass, and humiliate. In J. M. Coetzee's *Waiting for the Barbarians* (1980), a torturer describes his method: "First I get lies, you see—this is what happens—first lies, then pressure, then more lies, then more pressure, then the break, then more pressure, then the truth. That is how you get the truth. Pain is truth, all else is subject to doubt" (5). But quite often that "pressure" is intensified by etiquette. Take the moment in *Marathon Man* when, after drilling holes in Dustin Hoffman's character's teeth to interrogate him on the "safety" of some undisclosed "it," Laurence Olivier's torturer tenderly applies clove oil and apologizes. Even before he began the malicious dentistry, Olivier meticulously washed his hands for several seconds—an adherence to hygiene seemingly at odds with his desire to inflict pain. In *The Maltese Falcon* (1941), the villain played by Sidney Greenstreet insists on formal manners while threatening Humphrey Bogart's private eye with torture: "Well, sir," Greenstreet says (quite charmingly), "there are other means of persuasion besides killing and threatening to kill." Why not say "torture" instead of the euphemistic "persuasion"? Why use the polite and respectful "sir?" When screen villains sigh and warn that their "patience is wearing thin," we might wonder why there is any patience in the first place? Here we have a threat system ("Give to me, or I'll *do* you") but with an insertion of gentility ("Give to me, if you'd be so kind, or . . ."). Such mannered rituals in torture were so cliched by 1964 that Sean Connery's James Bond knew he was in trouble during an interrogation in *Goldfinger*. Strapped to a solid gold gurney through which a laser was slowly burning a hole toward his groin, he asked his captor (Gert Fröbe) if he expected him to "talk." "No, Mr. Bond," came the chillingly cheery reply, "I expect you to die!"

Fourth, torture is entertaining. As Michel Foucault (in *Discipline and Punish*) and Friedrich Nietzsche (in *Genealogy of Morality*) pointed out, the spectacle of public torture and execution was not only about seeing "justice done," but finding a means to satisfy our repressed instincts to see our fellows in pain. This also accounts for the interest in Sade's libertine novel *The One Hundred and Twenty Days of Sodom*, and the enduring fascination with Foxe's *Book of Martyrs*—both of which depict highly graphic and detailed accounts of rapturous torture. In high society, we might not see torture in the sense of fingernails being pulled (*Syriana*), or unnecessary dentistry being performed (*Marathon Man*), or the beating of a man's genitalia (*Casino Royale*), but we do find humiliation (*Emma*), shaming (*The Age of Innocence*), coercion (*Romeo and Juliet*), condescension (*Barry Lyndon*), and mortal threats (*Titanic*)—all techniques in the torturer's "playbook"—all part of a system of "laying low." All screened for our viewing pleasure.

All this said, I want to keep one crucial distinction crystal clear. The narrow definition of torture—to torture as punishment or revenge, to extract information or a confession, or for sheer sadistic cruelty—is much less the focus of this book than the broader, linguistic one. Several books on torture in film have been recently published.[2] While there might be some overlap with a few of my examples of torture, my central intention is to approach the subject from another angle (social form). Since the banning of torture across Europe in the eighteenth century, calls for its reinstatement have gathered apace in the twenty-first—principally to deal with terrorism (see Langbein 93). I conjecture that the coincidence of these two moments in history with the rise and fall of etiquette is no accident. We increasingly hear complaints that the tenor of political debates and discussions in online forums have become undignified, divisive, and abusive. Perhaps my approach will open the door to torture in the narrow sense, and certainly some of the examples herein constitute torture of that type. But this book intends to look more broadly at suffering, of different forms of suffering, and the suffering that form itself can engender. In any case, I hope I don't seem to be riding roughshod over Jean Améry's sober warning: that "if one speaks about torture, one must take care not to exaggerate" (22).

Performance, Inside-out

In his posthumously published *Untimely Meditations* (1910), Nietzsche regarded the "power" of forgetfulness as intrinsic to a quiet mind. Or, rather, he described the human capacity to dwell on mishaps, rue misfortunes, and stoke the fires of failure, as an evolutionary error. "There are people who . . . can perish from a single experience, from a single painful event, often and especially from a single subtle piece of injustice, like a man bleeding to death from a scratch" ("On the Uses" 62). If that injustice were a faux pas or other public embarrassment, we might describe our suffering in terms of "social death" (as when one is "mortified" by a blunder). One might declare that one's "face" (persona) can no longer be shown in those circles. By contrast, those who find themselves so at ease in their social milieu (as do snobbish elites), or who, by contrast, hold manners in such contempt (as do proud vulgarians) as to be indifferent toward and disdainful of them—well, such people are "so little affected by the worst and most dreadful disasters, and even by their own wicked acts, that they are able to feel tolerably well and be in possession of a kind of clear conscience even in the midst of them or at any rate very soon afterwards" (62).

This book is about the former group—those who (I include myself) feel they might perish from a single faux pas, bleed to death from a social scratch. We meet them regularly onscreen. They are the characters whose gestures depict what Murray Pomerance calls the "tiny moments, tiny gestures, yet gestures at the same time fully potent, upon which the whole structure of a film might stand" ("Three Small Gestures"). Think of Jack Lemmon's urgent patience in *Glengarry Glen Ross* (1992), or William H. Macy's squirming assurances in *Fargo* (1996). Both are salesmen with their necks on the block. Think of Kirsten Dunst's forced smile in *Melancholia* (2011), or Jennifer Lawrence's frustrated acceptance in *Mother!* (2017). Both are aggressively imposed upon by others and demonstrate simmering restraint. In each example, the actor performs a kind of wretchedness inflicted by the need to maintain decorum when they are, in fact, suffering. It is a performance within a performance: the performance of decorum for the other characters in the drama, and the performance of how torturous that "performance" is for us, watching the film. To communicate the "inner torment," as it were, they must reveal the minutiae of tensions in the body without betraying too much to their fellows. It might be an eye strain or a clenched jaw, the pursing of lips, strumming of fingers, or brief sagging of shoulders. To return to MacPherson's swan, the actor must perform the mannered impression of effortlessness and, at the same time, communicate the torturous effort of maintaining that impression.

To analyze such "torturous etiquettes," this book begins in Chapter 1 by exploring manners in terms of encountering strangers in public spaces via a series of territorial negotiations. In Chapter 2, the problem of engaging strangers raises new issues when moved to the private domestic space, giving rise to the paradox of hospitality. In Chapter 3, the suspension of manners to develop a friendship out of the purely formal modes of interaction is considered, along with the associated risks of (potentially offensive) forms of banter. Chapter 4 picks up the problem of banter by considering the way a joke can either diffuse or introduce tension in the social situation. Chapters 5 and 6 offer complementary views of the impact on etiquette of civil rights. Both chapters explore racist etiquettes, first from the perspective of service, and then through the perspective of disservice. Chapter 7 focuses on the relationship between etiquette and clothes and considers the construction of the "gentleman" and the dismantling of a "lady" on account of fashion faux pas. Chapter 8 considers table manners, and especially moments onscreen when dining etiquette is either jettisoned to make a "pig of oneself," or else coopted to torture one's guests. And the final chapter, Chapter 9, considers the importance of intimate gestures in human interaction, which cannot be governed by etiquette and hence are wide open to abuse. The nine chapters are split into three parts that move from relatively distant encounters inviting first contact ("Initiation"), through more intimate spheres of interaction ("Exchange"), to a final part in which the decorous center no longer holds ("Dissolution").

The book intends to show that much of the nuance in cinematic performance stems from negotiating the tensions inherent to social form. The screen actor allows us "backstage" to glimpse the fury of her pedaling feet in social interactions, to satisfy our instinct for cruelty regarding any social failing. It realizes the suppressed urge in us all to burst from the strictures of etiquette and unleash (and delight in) the destructive consequences. In such lapses, I will argue, is a truth we ignore at our peril.

Part I

Initiation

1

Close Encounters

Greetings

THE ORIGINS OF ETIQUETTE can be traced back to the chivalric and courtly behavior of the Middle Ages, as set out in texts such as Raymond Lull's *Book of the Order of Chivalry* (c. 1279–1283) and Geoffrey de Charny's *Book of Chivalry* (c. 1350). Their contemporary popularity, writes J. S. Bothwell, demonstrated "the importance of the rules and symbols of class, and social order, in the Middle Ages, and especially the later medieval period," in which "to neglect such matters, even to the smallest degree, was to risk mockery and/or worse, social exclusion" (112). Out of these works of instruction on chivalry emerged manuals on civility (*civilité*), genteel behavior, and honor, which became especially popular from the sixteenth century onward among Europe's elite.[1] As Europe plunged into the uncertainty and tumult of the Renaissance period, societies underwent unprecedented transformations necessitating more detailed manuals on civility to ensure social order was maintained.

This development was famously coined the "civilizing process" by Norbert Elias in his monumental work from 1939, in which he charted the gradual process by which European societies, disparate though they were, changed from the hot, explosive liquid magma of early chivalric societies to one cooled under the social pressures of the renaissance period into the hard rock of contemporary social form. Elias described the "civilising process" as one in which "socially undesirable expressions of drives and pleasure are threatened and punished with measures that generate displeasure and anxiety." Such mechanisms set in motion "frontiers of shame," a "threshold of repugnance," and "standards of affect" (172) that result, over time, in the gradual modification of our "human, all too human" (as Nietzsche put it) nature. But Elias was not exactly the easy optimist who viewed the history of Western civilization as unproblematically progressive: somewhat poignantly (and chillingly), when his book was republished after the war, he added the following dedication to the memory of his parents: "Hermann Elias, d. Breslau 1940" and "Sophie Elias, d. Auschwitz 1941(?)." A grim reminder that undergirding much of what we might be tempted to disregard as civilization was the real and recent horror of unimaginable pain and suffering and contemporary barbarism.

Elias passed the torch to the sociologist Erving Goffman, who wrote that a "status, a position, a social place is not a material thing, to be possessed and then displayed; it is a pattern of appropriate conduct, coherent, embellished, and well articulated. Performed with ease of clumsiness, awareness or not, guile or good faith, it is none the less something that must be realized" (*Presentation* 81). To "realize" one's social place one must carefully negotiate the close encounter of "first contact" with strangers. C. Dallett Hemphill's *Bowing to Necessities* models conduct literature on what she calls the "progress of an encounter." First, she looks at the duration of meetings between people of varying status. Second, the "proxemic" angle of their interaction regarding the rules of the spaces they meet in. Third, their "first impressions," including general demeanor ("air"), posture and deportment, and the management of their "faces." Fourth, greetings, including physical acts which frame and punctuate an encounter (shaking hands, hugging, and so on). Fifth, conversation, including sensitivities around subject matter and the "rules" of engagement (turn taking, interruption, language choice, and so on). And finally, physical contact, a category which is "quite broad," Hemphill noted, "because rules on touching include acts as disparate as spanking and hand-holding" (7). These five modalities of the "close encounter" are what drive etiquette. They are the stuff of etiquette. In the following examples, such encounters involve torture often by degrees. All five examples abuse etiquette to infantilize or feminize and exhibit an aggression that is conspicuously masculine. We look at the torture of a lingering imposition (*Schindler's List*) and of a territorial violation (*Cape Fear*). The tactical use of "codeswitching" in public debate (*Frost/Nixon*) and the "contaminating" touch in greetings (*Philadelphia*). And, finally, the use of verbal slurs (*The Irishman*). In each example, it is not simply that the formal behaviors governing close contact with strangers (or enemies) have broken down; those very formalisms have themselves become instruments of torture.

Say Thanks: Torturous Repetitions in *Schindler's List*

> Time, operator of punishment.
>
> —Michel Foucault, *Discipline and Punish*

In *Schindler's List* (1993), Oscar Schindler (Liam Neeson) is a *bon vivant* industrialist and member of the Nazi Party whose profiteering instincts and talent for palm greasing open the door to him establishing a factory supplying the war effort. Having cozied up to SS officers and wheedled his way onto their books as a supplier of pots and pans, Schindler makes huge profits by taking advantage of cut-price Jewish labor, cheap because of the prohibition on Jewish enterprise and the worthlessness of money in the Kraków ghetto. Schindler is work-shy (a man of "panache," not labor, he describes himself) and so hires a local accountant and community leader, Itzhak Stern (Ben Kingsley), to recruit workers for the factory. There are two early scenes in which a simple "thanks" is figured as a key turning point in setting Schindler up for a moral revaluation of his role in the unfolding genocide. The first scene opens with a jubilant Schindler inviting Stern to raise a glass with him to celebrate their soaring profits.

The scene is punctuated by a humorous clash of personalities as Stern neglects to pick up his drink for the toast, staring blankly (even uncomprehendingly) at Schindler's raised glass. He appears not to grasp (both literally and figuratively) the point of the gesture. "Just *pretend*," Schindler playfully urges, at which Stern (who doesn't drink) feebly picks up the glass, raises it and almost immediately replaces it on the table. "Is that all?" he adds (that is, might he be dismissed?). Furrowing his brow, Schindler leans in to patronizingly point out the meaning of giving and receiving thanks: "I'm trying to thank you," he contends. "I'm saying, 'I could not have done this without you.' The usual thing would be to acknowledge my gratitude. It would also, by the way, be the courteous thing." Stern (who does, of course, understand the gesture but is fearful enough of Nazis at this point to be chary of potential snares) caps off his failure with a weak reply, "You're welcome," leaving Schindler to pointedly down both drinks before summarily dismissing the hapless accountant.

The second scene of thanks occurs a little later, as Stern reports on the continuing success of the factory while Schindler prepares to enjoy his supper. Having delivered his report to Schindler—who stressed his preference for receiving a precis rather than reading it for himself, given he wished to enjoy his hot meal—Stern lingers on in silence. His refusal to leave puts Schindler off his meal; he urges Stern to speak his mind. A factory worker, Stern quickly informs him, is extremely keen to thank his employer personally for giving him a job. Schindler is bemused and more than a little reluctant but allows the imposition. He stands to warmly greet the elderly worker who enters but is taken aback to find the man has only one arm (and is patently unsuitable for factory labor). The worker initially offers a simple thanks to which Schindler generously smiles and shakes his hand. However, instead of leaving, the worker lingers on in the office to give Schindler a (too detailed) description of the mistreatment he had previously received at the hands of the SS. As he speaks, Schindler's smile (along with his food) begins to cool. Still, the worker remains, now keen to impress on Schindler how hard he works, how hard he will go on working. Schindler subtly gestures for the machinist to leave by patting him on the shoulder, before turning his back to conclude the meeting. The worker remains. Schindler's smile now conveys agitation, as does his clipped reassurance that the old man's message has been well received ("That's great, thanks," "All right," etc.). Schindler returns to his meal, but instead of leaving the infernal worker now turns to Stern, declaiming Schindler as a "good man," the man who has saved his life. Sensitive to Schindler's increasing agitation, Stern tries to usher the worker from the room at which the man returns, now quite emotional, to heap more praise on Schindler, the "good man," and to offer him a blessing. His food now cold, Schindler stares determinedly out of the window and raises a brief hand until the worker, at long last, departs.

"By the way, don't *ever* do that to me again," Schindler warns Stern as he leaves the office for an engagement. As with the first scene of "thanks," his corrective implies that Stern has failed to observe the proper etiquette. But the scene reads differently. We notice something to which Schindler seems blind: that the extraordinarily perceptive Stern knows only too well the correct etiquette. Like before, he is wary of Schindler who is, after all, a Nazi (with a shiny Swastika pin on his lapel). At any moment Schindler might interpret Stern's behavior as an affront and have him executed. But we also notice that Schindler appears bothered by more than just the intrusion on his dinner. "Did you happen to notice that that man had only one arm?" he adds when rebuking Stern. "What's his *use?*!" The penny has dropped that Stern has been stocking Schindler's factory with Jews officially deemed "essential to the war effort" but who are incapable of working, to spare them from deportation to labor camps from which rumors of torture and death have reached ears in the ghettos. Schindler's "skilled" factory workers are a bunch of ex-scholars and intellectuals, men and women with disabilities, the elderly, and so on. No wonder Stern begins to look nervous.

In the next scene, Schindler's overly demonstrative machinist is picked out of a crowd by two young grinning soldiers. They josh about with the old man—who keeps repeating his mantra of being "essential" to the war effort—while steering him convivially to one side. The soldiers execute him. Observing from a window, Schindler quickly moves away but cannot avoid hearing the gunshot. He (all-too) casually complains to the soldiers about the loss to his business, and when one of the soldiers questions the usefulness of a one-armed laborer, Schindler, now, insists on the old man's qualities as a machinist. For whom is he covering, we wonder: himself or Stern? If we return to the second scene of thanksgiving, Schindler's dismissive gesture might be regarded as that of a man impatient to resume his cooling meal. He seems tortured by the time it takes the worker to express a simple gratitude, the extension of which renders his gesture of thanks a rude imposition. But something else is stirring besides Schindler's irritation. This is arguably the moment he has his moral epiphany. His business not only exploits the miserable circumstances of the ghettoized Jews but feeds their dehumanization, erodes the foundation of his prideful sense of "courtesy." Later in the film, Schindler will not only come to accept but actively aid Stern's efforts to circumvent and counteract the misery meted out to the Jews, and at immense personal risk. Already by this point, however, it is no longer a question of good or bad business for Schindler, but treason punishable by execution.

These two scenes of thanks are, of course, reflected in the film's emotional climax in which Schindler, having saved many Jews from deportation to death camps, is confronted by those he has saved. Humbly, he insists they not thank him, but thank Itzhak Stern instead. He then breaks down and weeps over the many men, women, and children he and his list have failed to spare from the gas chambers. The moment confirms for Peter Krämer that Spielberg's film "deeply implicated the viewers as guilty bystanders" (138), a moral challenge to "address our relationship to the suffering of other human beings more generally: What are we doing about this suffering?" (140).

In the second scene of thanksgiving, the disabled worker's rude imposition on Schindler's meal marks the moment Schindler sees his workers for who they are. The man's persistent irritation brings his employer to the point Hegel described as *Anerkennung* (moral recognition). He sees the worker not just as a worker but as a man—a *Jewish* man. Likewise, Stern's apparent failure to understand basic courtesy is recast. He cannot accept Schindler's gratitude in the first scene of thanks because Schindler is being duped, is not yet consciously committed to the act of saving Jewish lives. As Kwame Anthony Appiah puts it, Hegel's concept of moral recognition is about the need for "others to recognize us as conscious beings and to acknowledge that we recognize them," such that "when you glance at another person on the street and your eyes meet in mutual acknowledgement, both of you are expressing a fundamental human need, and both of you are responding—instantaneously and without effort—to that need you identify in each other" (xiii). It is for this reason as much as fear for his safety that Stern cannot meet Schindler's gaze. The problem with Schindler is there is no instantaneousness or effortlessness in recognizing the plight of his workers. It is only through two acts of discourtesy that the conscience of the master is pricked by his slaves, thereby reconfiguring their relationship. Some might counter that Schindler's dismissal of the worker shows nothing of the sort. That his averted gaze telegraphs a patience thoroughly worn out, his raised hand even reminiscent of the Nazi salute. But as Stern and the fawning worker finally leave, Schindler goes on staring out of that window (see Figure 1.1). Staring, and thinking. Director Steven

Figure 1.1. Liam Neeson realigns in *Schindler's List*. Steven Spielberg, Universal Pictures, 1993. Digital frame enlargement.

Spielberg lingers on this moment, too. He centers Neeson in the frame as Schindler realigns his scruples with a frightening new world, his dinner now forgotten.

You're in My Space: Territorial Offenses in *Cape Fear*

While being in a "public place" used to mean "being safe"—as when gangsters arranged to meet "somewhere public" to limit the likelihood they would be murdered before potential witnesses—the sociologist Erving Goffman demonstrated that it is in public spaces that contact with others opens us onto a spectrum of interpersonal relations requiring careful consideration, lest we find ourselves subject to any number of public violations. These range from minor infractions (bumping into someone, for instance) to major offenses (such as sexual assault). The establishment and maintenance (not to mention, at times, defense) of what Goffman called "territories of the self" constitute a crucial means of securing our presence in the social world. To put it one way, while it is said of the Englishman that his "home is his castle," he will find no moat, no ramparts with which to defend his personal space when out in public. One must stake a claim on a municipal space: with one's body (by occupying a space), with a gesture (by waving one's hand to indicate a seat is taken), with a personal effect (by placing a possession down to indicate a space is taken), or with one's voice ("Hey, I'm walking here!" adlibbed Dustin Hoffman, remaining in character as "Ratso," when a New York cabbie nearly ran him over while filming *Midnight Cowboy* [1969]). When we move from a "fixed" territory (an owned property: one's home, for instance) to a "situational" one (a temporary tenancy in a public place), we find ourselves engaged in more complex interactions with others who may wish to claim the same space for their own use. We also find ourselves subject to a raft of (often unwritten) etiquettes designed to prevent us from coming to blows, or else find ourselves subject to violation.

A good example of an etiquette that has emerged from our situational usage of public spaces is the rule that one ought to refrain from sitting next to a stranger in an empty setting—a cinema, for example. While it is perfectly permissible to do so (and would of course be entirely expected when the auditorium is full), sitting next to a stranger when vacant seats elsewhere are available would be regarded as an infringement of "personal space," irrespective of the technical legitimacy of its use (*Relations* 31). The most extreme example of this kind of infringement is found in Lars Von Trier's *Nymphomaniac*, in which two adolescent girls work their way through the men on a train, seducing each one in turn. When one of the passengers (Jens Albinus) refuses, one of the girls (Stacy Martin) persists in her attempts to arouse him until, unable to resist any longer, he succumbs to what she calls an "unequivocal provocation"—forcibly performing unwanted fellatio. Personal space is the first in Goffman's list of potential areas for territorial dispute, to which he added: occupancy of a "public stall," which he described as the well-bounded space to which individuals can lay a temporary claim (a seat in a cinema, for example); the integrity of a "use-space," such as the territory immediately surrounding the body of an individual (one's view of the screen, for example, which might be compromised by an errant child refusing to sit down in the seat up front); observance of "the turn," in which one's claim on a space begins at and then elapses after a period time (for example, turn-taking in the queue to buy a ticket for the film, as well as vacating one's seat at the end of the screening).[2] Finally, Goffman added the bodily "sheath," which referred to the skin and clothes protecting the body itself (control over which is often ceded by horny teenagers in the back row) and "possessional territory," such as personal effects (an overcoat stashed under one's seat—or on top of it, to lay claim to a use-space).³

Such territorial etiquettes are violated in a scene from Martin Scorsese's *Cape Fear* (1991), in which a lawyer, Sam Bowden (Nick Nolte), takes his wife, Leigh (Jessica Lange), and daughter, Danielle (Juliette Lewis), to watch a film at a cinema. This pleasant family outing is ruined when a nuisance viewer (Robert De Niro) arrives late to the screening, sits directly in front of the Bowden family (his head partially blocking their view of the screen), and then proceeds to light a fat Cuban cigar (the end of which he bites and spits to one side) before blowing smoke into their faces. When Sam politely coughs to express his annoyance, the nuisance viewer begins laughing raucously (and unreasonably) at the movie (see Figure 1.2). He alone in the cinema seems to find the scene funny enough to laugh aloud. Sam leans forwards to get the man's attention and request he curb his enthusiasm, but his (all-too) polite "excuse me" is not just ignored—the vexing viewer takes Sam's irritation as a sign to stretch his body out even more across the seats, spreading his exasperating presence. Unwilling to provoke a confrontation, Sam moves himself and his family to another row as the man briefly glances after them and continues to cackle away.⁴

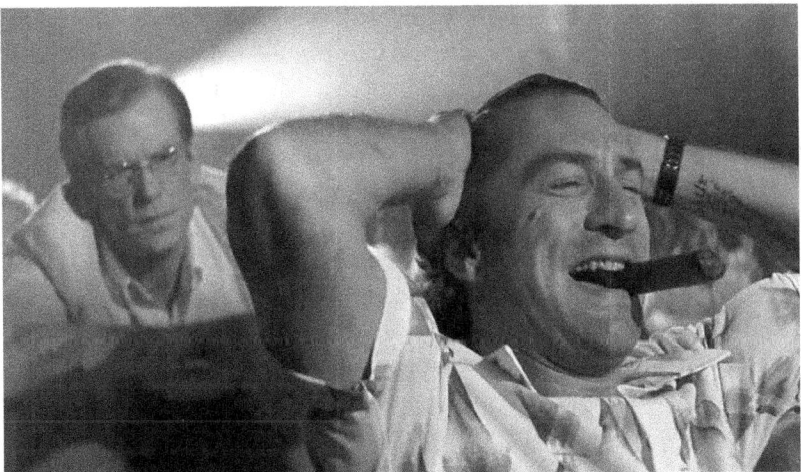

Figure 1.2. Robert De Niro violates space in *Cape Fear*. Martin Scorsese, Universal Pictures, 1991. Digital frame enlargement.

The nuisance viewer clearly (and pointedly) stops short of breaking any of the "house rules" that govern acceptable behavior: the seat in front of the Bowden family is available to him, smoking was allowed (at least it was back in 1991), and the film being screened is a comedy—laughing is, to an extent, to be expected (and, for the filmmaker, hoped for). Sam can hardly complain to the management, much less have this viewer removed. But something about the viewer's behavior seems malicious, designed not to express his own enjoyment but to inhibit others'. He seems deliberately to have violated the Bowden family's "territorial preserve" yet has broken no "rules."

After the screening, the Bowden family enjoy an ice cream and joke about the nuisance viewer, whom Danielle refers to as that "annoying, loser guy." She expresses a wish that her father had just "punched him out!" The mirth is soon wiped from Sam's face, however, when he comes to settle the bill only to be told by the teller that it has been paid . . . by the "loser guy." Sam rushes outside and, squinting, catches sight of the man from the movie house who is, it turns out, not a stranger after all, but someone from his past. Sam anxiously ushers his family back inside the ice cream parlor, his furrowed brow betraying his uneasiness about this man.

We soon learn that this man is Max Cady, newly released from prison, whom Sam defended at his trial for the rape and battery of a minor, which saw Cady sentenced to fourteen years. While defending Cady, Sam discovered evidence of the victim's promiscuity. So disgusted was he with his client's crimes, and knowing this report would mitigate Cady's sentencing, Sam buried the file. In jail, however, Cady taught himself to read. He then studied law, and eventually discovered the files regarding his case (thereby uncovering Sam's sabotage of his defense). Cady has returned to exact a highly calculated revenge on Sam, which rests on his understanding of the strict limits of his parole and the legal limits of criminal harassment. That is, Cady begins a campaign of violent intimidation on the Bowden family without ever (provably) violating the terms of his release. He lures Bowden's dog to the perimeter of the house and poisons him. But when Sam complains to the police, he is forced to admit he has no evidence Cady trespassed on their property. Later, Cady stalks the Bowden family at a parade (this moment recapitulates the scene in director Martin Scorsese's *Taxi Driver* when De Niro's mohawked menace stares threateningly at the senator he intends to assassinate). When Sam confronts him, Cady makes a lewd reference to Danielle, prompting Sam to grapple with him. But it is Sam who draws looks of disgust from outraged bystanders (none of whom caught Cady's provocation). They see Sam as the aggressor. Throughout these early scenes, Cady uses what Goffman called the "modalities of violation," that is, the violation of a territorial preserve through incursions, intrusions, encroachments, presumptions, transgressions, defilements, besmearing, or contamination (see *Relations* 44). Among the modalities of violation, Goffman lists the penetrating glance: "Although in our society the offense that can be committed by intrusive looks tends to be slighter than other kinds of offensive incursions, the distance over which the intrusion can occur is considerable, the directions multiple, the occasions of possible intrusion very numerous, and the adjustments required in eye discipline constant and delicate" (45). Cady is never more terrifying in the film than when he simply stands on a boundary staring into the Bowden family territory, penetrating their "territorial preserve" with his threatening gaze. Such territorial violations disturb precisely because they violate within the law. They are mere "etiquette violations," hence not legally enforceable.

Leighton Grist writes that Cady's etiquette violations rachet up from these early territorial incursions to more violent and disturbing infringements, including the violent rape of Sam's colleague and lover, who refuses to press charges against Cady because she knows how the system "works," how humiliating a rape trial can be (Sam, of course, knows this is true—and knows that Cady knows it, too). "The law," writes Grist, "is accordingly placed as being complicit with violent misogyny . . . is represented as effectively corrupt and corruptible" (*Films* 145). The irony of the film is ultimately that while Cady operates within, or else manipulates, the legal parameters set by society, Sam is increasingly drawn to violate those very same laws to stop him. He tries to convince a sympathetic detective (played by Robert Mitchum, who starred as Cady in the 1962 original) to arrest Cady. "With what?" comes the incredulous response. "You know the law," the detective adds, somewhat huffily. He hires a private detective (Joe Don Baker) to keep tabs on Cady, but his cover is quickly blown. Desperate, Sam hires a gang to do a "hospital job" on Cady, but he bests his assailants and files a restraining order on *Sam*, whom he surreptitiously recorded issuing a threat to have him attacked. Finally, Sam buys a gun.

Max's torture of etiquette is by extension a torture of the law. But what is most interesting about the film is the way Sam's own moral standards deteriorate. His dove-like, liberal attitude is stripped away to reveal a baser, more barbarous nature that Grist points out renders him Cady's effective "doppelganger" (*Films* 139). In many ways, it is a film about the hypocrisy of such men, for whom the laws by which they live and (in Sam's case) work can be abandoned in the name of protecting their privileged lives. When Cady eventually discards his tactical territorial violations to brazenly invade the Bowden family home, the film correspondingly reflects the horror tropes associated with the home invasion film. But, as Grist points out, Cady's menacing presence on the periphery of the Bowden home "exacerbates strains implicit in the relationships between" them, strains that quickly draw from the home its homeliness, just as they draw from the polite and civilized Sam a monster comparable to Cady himself (*Films* 137). After a final battle, the Bowden family survive their close encounter with that particular monster (who is finally vanquished), but the damage to Sam's moral character is done. The family physically survive Max Cady, but the final shot of them embracing is an uneasy and ambiguous one.

Do You Mind? Codeswitching in *Frost/Nixon*

Some breaches of etiquette are less egregious and might be intended as a light-hearted remark. Such miscalculations tend to be easily forgiven, less so when the individuals concerned don't share equal "footing." Footing, Goffman wrote, concerns the social position of an interlocutor when engaged in conversation with others, and it can matter intensely when shifting from a formal relationship (for example, the employee in relation to their line manager), to an "unserious" remark inviting the temporary alleviation of workplace hierarchies. In doing so, the ordinarily serious professional setting undergoes a "change in gears," which sociologists call "codeswitching." But Goffman illustrates how codeswitching might lead to a more damaging change in footing if it isn't carefully considered. He gives the example of a briefing once given by President Richard Nixon to reporters in the Oval Office, which Nixon ended by standing up and adopting a "teasing voice" to call out one of the female reporters for wearing slacks instead of a skirt. A 1973 edition of the *Evening Bulletin* reported that the president ("a gentleman of the old school") then asked if pants cost less than gowns. The reporter responded that they did not. "'Then change,' commanded the President with a wide grin as other reporters and cameramen roared with laughter" (qtd. in Goffman, *Forms* 125). Aside from the flagrant chauvinism of the president's remark, Goffman was interested in the complexity of Nixon's switching codes from a formal (professional—which here means presidential) to an informal (blasé, even familiar) mode of address. The effect was to single out this reporter, thereby objectifying her for the patronizing laughter of her male peers. However, Goffman was as interested in the effect of Nixon's remark on this reporter's footing, especially when the president subsequently shifted back into "professional mode." When "a change of gears occurs among more than two persons, then a change commonly occurs regarding who is addressed" (*Forms* 126), by which Goffman meant that Nixon's off- (indeed under-) handed remark continued to hang "in the air," as it were, even after he had switched back into presidential mode. What was undoubtedly intended as a playful criticism (that is, light joshing) to introduce a little levity into an officious meeting ended up undermining this female reporter's professional position in relation to her male peers. Playful ribbing turns into a serious diminution of the reporter's professional footing.

In Ron Howard's *Frost/Nixon* (2008), "codeswitching" is used more tactically by the fictional Nixon (Frank Langella) during his first televised interview with an opportunistic young broadcaster, David Frost (Michael Sheen). The ex-president has agreed to the series of interviews, hoping to use them to rinse clean his public face following the Watergate scandal that forced him to resign the presidency.[5] For both men, the stakes are high. If Nixon fails to win public sympathy by steering the agenda, his political future will be irrecoverable. For Frost's team, the interview is an opportunity to coax a confession from the disgraced former president and achieve closure for the American people following an unprecedented constitutional crisis. But the stakes for Frost personally are high, too. If he fails to get an apology from Nixon, he will lose the money staked by private investors (much of it raised himself), and his broadcasting credibility will lie in tatters.

Ahead of the first interview, the two men focus on last-minute preparations as a large room bustles with producers making final adjustments to the set and technicians check and recheck sound and light levels. Makeup artists fussily apply finishing touches to both interviewer and interviewee, as Nixon cordially sidles up to Frost to express his gratitude that he managed to pull the interviews together.

Frost smiles with reciprocating warmth. However, Nixon then subtly switches codes. He leans in conspiratorially to brazenly ask the Brit how much it all cost. At the mention of money, Frost freezes, his toothy smile now fixed in his heavily made-up face. "Oh, d'you mind me asking?" Nixon wonders, before pressing again for an answer, ". . . c'mon, c'*mon*, it's just between us." Leaning even closer, Nixon signals to Frost that they are speaking in confidence. Seemingly incapable of refusing (perhaps wary of appearing rude), Frost answers through his still-grinning/gritted teeth that it cost two million dollars, at which Nixon raises his eyebrows in surprise, gasping (rather more audibly than discretion allows), "Jeez, I didn't realize we were making *Ben Hur*!"

In terms of etiquette, Nixon has already transgressed. A man with his worldly wisdom and experience would almost certainly have known that it is a serious taboo to talk to an Englishman about money (even, perhaps especially, when conducting business). When raising what they call "the sordid subject of money," writes Kate Fox, the English "tend to become tongue-tied and uncomfortable," which they might then try to cover by joking, blustering, being over-polite, or even *apologizing* (288). "Money," "cost," "price," "fees," "payment," etc.—all are "dirty words" to the English. Howard emphasizes the transgression by moving from the intimacy of the closeups previously framing Nixon and Frost to a medium long shot of Nixon's expressive posture as he makes the *Ben Hur* comment (drawing the attention of others who, inevitably, eagerly listen in). The next code-switching "assault" comes when Nixon asks *how* Frost raised the money (the answer to which—we know from the previous scene with his chief of staff—Nixon already knows). Frost confesses that the money has not all been raised but demurs that "everyone's been kind and deferred fees," to which Nixon casually responds, "Well, not *quite* everyone" (in reference to his own $600,000 fee). Nixon's casual pre-interview chit-chat has been quite mistaken by Frost as "backstage," if not entirely separate from the interview to come. He has miscalculated, however. This is, by contrast, a masterful means of undermining the "footing" of the inexperienced broadcaster prior to going live, designed to put to the front of Frost's mind all that is at stake in the interviews.

But Nixon is not finished unnerving Frost. Having failed to parry Nixon's "money-talk," the broadcaster becomes defensive. To (at least momentarily) regain some goodwill, the former president changes tack, showing a little deference by asking permission to dab his upper lip before answering each of Frost's questions during the interview. He wryly notes his "history with perspiration," a reference to his 1960 electoral defeat to John F. Kennedy, which some attributed to the presence of perspiration on his upper lip during televised debates (said to have made him look disingenuous next to the cool, dry Kennedy). "Moisture on my upper lip," Nixon chummily laments, "cost me the presidency," to which he adds (as Howard cuts to show Nixon's face on a television monitor), "Television and the closeup . . . they create their own sets of meanings." Having made this self-deprecating remark, Nixon switches codes again. "So, now they insist I bring a handkerchief, and that I trim my eyebrows," he casually notes. A producer announces they have sixty seconds until they begin taping, at which Nixon asks Frost, "Do you trim yours?" Frost answers no. "Course not," Nixon replies, "You're light-skinned. You've got blue eyes. You've got no troubles with perspiration, I imagine? You were obviously born to be on the tube," he adds. Once again, Frost's toothy smile falters—just what is the former president implying? As the producer now tells them they have just thirty seconds remaining, Nixon makes his insinuation unambiguous. While Frost attempts to clear his head by focusing on his interview notes, Nixon observes the Brit's shoes (which are laceless, Italian-style dress shoes). As the lights dim, he interrupts Frost's concentration by asking him if his shoes are Italian, to which Frost distractedly confirms that they are. "Huh, that's interesting," he nonchalantly observes, allowing his comment to trail off into silence before, after a pause during which the seconds tick down to the moment they start taping, he asks, ". . . you don't find them . . . too effeminate?" Jolted out of his notes, Frost uncertainly answers "no," at which Nixon delivers the killer blow: "Well, I guess somebody in your field can get away with them, y'know?" By "your field," Nixon means "presenting," not "debating." He implies that Frost is a man of appearances, not substance. The producer signals the final countdown as Frost's face is now plastered with self-doubt. Nixon has managed to weaponize an otherwise relationship-building, self-deprecatory comment to suggest an ad hominem attack on Frost's masculinity, all through subtle degrees of codeswitching. His apparently casual chit-chat constitutes a minor "offscreen" violation that, when the pair shift into professional mode (that is, start the interview), reframes Frost's juniority as juvenility. He is not merely less experienced than Nixon; he is inexperienced. He is not just the younger man, but unmasculine. They are not just different, but mismatched.

These early salvoes clearly rock Frost, as Nixon dominates the first interview (for which Frost has not prepared). Now, with his creditors worrying about their investment, the pressure falls on the broadcaster. Can he regain control over the agenda for the remaining interviews, or will he be cowed into submission? Again, Howard introduces the second interview by focusing on the "backstage" moments leading up to the recording. This time, Nixon bursts into the room and grandly beholds Frost, "Ah!" he exclaims, "the Grand Inquisitor," to which Frost (clearly more wary than before—but still smiling) claims he is more like the "friendly neighborhood confidante." Apparently ill at ease with the idea that these might become adversarial encounters (perhaps sensing that if they do, he will lose), Frost appears keen to reframe the interviews as collegial—to lull Nixon, perchance, into a false sense of security. Nixon, however, remains brash and upbeat, and is soon gifted an opportunity to take up his earlier line of attack when a blown lightbulb induces a moment's panic in the inexperienced broadcaster (who, mistaking the loud bang for a gunshot, briefly imagines they are under attack). Nixon's eye is then caught, however, by an attractive brunette in the background. Momentarily distracted, his chief of staff (Kevin Bacon) reminds him to "focus, sir." As a producer announces that they have thirty seconds until they begin taping, Nixon hits on a new line of attack. They sit down and this time Frost studies his notes, keen to focus. His concentration is broken, however, when Nixon asks if he had a pleasant evening the previous night, to which Frost curtly responds, "Yes, thank you," quickly returning to his notes. As before, Howard's camera studies Nixon studying Frost (who studies his notes). The former president looks away, biding his time as the seconds tick down to the start of the interview. Then, with just moments to go, Nixon raises his eyes to look penetratingly at Frost before asking, *sotto voce* and with one eyebrow provocatively raised, "Did you do any fornicating?" Howard zooms in on Michael Sheen's face as Frost looks up from his notes, shocked at the remark. The producer counts them down and Frost clears his throat and gives a shake of the head, trying to shake off the impertinent question, clearly ruffled. Howard cuts back to Langella, who, with his twinkling eyes narrowing (as if homing in on prey), looks comfortable, ready.

Goffman wrote that "to interrupt someone is much like tripping over him; both acts can be perceived as instances of insufficient concern for the other," just as "to ask an improperly personal question can be equivalent to making an uninvited visit; both constitute invasions of territoriality" (*Forms* 37). During the interviews, Nixon's strategy is to "drown out" the broadcaster with unceasing talk, reliant on Frost's gentlemanly instinct to resist interrupting. But before the interviews, he uses the impropriety of personal questions about money, masculinity, and even Frost's sex life (the subject of much gossip and media speculation) to unsettle and disturb his thoughts. He breaches what Fox describes as the "English obsession with privacy" (76). Even the odd choice of word, "fornicate," seems carefully chosen to provoke. It is not a swear word as such (at least not according to Geoffrey Hughes [*Swearing* 1991]) but is derived from *fornix*, meaning arch (that is, an underground brothel). Hence, "to fornicate" specifically implies *unmarried* sexual intercourse (Frost is unmarried and has gained a public reputation as a bachelor and playboy). Was Nixon (who was married) inspired by his own desire to "fornicate" with the attractive brunette? The word "fornicate" hangs over the interview like "ritualistic profanation," as Goffman called it (*Interaction* 87). Despite his more assiduous preparations for this second interview after the disastrous first, Frost fumbles his opening question (then this fumbling preoccupies him). He then fumbles the interview (like a teenager in his first sexual encounter). It marks yet another victory for Nixon, whose bullishness turns to overconfidence as the tide turns in the final two interviews.

I won't explore those later interviews here, which do end with Frost eliciting Nixon's famous "confession." What interests me is the way Nixon's "codeswitching" affects Frost's "face." A person may be said to *be in wrong face*, Goffman wrote, when information gleaned from the social encounter cannot be integrated with the "line" being sustained by them. They can be considered *out of face* when this line falters altogether: "The intent of many pranks is to lead a person into showing a wrong face or no face . . . [and] should he sense that he is in wrong face or out of face, he is likely to feel ashamed and inferior because of what has happened to the activity on his account and because of what may happen to his reputation as a participant" (*Interaction* 8). Frost's toothy smile and peppy congeniality ironically betray his inexperience, allowing Nixon to attack his footing. However,

Nixon proves a master at exposing Frost's insecurities because he shares those insecurities. It is a case of what Thomas Hobbes described as the "sudden glory arising from some sudden conception of some eminency in ourselves, by comparison with the infirmity of others, *or with our own formerly*" (qtd. in Morreal, emphasis mine). When Frost recognizes he is in danger of bungling these interviews, he begins to knuckle down and study his opponent, and he is gifted a key insight prior to the final interview (on Watergate) when an inebriated Nixon drunkenly phones him to remark on how similar they are, having both risen from modest backgrounds. Ironically, this exposes Nixon's pridefulness, his "Achilles's heel," enabling Frost to elicit the famous confession (in response to being pressed on the legality of his actions, Nixon finally snaps: "I'm saying when the president does it, it's not illegal!").[6] Frost ultimately uses Nixon's hubris against him (that is, Nixon fails because he doesn't regard himself as disgraced).

Howard's film ends with Frost visiting Nixon in his later years, who warmly receives and acknowledges his former rival. As a parting gift, Frost leaves a pair of the same Italian-style dress shoes Nixon had earlier mocked for being "too effeminate." Nixon smiles and accepts this touching gesture from a worthy opponent.

Hands Off: Contamination Fears in *Philadelphia*

It is no great surprise that laying hands on a stranger raises etiquette problems. To "lay one's hands on" an object means to find and take possession of it. When said of a person, "the laying *on of* hands" means to bless or heal (invoking the Holy Spirit). However, to "lay a hand on" also means to touch (inappropriately) or harm (as in the threatening expression, "When I get my hands on you . . ."). In one of his essays, Michel de Montaigne marveled at the range of meaning conveyed by the hands. "How they promise, conjure, appeal, menace, pray, supplicate, refuse, beckon, interrogate, admire, confess, cringe, instruct, command, mock and what not besides," he gushed, adding, "with a variation and multiplication of variation which makes the tongue envious" ("Apology for Raimond Sebond"). Montaigne echoed Quintillian in AD 80, who observed that while "other portions of the body merely help the speaker, the hands may almost be said to speak. . . . In fact, though the people and nations of the earth speak in a multitude of tongues, they share in common the universal language of the hands" (qtd. in Bates 175).[7]

Hands are used to establish a bond and suggest the development of that bond in a future relationship ("O then dear saint, let lips do what hands do, / They pray, grant thou, lest faith turn to despair," ventures Romeo to a game Juliet in Shakespeare's tragedy [1.5.101]). Shaking hands is considered one of the most fundamental of gestures. It signifies peace and companionship the world over, is used in greetings and farewells, as well as to conclude business transactions, make truces, and establish pacts (sometimes with spit—or, if one really is serious, blood). The "bond" might be symbolic, to signify the relationship between people who share feelings, interests, or experiences. It can be (quasi-legally) binding, as in the promise or the pledge. An oath or word of honor might have signified that a bond had been established, but to confirm it required the meeting of palms. It still is often with a handshake that a deal is "sealed." The symbolic importance of such bonds is often more than just trifling or purely ceremonial. Handled badly, it can end in bloodbath. Consider the moment in *Django Unchained* (2012) when, after a thoroughly acrimonious dispute over the purchase of slaves, an abolitionist bounty hunter, Dr. Schultz (Christoph Waltz), and a hateful slaver, Calvin Candie (Leonardo DiCaprio), finally conclude a business deal to release a slave from bondage. However, as Dr. Schultz makes to leave in disgust, Candie mischievously insists on their shaking hands, claiming that in the South no deal is done until it is shaken on. Knowing well that such a gesture of cordiality between men of equal standing will abhor this abolitionist man of morals, Candie finds in it a puerile victory (one snatched from him when Schultz, instead of shaking, shoots the slaver dead). A refusal of a handshake can also signify the dissolution of a previously strong bond. When gangsters Tom Powers (James Cagney) and Matt Doyle (Edward Woods) refuse to shake hands with their old mentor, "Putty Nose" (Murray Kinnell), in *The Public Enemy* (1931), we already suspect (as does he) that the reunion will not end well. Here, the refusal of a handshake not only marks a refusal to renew the vow of friendship. It constitutes an overture to Putty's execution for earlier ratting them out. Putty Nose has broken his word and thus broken their bond. Hence, no handshake.

Most traditional mannered gestures have had their origin traced, however contested (or potentially apocryphal). The custom of doffing one's hat in greeting, for example, comes from knights raising their visors as a show of amity. Should the gesture reveal a foe instead of a friend, notes Richard Duffy, the knights would fight on the spot (xvi).[8] It is somewhat baffling, then, writes Herman Roodenburg, that the provenance of the handshake is so difficult to source. This is doubly mystifying given the word "manners" itself comes from the Latin *manus*, meaning "hand." With our manners, we figuratively handle (or mishandle) relations with others. But while one can find many references to bowing, doffing, and curtseying in early works on civility, on handshaking the early modern manuals are silent.

In Charlotte Brontë's *Jane Eyre*, a handshake can convey much that is unspoken. After initially struggling to see eye to eye, Jane and Hannah eventually overcome their initial mistrust to bond over a handshake—following which, Jane remarks, they were friends. By contrast, after she rejects the (cynical) offer of marriage from St. John, Jane is then snubbed by the latter, who pointedly refuses to kiss—or *even* shake hands—goodnight. Jane insists on their shaking hands but finds the experience disquieting: "What a cold, loose touch he impressed on my fingers!" St. John assures Jane that he bears her no ill will, but his handshake betrays him. A gentleman should always shake hands, noted Emily Post, and he should be aware that the "personality of a handshake" conveys the sincerity of his intent:

> A handshake often creates a feeling of liking or of irritation between two strangers. Who does not dislike a 'boneless' hand extended as though it were a spray of sea-weed, or a miniature boiled pudding? It is equally annoying to have one's hand clutched aloft in grotesque affectation and shaken violently sideways, as though it were being used to clean a spot out of the atmosphere. What woman does not wince at the viselike grasp that cuts her rings into her flesh and temporarily paralyzes every finger? (20)

The passing feeling of strength and warmth in the briefest possible clasp, along with a deep but equally succinct look into the countenance of the person one is embracing, makes for the best introduction to a stranger.

Hands communicate much that cannot be said in Jonathan Demme's *Philadelphia* (1993). In an early scene, a successful lawyer,

Andrew Beckett (Tom Hanks), is invited by the partners of his law firm to an informal meeting. They give Andy a high-profile case before announcing he is to be promoted to senior associate. They celebrate with much backslapping, handshaking, and, pointedly, an embrace from the most senior partner, Charles (Jason Robards). But another of the partners, Walter (Robert Ridgely), notices a lesion on Andy's forehead. Andy explains it away as a bruise. The lesion is, in fact, a symptom of the AIDS virus Andy has kept from his employers. However, when Andy is unexpectedly sacked for "gross negligence" after a crucial file he had left on his desk for his assistant goes missing, Andy deduces that he has been the victim of sabotage by the partners, who wanted a pretext to fire him, having learned of his illness.

The partners are not the only ones with prejudices, however. When Andy struggles to find a lawyer to represent him, he ends up at the office of a small claims lawyer, Joe (Denzel Washington), who warmly shakes Andy's hand on their introduction (clearly an overture to his sales pitch). When Andy explains why he needs representation, however, Joe visibly recoils. As Andy explains about his unfair dismissal, director Jonathan Demme uses point-of-view shots to give Joe's perspective as he worriedly looks at all the things in his office that Andy is handling. Andy's hands represent contaminants that not only threaten to undermine the sanctity of the office space (Joe's work territory) but what Goffman calls the "territory of the self." Clearly unsettled by the encounter, Joe refuses to take on Andy's case, who leaves disappointed but unsurprised (it is his tenth rejection). Once Andy is gone, Joe rushes to his doctor to confirm that he is not infected, and that he does not pose a threat to his baby daughter should he touch her on his return home. The doctor mockingly reassures Joe before explaining the basics of HIV transmission. Later that evening, Joe admits that his prejudice stems not just from ignorance about the virus but from his homophobia. He asks his wife, "Would you accept a client if you were constantly thinking: 'I don't want this person to touch me, I don't want him to even *breathe* on me'?"

However, Joe's mind is changed when he witnesses Andy being discriminated against by a librarian (Tracey Walter) while researching his case (unable to find a lawyer willing to take his case on, Andy intends to represent himself). The librarian very gently, timidly even, asks if Andy would like to move to a research room. "No, thanks," Andy brightly responds, missing the inference. The librarian nervously looks around at a room filled with equally nervous-looking researchers before reiterating the request, "Wouldn't you be more . . . *comfortable* in a research room?" Andy finally catches the implication. "No," he responds firmly, "would it make *you* more comfortable?" Joe is watching from a nearby table, hiding behind a screen constructed from legal files. He is visibly appalled at the librarian's microaggression. Flushed with rage, Joe stands and strides over to Andy, glowering at the librarian (who shamefacedly scurries away) and the onlookers (who return to their studying) before warmly acknowledging Andy. We then get a second handshake (of sorts). Joe sits, and Andy uses his hands to share a file across the table. After a brief hesitation, Joe takes the file (Demme cuts to and lingers on a closeup of Joe's hands, immobile, before they move to grasp the file Andy has been touching).

Susan Sontag noted that the hysteria surrounding AIDS hinged on ignorance concerning the nature of its transmissibility. By the late eighties and early nineties, wrote she, AIDS had supplanted cancer as the central stigmatizing illness, one that marked sufferers with a "spoiled identity" (to use Goffman's expression). "It seems that societies need to have one illness which becomes identified with evil," Sontag wrote, "and attaches blame to its 'victims' " (*Illness as Metaphor* 101). Moreover, "infectious diseases to which sexual fault is attached always inspire fears of easy contagion and bizarre fantasies of transmission by nonvenereal means in public spaces" (112). We see this when the partners voice their disgust at the thought of all those handshakes and workplace intimacies with Andy. Charles especially vents about how Andy "brought *AIDS* into our offices, into our men's room." He pauses, before raging further, "he brought AIDS *into our goddamn family picnics!*"

This film hinges on Joe's slow but steady recognition that his fear of contamination is not just rooted in health fears, but the general feeling that touch can be contaminating if it belongs to the wrong *kind* of person. The librarian provokes Joe not just because of the injustice of his microaggression, but because he, a black man, recognizes in it the same persecution by the softly spoken racist shopkeeper, who gently points out, before asking what he needs, that the store doesn't stock or won't sell what he wants to buy. The idea is expressed in a scene from the (much maligned) *Green Book* (2018), in which an Italian American nightclub bouncer, Tony (Viggo Mortensen), notices one of the African American laborers working in his house drinking water from one of his glasses. Once the workers have left, Tony carefully takes the glass and discards it in the trash. Even washing with detergent is insufficient in Tony's eyes to cleanse this tainted object. "Etymologically," noted Susan Sontag, "patient means sufferer. It is not suffering as such that is most deeply feared but suffering that degrades" (123). The library scene complements the notion: here we have a degradation that induces suffering. By reaching out to grasp that folder being offered by Andy, Joe's hand "speaks" more than he knows. With his hands he already says, "I'm with you."

When my hand reaches out to grasp another's, I experience both my own and my partner's flesh in two dimensions. The first is the feeling that I am "touching," with the complementary sense that the one I touch is "tangible." But this relation is reversible: by touching another, I feel my own hand in its tangibility, my own flesh as flesh. I become a subject who touches, who seizes an object; in the same gesture, I recognize myself as touched—as an object in another's grasp. This idea, from Maurice Merleau-Ponty (*Basic Writings* 250–52), asserts that one cannot hold both dimensions in the mind simultaneously. And what is good for the hands is good for the eyes, too. Merleau-Ponty points out that the same relation appertains to looking. I see another and as our eyes lock, I behold them with my gaze. I also behold them beholding me. I don't just see this person, but see "myself seen from without, such as another would see me." I become "installed in the midst of the visible," and to possess the visible, I must already be possessed by it (252). And this is how *Philadelphia* ends. After winning their wrongful dismissal lawsuit, Joe visits Andy at the hospital as he prepares to die. Demme shoots the pair in a traditional shot/reverse-shot as they congratulate one another. Then, as Andy's breathing struggles and he fumbles for the oxygen mask, Joe gently lays a hand on top of Andy's, at which Demme cuts to Andy's point of view.[9] Demme then cuts (with editor, Craig McKay) to Joe's point of view as his hands bring the oxygen mask up to Andy's face (see Figure 1.3). As he carefully positions the mask over Andy's mouth and nose and smooths the elastic strap over Andy's ears, Joe brings his hands down to briefly caress Andy's cheeks. Demme cuts back to Joe, who lifts his eyes up to meet Andy's, before cutting back to Andy, who smiles.

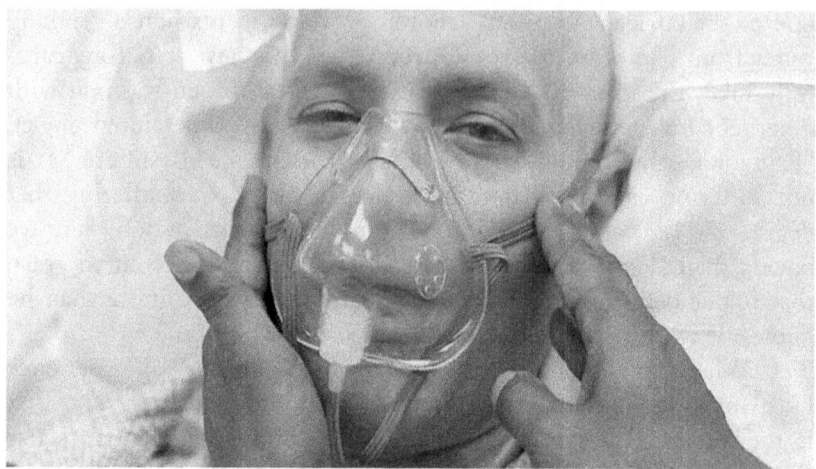

Figure 1.3. Touching distance in *Philadelphia*. Jonathan Demme, TriStar Pictures, 1993. Digital frame enlargement.

Despite the platitudes they give about seeing one another again, both men know this is goodbye. But it is a goodbye that recapitulates (and transforms) their first meeting. From Joe's initial recoil at Andy's contaminating hands and his fear of Andy's infectious breath, to this caressing touch and the care with which he helps Andy breathe, Joe repudiates not only the "metaphors" (as Sontag puts it) around the AIDS virus at the time, but also the homophobia such metaphors sustained.

You People . . . : Speech Violations in *The Irishman*

> A public back-down is an unfinished thing,—for some natures at least.
>
> —Owen Wister, *The Virginian*

A memorable (and poignant) example of a speech violation occurs in Stanley Kubrick's *The Killing* (1956). During a daring heist at the racetrack, sharpshooter Nikki Arane (Timothy Carey) is tasked with shooting one of the racing horses to provide a distraction for Johnny

Clay (Sterling Hayden) and his accomplices to rob the bookkeepers. To gain a good vantage point, Nikki smooths his way into a private parking lot by chatting amiably with an African American parking attendant (James Edwards). He succeeds in charming his way through, but his breezy manner comes back to bite him. Time is of the essence: Kubrick presents the heist from multiple perspectives, always coming back to the ever-ticking clock, and if Nikki fails to take the shot the entire plan is kaput. The problem for Nikki is that he was too chummy with this parking attendant, so much so that the (presumably bored) young man sidles up to his vehicle to pass some time, obviously oblivious that Nikki has no time to pass. The shootist initially tries to shut down the conversation politely, but when it becomes apparent that the attendant is keen to stay and chew the fat, Nikki aggressively insists on being left alone. "Is something wrong?" the attendant asks, confusion etched on his face. "You're wrong, n——r," Nikki spits, his face full of snarling menace. Wounded, the attendant withdraws, turning his back on Nikki whose face immediately sags under the weight of his vile, racist remark (which despite intending it, he did not mean). Like the actor playing him, Nikki appears to be of Italian descent. One might reasonably suppose that he is himself no stranger to prejudice. The racist remark is effective (the attendant leaves him alone), but he has offended against his own sense of moral order.

Nikki's offense is echoed in the "seventeen pantomimes" scene from *True Romance* (1993), in which a security guard, Clifford (Dennis Hopper), finds himself beaten and bound by mafia gangsters who intend to torture him until he divulges the whereabouts of his son (on the run with his girlfriend and a suitcase full of stolen heroin). To provoke the mobsters into giving him a quick death (thereby avoiding painful torture and the likelihood he will betray his son), Clifford tells them that "all Sicilians have "n——r blood." The mafia boss is so outraged, he immediately executes Clifford personally.

In both examples, vile racism becomes necessary to sufficiently provoke an interlocutor into breaking the spell of (torturous) etiquette. While the exigency of the situation demands they "speak their worst," such offensive remarks clearly fall within a "repertoire," so to speak—that is, both men are capable of not only calling up but (convincingly) delivering these racist retorts. However, while both willfully perform "the Racist," as if it were a role, Clifford raises a suspicion that part of him delights in this provocation. While Nikki's falling face suggests his remarks are at odds with what he really thinks, Clifford, by contrast, delivers his anecdote about Sicilian blood a little too well. He has the intricacies and details not only committed to memory—he delivers them with practiced aplomb. Nikki's offense in *The Killing* always inspires my sympathy, whereas Clifford's in *True Romance* leaves me cold.

In Martin Scorsese's *The Irishman* (2019), a similar speech violation skirts a fine line between mannered speech and racist provocation. On the surface of it, professional conflict alone is sufficient to explain the antagonism between Jimmy Hoffa (Al Pacino)—head of the International Brotherhood of Teamsters—and Anthony 'Tony Pro' Provenzano (Stephen Graham)—a mafioso rival vying for Hoffa's position. But beneath these surface tensions something personal boils. Jimmy wants to extricate his union from the mafia's pervasive hold, and Tony represents the worst of the mobster type. He is disrespectful, presumptuous, and (perhaps worst of all for Jimmy) rude. While diplomacy comes naturally to neither man, their mutual loathing arises from deep-seated prejudice that boils over in two interconnected scenes. Both are structured around one man having to swallow his pride to ask a favor of the other, while ending up committing minor solecisms leading to a major brawl.

In the first of the two scenes, Jimmy and Tony are doing time together. As Jimmy enjoys a bowl of ice cream alone in the prison cafeteria, Tony, without waiting to be invited, joins him at the table, blurting, "I gotta talk to you about a problem." His "problem" is that his generous pension with the Teamsters has been forfeited because his crime (extortion) involved violence. While savoringly spooning ice cream into his mouth, Jimmy coolly responds that there's nothing he can do. "It's *federal*," he commiserates. Unconvinced, Tony asks how Jimmy kept his lucrative pension. Jimmy explains that his crime (fraud) was nonviolent. Tony continues his entreaty, suspecting Jimmy won't rather than can't help. He never once says "please," and he obdurately persists in refusing Jimmy's refusal. The tone of their discussion disintegrates when Jimmy gives a derisory shake of the head at Tony's unwillingness to concede the point. "Don't fuck with me, Jimmy," Tony menaces, "just *do* something about it." What started out as a demand thinly dressed as an impolite request is now a simple rude demand. Jimmy stops eating his ice cream and raises his voice, at which Tony brings his finger (already wagging at Jimmy) to his lips. "Shh!, lower your fuckin' voice!" he snarls. The conversation turns decidedly less civil. Jimmy lowers his voice (to menace rather than acquiesce to Tony's hushing gesture) and contemptuously fires back, "You tellin' *me* to lower my fuckin' voice," adding: ". . . *cocksucker* . . . fuck you." Tony's demands now sound like threats ("I want what I'm *fuckin'* owed") punctuated by a now jabbing finger. Jimmy derisively scoffs, "You people . . . *you* people, oh my God . . . I am done . . . with *this*." He snorts and with a dismissive sweep of the hands indicates that their meeting is concluded. Tony, however, takes "you people" to be an ethnic slur. "What'd you say, 'You people,' you said '*you people.*' What does that fuckin' mean, 'you people'?" he asks. The scene ends with Tony smacking Jimmy's ice cream bowl across the room and hurling the union man to the floor to lay on a savage beating.

The second scene takes place some years after their release from prison, only this time the power relation is reversed. With his parole conditions and time in prison damaging his position in the Teamsters, Jimmy now requires Tony's endorsement to regain a foothold in "his" union. The scene begins with Jimmy waiting for Tony in a café alongside his friend, Frank (Robert De Niro), who is backing Jimmy up. Tony is late by more than ten minutes, and Jimmy is agitating to leave. "This isn't right," Jimmy huffs, "this isn't *right*. You don't do this. You don't keep a man waiting." He reiterates the point, "You *don't* keep a man waiting," adding, "the only time you do is when you want to say something. When you want to say, 'fuck you.'" When Tony finally arrives with his pal, he adds insult to injury by swaggering into the café wearing an open aloha shirt, white shorts, and Gucci loafers. Breezily passing a comment on the sweltering LA weather, he makes no attempt to apologize for being late. Jimmy scornfully derides Tony on dressing down for a business meeting before accusing him of being late. However, when he asks Tony for this favor, Jimmy can barely get the words out: "I want you . . . I, um . . . I want you to endorse me . . . for . . . you know what." Before he will endorse Jimmy, however, Tony demands an apology for the "you people" slur all those years ago. "That's what you said, right Jim? 'You people.' Am I beneath you?" asks Tony. "Definitely," responds Jimmy. As their pals attempt to laugh it off, Jimmy doubles down. "Who the fuck are you to apologize to?" at which Tony makes to leave. He is coaxed back to the table to await Jimmy's apology. The union man, however, simply sits in silence, thinking. He cracks wise about the altercation and brings a smile from Tony. But just as the meeting appears to have been saved, Jimmy responds thus: "I'll apologize for it, *after* you apologize for being late," adding, "you motherfucking *wop* cocksucker." (To which Tony rages, "I'll apologize for being late after I kidnap your granddaughter, rip her guts out, and send them to you in a *fuckin'* envelope!") The second scene ends as the first did, with the pair brawling on the floor.

In her *Guide to Excruciatingly Correct Behavior*, Judith Martin gives four examples of what she calls "etiquette orders." " 'I want you to apologize right now' and 'Don't speak to your father that way' and 'Do you consider yourself properly dressed?' and 'I would appreciate it if you would show more respect' " (16). One can tick each one off as they appear in these two scenes from *The Irishman*. The etiquette orders become impossible not just because Jimmy and Tony are adults (hence cannot be ordered to obey the parental authority who teaches manners), but because unlike the child, who is like a malleable material being shaped by etiquette, each man regards the other as beneath him—beneath etiquette. Here, we have the difference between "People Who Should Know Better" (as in the professional who knows but disregards the rules), and "People Like That," as in the slur, "What can you expect of People Like That?" Treated like children, such "people" tend not to be the downtrodden, Martin points out, but "the newly rich" (21). What Jimmy Hoffa hates is the ascendancy of the Italian Americans. Unlike Nikki and Clifford, Jimmy uses the ethnic slur despite himself. He cannot resist it.

We are vulnerable in language, claims Judith Butler in *Excitable Speech*. But that vulnerability is not straightforward. "We ascribe an agency to language, a power to injure, and position ourselves as the objects of its injurious trajectory" (1). And if language can injure our sense of self, that self must have been (at least partly) constructed *by* language, reasons Butler. If so, its formative power preceded and conditioned any decision we might have made about it, "insulting us from the start," as it were (2). We have already been called a name, are called into being by a prior act of naming. Hence, to be insulted now, calls up that condition of being constituted in language (what Louis Althusser called "interpellation"). Which are the words that wound? Beyond the words themselves (those that are "uttered, utterable, and explicit"), linguistic injury is also sustained by the "mode of address." "One is not simply fixed by the name that one is called," writes Butler. "In being called an injurious name, one is derogated and demeaned" but at the same time one is "given a certain possibility for social existence, initiated into a temporal life of language. . . . Thus the injurious address may appear to fix or paralyze the one it hails, but it may also produce an unexpected and enabling response" (2).

Jimmy's problem is that if he doesn't make clear his injurious intentions with the "you people" comment, he cannot interpret Tony's intentions (was he simply running late, or saying "fuck you"?). It matters because there is not room enough for both men in their political struggle, hence their language game is a zero-sum game. The effect of Jimmy's words is intended to "hit the gut," as Mari J. Matsuda puts it (qtd. in Butler 75), since "hate speech is understood not only to communicate an offensive idea or set of ideas but also to enact the very message it communicates: the very communication is at once a form of conduct" (Butler 72). For Jimmy, "you people" both proclaims the inferiority of Italian Americans and effects their subordination. However, the line demarcating "speakable" from "unspeakable" words instantiates, Butler writes, "the current boundaries of the social" (121). This circumscription is the work of etiquette. Ethnic slurs are "unspeakable" only because they have been put beyond the pale. But what if, rather than immobilizing the addressee (as slight, as injury, even as offense), speaking the unspeakable constitutes the very "act" that "outs" the speaker as an agent making a clear, unambiguous, choice (129)? Butler stresses the potential subversiveness of such speech, for it informs the "influential rituals by which subjects are formed and reformulated" (160). Therefore, to "speak one's worst" can, paradoxically, counter-mobilize those excluded in a political system, as these scenes in Scorsese's films dramatize.

∼

In each of the examples in this chapter, we have what Trent H. Hamann describes as the function of etiquette "to operate as an important set of techniques through which individuals actively participate in the social constitution of themselves as subjects living within complex relations of power—what Foucault calls 'technologies of the self'" (61). As such, Hamann claims, they constitute an "ethics." The point is worth emphasizing, because as Ron Scapp and Brian Seitz argue, manners tend not to be seen on a par with their more dignified sibling, morals (and correspondingly, etiquette with ethics)—but they should be. Manners are "vital" in every sense of the word. The mere style in which one says "hello," Scapp and Seitz write, "may initiate patterns of inclusion and exclusion, distance and intimacy, as we negotiate all of the names we have for each other, whether names of respect or of flattery, names of love and of optimistic expectations, hospitable names, the names by which we address our hosts, names of disdain or derision, even the insults we hurl at those who have offended us" (3). To remove manners from the frame by which we seek to consider how we treat one another does nothing less than strip from that frame the "flesh" with which we communicate our intentions, good or bad. "Etiquette is about the execution and performance of those opportunities for consideration of the other," Scapp and Seitz continue, "whether stranger or friend, that emerge in everyday lived experience." As such, public etiquette "duly acknowledges the existence and necessity of boundaries while negotiating, respectfully traversing, and even transforming the conditions that allow one to become presentable, and thus allow one to extend oneself to the world" (5). When we proceed without etiquette, or else abuse it, that "small world" can quickly become a claustrophobic, crowded, torturous place to live.

2

Home Invasions

Hospitality

> Whatever possessed you to ask these people to your horrible house.
> —Emily Post, *Etiquette*

∽

THE TORTUROUS ETIQUETTES explored in Chapter 1 hinge on the problem of sharing municipal spaces to which different members of the public are entitled to make claims. Within those spaces, rules and manners ensuring cohabitation are easily violated for any number of reasons . . . unintentionally, prejudicially, maliciously, and so on. As such, certain structural issues materialize in and through one's use of a space. However, such structures shift in emphasis when we turn to look at the problem of hospitality. Judith Still observes that hospitality is, by definition, a structure regulating relations between inside (private) and outside (public) in a manner that changes the conditions of our sharing a space with others (11). Hospitality is not merely offering someone a glass of water or a bed for the night; it depends on the relation between the "host" who offers and the "guest" who accepts (or refuses) it. If the guest joins the household—that is, makes it their home—we cease to be in a situation involving hospitality. The host occupies a space that is more concretely "theirs." It is a space in which "home rules" apply. When entering a private space, then, a guest brings the outside in. The public comes into the private. Hospitality marks the principles underlying this process of crossing a threshold. Much is at stake here, argues Still, for no guest can make a claim on a private space that doesn't belong to them, yet this is precisely what hospitality extends. Sentiments like "*Mi casa, su casa*" (literally, "my house is your house") or "make yourself at home" don't take much stress-testing before they break. Your house is not, it turns out, my house. I cannot behave exactly as I want in it.

The paradox of "hospitality" constitutes one of Jacques Derrida's famous "undecidables." One cannot maintain control over one's home *and* extend unqualified hospitality to one's guests. Drawing on Derrida, Karin Wagner notes that "for there to be hospitality, there must be a door. But if there is a door, there is no longer hospitality," since a door implies a key, and a key implies that a guest remains an outsider (26). Derrida makes a distinction between being invited into another person's home, meaning guests are expected (and prepared for), and a "visitation" in which guests arrive unannounced, and thus are unexpected. Wagner writes that the "absolute guest" is one for whom there is no "horizon of expectation," no imposition at all. If they burst in on my privacy and unsettle the boundaries of my intimate space, it must be accepted, *tout court*.

The same paradox is found in etiquette. Emily Post wrote that "the entrance of the outsider"—meaning low-born or vulgar—into what she called "best society" requires them to climb a path that is "steeper and longer because there is an outer gate of reputation called 'They are not people of any position' which is difficult to unlatch" (70). For such people, rattling the gates will not unlock them any more than plaintively peering in. If she "has not the key of birth," Post concluded, then gaining entry to high society is a matter of "study to make herself eligible" (70). But once inside, does the outsider truly become an insider, no different to those born with "poise" ("position") in the architecture of high society, or do they remain a trespasser, tolerated as one tolerates the uninvited guest? And what if the outsider refuses to make themselves eligible (by reading Post);

what if they simply turn up (bypassing the gates altogether)? When Post discusses hospitality, she calls this "descending on a house," and it is considered the height of rudeness.

Hostile hospitality blends these two thoughts and exposes the etymological tortures at the heart of bringing the outsider in. For instance, the word "guest," *hostis*, links both "stranger" and "enemy." Likewise, "hospitality," *hospitāre* (to receive a stranger as a guest), shares a root with *hospes*, from which "hostage" is also derived. This sense is reflected in the opposite of the torturous guest: the overbearing host. Jonathan Swift complained of such a host, in whose presence "a man must reckon upon passing an hour without doing any one thing he has a mind to, unless he will be so hardy as to break through all the settled decorum of the family." At their most tyrannical, Swift grumbled, an honest gentleman might find himself kept for days against his will in the home of friends who, doubtlessly well intentioned, insist on "hiding his boots, locking up the stable, and other contrivances of the like nature . . . as if the whole family had entered into a combination to torment him" (34–35). Taken to the extreme, we find another etymological root for this type of torture: *hostis* also yields *hostia*, which refers to the expiatory victim offered to the gods—*a sacrifice*.

There are so many examples of this. In Darren Aronofsky's *Mother!* (2017), a stranger (Ed Harris) appears at the door of a young woman, Veronica (Jennifer Lawrence), and her husband (Javier Bardem), having mistaken their home for a guest house. Without asking his wife, the husband invites the man to stay. The stranger is apparently without grace, as he proves when he lights up a cigarette indoors without asking. When Veronica delicately observes, "We don't smoke," the stranger misses the hint, replying, "Good for you." "We don't smoke . . . *in the house*," she clarifies. He huffily flicks the offending smoke out the door, but Veronica later finds an ashtray brimming with dog ends (indignant, Veronica petulantly flicks the stranger's lighter behind a chest of drawers). Eventually, the stranger leaves, but soon returns with his wife (Michelle Pfeiffer)—who is even worse. "Why don't you have kids?" she drunkenly blurts out during a meal. "Then you can create something together," she remarks. "This," she gestures to the house that Veronica is painstakingly renovating, "this is all just . . . setting." Between them, the guests terrorize Veronica while her husband blithely ignores them (either because their behavior doesn't affect him or because he doesn't see it). It is, as Nick Pinkerton puts it, "a kind of death-by-a-thousand-impositions," not unlike Eugène Ionesco's *The New Tenant* (1953) or Roman Polanski's "apartment" trilogy.

This chapter begins by looking at the guests, strangers, and villains who abuse hospitality as an overture to a more comprehensive invasion of the family home (*Mother!* ends with a surreal invasion by hordes of cultlike barbarians, who destroy everything Veronica has been building, including her newborn child). The chapter ends by also thinking about hostile hosts, whose dominance in the hospitality dynamic affords them the power to subject the hateful stranger to torture justified by their initiatory breach of the inner sanctum of the home—which, as the chapter will show, can be seen as an extension of the self in its privacy, a self that contains our deepest desires, desires that are disturbed and perhaps violated by the arrival of the impudent outsider.

Rooms within Rooms: *Romeo and Juliet* and *Beguiled*

In Franco Zeffirelli's *Romeo and Juliet* (1968), the ever-irascible Tybalt (Michael York) is horrified when among the masked guests at a lavish party for the Capulets, he notices one of his family's sworn enemies, Romeo Montague (Leonard Whiting), among the revelers. He explodes, rushing to his uncle, Lord Capulet (Paul Hardwick), to beg permission to kill the interloper, come to "fleer and scorn at our solemnity." However, Lord Capulet is unmoved. He registers Romeo and generously remarks on his reputation as "a courtly gentleman, and to say truth," Capulet adds, "Verona brags of him to be a virtuous and well-managed youth." He instructs Tybalt to "have patience, take no note of him!" Bitterly disappointed, Tybalt reluctantly withdraws. The dancing and merriment continue. Unaware of the drama surrounding his presence at the party, Romeo joins the Morisco dance having espied Juliet (Olivia Hussey) from afar (this, his pretext to get close to her). The rage in Tybalt's eyes blazes. He scowls at this "villainous guest" from the periphery until, able to contain his rage no longer, he returns to his uncle to renew his *cri de coeur* ("'tis a shame!" he cries). Capulet loses his patience, snarling that Tybalt is a "saucy boy!" before accusing him of wishing to "make a mutiny amongst *my* guests. Am *I* the master here or you?" Tybalt will not, however, be calmed. "I will *not* endure him!" he fumes, at which Capulet bellows that Romeo "*shall* be endured . . . or I know what!" Both men are silenced, however, by the arrival of Lady Capulet (Natasha Parry), whose sharp castigating gaze brings both of these saucy boys to heel. Having restored a semblance of order, Lady Capulet casts a calm, smiling gaze around the room as Zeffirelli (and editor Reginald Mills) cut to the faces of elderly onlookers (nosily enjoying the quarrel). Still smiling, Lady Capulet saunters over to Tybalt. "You're a . . . *princox*," she chides under her breath. "Be quiet, or . . ." (she leaves the threat unspoken). Finally put in his place, Tybalt ruefully trudges off as Lady Capulet smiles again for the benefit of the eager spectators before moving elegantly to her husband, his head bowed. She hisses at him: "For shame, I'll make you *quiet*!" She turns back to the dance, but not before refixing her scowl to that previous, warm, smile.

"To be courteously polite, and yet keep one's walls up is a thing every thoroughbred person knows how to do," wrote Emily Post. "A well-bred person always lives within the walls of his personal reserve, a vulgarian has no walls—or at least none that do not collapse at the slightest touch" (154). In this scene, Lady Capulet keeps her walls up, while Tybalt—the vulgarian—has none. But Lord Capulet is the one whose walls "collapse at the slightest touch." There are layers to the performance management of each character. In Tybalt, we have the epitome of the tension of the adolescent, young enough to throw a childish tantrum but old enough to know better. He is not indifferent to social form (he does, after all, beg his uncle's permission to tackle Romeo), but he cannot contain his contempt. Zeffirelli cuts from the film Tybalt's ominous final lines in the scene:

> Patience perforce, with wilful choler meeting,
> Makes my flesh tremble in their different greeting:
> I will withdraw, but this intrusion shall
> Now seeming sweet, convert to bitt'rest gall. (1.5.87–90)[1]

Instead, we *see* Tybalt meet "wilful choler" with "patience perforce" in the contorted expressed on Michael York's face.

In Lord Capulet, we have the master of the house, whose own decree that no blood will be spilled at his party is complex. He partly has the prince's decree ringing in his ears (following an earlier skirmish between the Montagues and Capulets, the Prince of Verona had warned that a cessation of hostilities must be observed, "on pain of torture"). He also wants to keep order in his own house and is pacified by Romeo's good reputation. But he, too, breaks form. By refusing to accept Capulet's decree, Tybalt implicitly challenges his uncle's authority (in addition to which most versions of *Romeo and Juliet* imply incestuous desires between Tybalt and Lady Capulet who, like Juliet, married young). Paul Hardwick plays Capulet as a man similarly prone to changing moods. His beneficence soon sours as he growls at Tybalt's impudence before exploding at the mutinous "saucy boy."

But it is in Lady Capulet that dissemblance is truly maintained and the management of decorum exercised. We see this in Natasha Parry's reassuring smile, which she can turn on and off at will. As she moves from the main party room into this side room (where the boys quarrel), she moves into a domain over which she must regain control. As Romeo falls in love with Juliet in the main room, different passions rage in this side space (which is not exactly a separate room, but a curtained-off area). The management of one's internal feelings and their outward expression proves critical in Zeffirelli's adaptation. Discomposure threatens the maintenance of social form (note that the word "shame" alone is used by both Tybalt and Lady Capulet to refer to two different threats to the party—the presence of Romeo for the former, and the squabbling men for the latter). Romeo himself, the masked stranger, is the "breathing breach of etiquette," to borrow Kenneth J. Saltman's phrase (41). He is the source of this discomposure and yet, ironically, it is he for whom the stars have momentarily aligned (only later will they "cross"). What threatens Tybalt is, first, Romeo's presence ("this by his *voice* should be a Montague," he sneers—indicating not only that Romeo is offensive because he is a Montague, but because of the way Montagues speak, for their social class). But more than that, it is his desire that enrages Tybalt, the look of desire in Romeo's eyes. It is wrong to deduce that Tybalt is enraged at Romeo's choice of desired object (Juliet, that is, his cousin), for he has no idea that this is who Romeo has seen. For Tybalt, the threat to the stability of their "house" is first the stranger's presence, then his desire.

The same idea resonates in Sofia Coppola's *The Beguiled* (2017) in an even more complex way. In rural Virginia in 1864, a young student at an all-female seminary, Amy (Oona Laurence), is out in the woods collecting mushrooms for dinner. As she listens to the sound of guns booming from the Civil War raging in the distance, she is distracted by a badly wounded soldier (Colin Farrell) wearing the colors of the Union Army. She offers to take him to safety, and he gratefully accepts. When Amy presents the soldier to her teachers at the seminary, they are understandably wary. The matriarch of the school, Martha (Nicole Kidman), gathers and loads a pistol after treating and dressing the soldier's wounds, and warns the students to keep away from him. She is aided in her teachings by Miss Edwina (Kirsten Dunst), an exemplary teacher who takes her duties too seriously. When the soldier wakes up, he offers his name, Corporal John McBurney, and insists he is not an ideologue—and will pose no threat when his strength returns. What he misses, he says, is home and all he wants now is to survive the war.

As trust begins to develop around McBurney, so does intrigue. Martha insists on formalities, calling him "Corporal McBurney" even when he asks to be called John. She coldly reminds him that he is "not a guest here" but a "most unwelcome visitor." Having initially resolved to turn him over to the Confederate Army, however, Martha softens and agrees to let him leave as soon as he is able. At dinner one night, Martha asks the students what they can learn from McBurney's presence. One of the adolescent students, Alicia (Elle Fanning), ironically describes him as a "dangerous enemy" before passing a sexual innuendo. A younger student, Janey (Angourie Rice), regards him as a hateful enemy—a reminder of the brutal conflict that has raged for over three years. In response, Miss Edwina reflects on how polite and considerate McBurney has been and regards him as a pleasant reminder of the outside world. Over a little time, these early responses to McBurney evolve into different relationships with him. For the pre-adolescent children, he becomes a paternal figure to impress with their budding skills (musical, culinary, and the like). The sexually precocious Alicia, however, takes to secretly flirting with McBurney in his room as he convalesces (and while not exactly reciprocating, his warm manner is far from discouraging). Edwina, too, secretly bares her soul to McBurney, telling him that she yearns to be taken from this place to see the world (implying he is the man to take her), lest her cake remain dough. Finally, we have Martha, who has lost her husband and misses a man's embrace. She remains aloof, (too) stiffly formal, and by far the most conflicted by McBurney's presence. In a powerful scene, Martha gives an unconscious McBurney a bed bath. As she runs a sponge over his naked torso, her hand begins to slow as she reaches his groin (covered by a towel). Embarrassed by her own arousal, she perfunctorily finishes and scampers off. The next time she sees him, Martha asks McBurney to leave the seminary.

In an apparent attempt to stave off leaving, McBurney nurtures relationships with each of the women and children, playing off their individual desires and insecurities. When Alisha learns of his impending departure, she responds that they will "have to make it so *pleasant* for him that he won't even consider leaving," adding that they should invite him to dinner, to "show him some *real* Southern hospitality"—a barely disguised double entendre. Desperate to leave with him, Edwina privately declares her love for McBurney, and he affirms his for her, promising she can go with him. At the farewell dinner, McBurney is the guest of honor and finds everyone around the table competing for his attention. He plays them all. Is this bare survivalism on his part, or does he get a kick from all this female attention? Either way, he has a knack for manipulation (blending charm with courtesy). At the end of the dinner, Martha declares that McBurney has taught them all a lesson in humility: the homogenous "enemy" is also a human "individual." She dismisses the girls (who shoot daggers) as well as Miss Edwina (who looks disappointed) and offers a whiskey to McBurney. They bond and he offers to stay and help tend the land. "Tell me to 'stay,' he asks. *No*, tell me I'm 'welcome.'" Martha beams, and stay on he does. For a time all is well, until one night the dream collapses.

An urgent undefinable sound (of a struggle?) wakes Miss Edwina, who hastens up to the girls' rooms. She bursts in on McBurney screwing Alisha. In her shock, Edwina screams and McBurney rushes from the room to explain, at which Edwina instinctively pushes him away. He falls down the stairs and breaks his leg. Miss Martha arrives in shock and incomprehension. She quickly assesses his wound and decides to amputate the leg before it infects. When he wakes, McBurney screams in horror and rage as the girls take cover. "You vengeful bitches!" he hollers from within his locked room. A little time passes and McBurney's bitterness grows. He accuses Edwina and Martha of acting out of spite because he had visited Alisha's room that night instead of theirs. McBurney presses Alisha to unlock his door. When she consents, he steals Martha's gun and terrifies them all with murderous threats. To pacify him, Edwina offers herself to McBurney and he aggressively fucks her. Afterward, Edwina tearfully restates her desire to leave with him.

Desperate to be rid of the now pugnacious McBurney, Martha consents when one of the students suggests that Amy returns to the woods to pick the kind of mushrooms from which she is usually forbidden—that is, toxic ones. (The scene recalls the arsenic-laced sugar sprinkled over blackberries at dinner in Shirley Jackson's novel *We Have Always Lived in the Castle* [1962].) Martha cooks a lavish dinner and they gather around the table to eat. They recite Grace, after which Martha asks if McBurney would like any mushrooms. He would be delighted to, he replies, seemingly keen to atone for his brutish behavior, and the dish is passed from Martha down the line of girls, each one passing the poisoned dish, hand to hand—it marks this as a shared venture, a pact. McBurney generously ladles mushrooms onto his plate and offers them to Edwina, who assents—not privy to the plan. The others exchange nervous glances. How can they dissuade Edwina without alerting McBurney? One of the girls reminds Edwina that she doesn't like mushrooms, and, to their relief, she confirms it and refuses the offer. McBurney ravenously digs in. After eating several mouthfuls, he asks if Amy ("Miss Amy," he politely calls her) picked the mushrooms herself. She nods, trying to conceal her guilt and bury her good conscience. "Delicious," he compliments, before declaring that he plans to stay no longer with them at the seminary. Before he leaves, he adds, he hopes to "make up for all the unfortunate things that happened." Coppola cuts to the girls' hands clasping under the table. Martha engages the girls in small talk as McBurney suddenly begins to struggle for breath. When his throat begins to close, Edwina looks around in panic as her man chokes to death in her horrified arms. She quickly deduces what they have done when she looks up and sees all but Amy has remained calm, holding hands in a show of solidarity. "Miss Amy," Martha prompts, jolting Amy out of her shock, before taking up Martha's outstretched hand (see Figure 2.1).

The film ends with them quietly sewing McBurney's corpse into a shroud and leaving him for the Confederate soldiers to retrieve. Edwina looks on, utterly devastated.

Critical reaction to the film was mixed (as it often is with Coppola). Despite being a fan of her work, Owen Gleiberman gave

Figure 2.1. Communion in *The Beguiled*. Sofia Coppola, Focus Features, 2017. Digital frame enlargement.

a negative review, arguing that while Don Siegel's original film (1971) worked on the strength of the characters and their motivation—especially the "grisly act of symbolic castration" marking a first departure for Clint Eastwood (who played McBurney) from the triumphant hero—Coppola's film was "muddled" regarding character motivation, "coldly ideological and abstract" (110). However, for me this "muddling" is what gives her version its power. In the first half of Coppola's film, McBurney's convalescence elicits from each of the women a passion that finds in the stranger a corresponding ideal object of desire. Yet he is an object that changes according to the light each woman shines upon him. He reflects the young girls' desire for the war to end (and their fathers to return). He reflects Alicia's desire for womanhood, Martha's desire for a husband, and Edwina's desire to escape. But McBurney is not only an object of desire. He is another subject, driven by desires of his own, and when his desire comes into play—and it is a crass, ignoble desire at that (i.e., his transgression with Alicia)—what was "in him, more than him," to paraphrase Lacan, dissolves on contact with reality.[2] As with Lacan's metaphor of a hand reaching for a ripe piece of fruit only to find another hand, reaching back, McBurney capacity to symbolize what the women want in desiring him turns to rot.

Hence, when McBurney (sort of) apologizes for the "unfortunate things" that have happened, we wonder if his murder will poison this community of women. But as each one grasps the hand of another in sisterly solidarity, Coppola conveys the opposite sense. Here is a unity in the renunciation of individual (male) desire in favor of a communal (female) one. By renouncing their individual desires they hope to be returned to the reassuring safety of codified, mannered behaviors and clearcut social mores free from the masculine desires that brought war in the first place. The motivation Gleiberman calls "muddled" is, for me, the very uncertainty that accompanies an unconscious desire that can neither be explained nor integrated into the social conventions governing our collective lives. Hence, despite agreeing substantially with her overall interpretation of the film, I resist Anna Backman Roger's central claim that Coppola's film is less ambiguous than it appears. After describing the sex scene between McBurney and Edwina as one that "obfuscates the boundaries between consent and violation," Rogers then unequivocally interprets it as rape. She says this contributed to her personal reaction to McBurney's demise, which, she recalls, left her feeling "gleeful" (perhaps inappropriately, she adds). Rogers finds in this interpretation a powerful reversal of "the pernicious myths upon which most romantic narratives are based and the psychological mores they harness as a form of control over the female psyche"—not least as expressed in Siegel's original adaptation (n. p.).

For me, however, the film is more powerful still with that ambiguity in play. As with Julia Kristeva's "problem of foreigners"—that is, when the stranger appears like a psychological "symptom," disturbing our composure—it is feminine ambiguity that deconstructs the dominant, decisive, sexual narrative of Siegel's original film. The stranger's appearance is an "invitation," writes Kristeva—not to reify or petrify him, but to analyze him by analyzing us. The stranger teaches us what is strange about our own self. Likewise, the foreigner confronts me with what is already foreign "inside" of me (that is, my ineffable sexual desire). "This by his voice": Colin Farrell speaks with his Irish accent in the film (Irish immigration to the United States being common at the time), and so as well as being a Union solider (that is, a Northman), he is also a migrant.

This confrontation with the unconscious is rooted in the erotic, in the Freudian "uncanny" (unhomeliness), and in a confrontation, ultimately, with death. What is uncanny about McBurney is not that he violates the home per se, but that he morphs that home into myriad, mutually exclusive ideas of what it means to be "at home." By symbolizing what each of the women desires, he invites each to expand the field of her desire—and to name it. "In naming it," wrote Lacan, "the subject creates, brings forth, a new presence in the world" (qtd. in Evans 36), a new idea of home. If welcomed, such a name can be integrated in the home (as occurs with a marriage). But as McBurney names so many desires at the seminary, and as no desire can be finished or satisfied (they go on expanding), this phantasmatic house of mirrors inevitably collapses. Only then does any clarifying choice emerge: either the relationships between these women, or the object of desire itself, must be poisoned. Whether right or wrong—for Coppola, it was mushrooms for McBurney.

Host(age): *Funny Games*

All guests raise a question about desire. Even in the most elementary of scenarios, the question of how to satisfy one's guests is bedeviling. The problem is inherent to etiquette. Often, when one asks one's guest what they would like to drink one receives the reply, "Oh, I'll have whatever you're having," or "I'm easy." Such a response can be insufferable—worse, even, than an overly demanding or fussy request. The situation resonates with the one described by Kristeva, who wrote of the stranger-guest that he "sets the difference within us in its most bewildering shape and presents it as the ultimate condition of our being *with* others" (*Strangers* 192). Should the host take the guest's answer at face value? What if he is just "being polite," and my efforts to make him happy in fact come nowhere close to satisfying or comforting him? For Lacan, this question, "*Che vuoi?*" ("What do you want?" or, as Lacan puts it, "What do you want from me?") amounts to an ethical one. Words become slippery, and intentions are often masked (rather than revealed) by social form.

When Derrida discusses desire, it is with a slightly different thrust. As the master of the house awaits the arrival of the guest, "anxiously on the threshold of her home," she is impatient for the stranger to arrive. As she sees him on the horizon, at the first sight of this guest, she might call out to him: "Enter quickly, as I am afraid of my happiness" (*Of Hospitality* 121–23). Enter quickly, she implores, for "desire is waiting for what does not wait." Enter without waiting, hurry up and come inside, "come within me." "It is *as if*," Derrida wrote, "the stranger or foreigner held the keys," as though the host were the prisoner in her own house; the guest his "liberator" (*Of Hospitality* 123, pronoun altered). It is in this sense that our traditional understanding of the terms of hospitality are reversed: the host becomes a hostage, and the invited guest invites, as it were, their host. Derrida glibly points out that everyone becomes someone else's hostage in this situation, since the stranger (*hostis*) is already a hostage of sorts. Such are the paradoxical laws of hospitality. "One cannot at the same time take and not take, be there and not be there, enter when one is within" (*Of Hospitality* 125). In short, the deceptively simple question, "What do you want?" becomes an impossible demand with no answers. Hence, the guest replies, smilingly, as if he knew what he wanted, and the master of the house relievedly finds herself "at home," in her own house, through the guest effectively taking control, exposing his desire. The situation is—on both sides—somewhat intolerable.

In *Funny Games* (1997), Michael Haneke offers an unbearable meditation on the ethics of the "torture genre" via this Derridean impasse in hospitality. The film targets the pleasure film viewers derive from seeing innocents tortured in "home invasion" films (especially in Hollywood), from Wes Craven's *The Last House on the Left* (1972) to Bryan Bertino's *The Strangers* (2008). Haneke's film especially skewers the "restorative justice" meted out in those films' finales—when the torturers are finally overcome and killed by their victims (often following a momentary lapse on the part of the home invaders, or else some equally implausible *deus ex machina*).

In Haneke's film, an upper-middle-class couple, Anna (Susan Lothar) and Georg (Ulrich Mühe), travel with their son Georgie (Stefan Clapczynski) and pet dog to their lakeside vacation house for a weekend break. However, not long after they arrive, two soft-spoken young men who call themselves Peter (Frank Giering) and Paul (Arno Frisch) arrive, claiming they are guests of the neighbors. At first, they seem friendly and innocent enough, but things take a nasty turn following a neighborly request to borrow some eggs. During an increasingly heated argument (engineered by the visitors), Peter and Paul use physical violence to overpower and psychological manipulation to intimidate and dominate the family. They tie them up and force them to play vicious "funny games" (a euphemism for sadistic torture), and as they play, the boys frequently chide the family for their lapses in manners, effectively for being rude hosts. Soon, in addition to etiquette, the desire to correct the family's rude behavior comes to play a prominent role in the torturous "games," including the moment Paul breaks the "fourth wall" to interrogate us, the viewers, on our own desire to watch this family's unrelenting torment. In effect, Paul accuses us of rudeness, too. By degrees, Haneke turns the screw on our spectatorial position, using and abusing the concept of social grace in relation to hospitality to facilitate a double violation. By acclimatizing us to Peter and Paul's increasingly violent "games," we become complicit (Haneke suggests) in wishing to see the family suffer, secure that by the end of the film the tables will be turned—the torturers will get their just deserts.[3]

I want to focus on the moment Peter and Paul cross the threshold of Anna and Georg's vacation home, a moment that begins not with some violent break in or forced compromise of a boundary, but with a very gentle and courteous request to borrow some eggs. The borrower is Peter, who alone turns up to beg some eggs on behalf of Anna's neighbors, with whom she and Georg are on friendly terms. Anna quickly consents, informing him she has eggs aplenty and can sure spare the six he requires. While Peter waits, he is meek and respectful as he stands just inside the doorway (over the threshold of which he was implicitly invited by Anna's breezy and friendly demeanor). She asks Peter if he would like the eggs wrapped (he declines, piling them instead into his cradling arms). She waves him off and returns to preparing dinner. However, no sooner than Anna turns her back, she hears something splat outside followed by mumbled cursing. Peter returns. "I'm so sorry," he explains, "but I've dropped the eggs." "Oh, well," Anna replies. There is a long pause. "May I have some more," Peter asks (still in a soft, courteous voice emanating from plush pink lips set against cherubic cheeks), recalling from their earlier conversation that she has plenty to spare. Anna is somewhat less charmed by klutzy Peter and bristles at the imprudence of his request for more to replace the ones he has broken. He simply waits, as though utterly insensible to her cooled manner.

But to fetch some more eggs Anna dutifully goes, this time sardonically asking if he would like them wrapped. He misconstrues the inference (she is not asking), and replies, "If you insist." "If *I* insist?" Anna replies, taken aback at the suggestion that it is she who is being difficult. She wraps them and Peter leaves for a second time. With the strange young man gone from the house, Anna bursts with palpable relief, shaking her head with a chuckle to herself. But then we hear a dog bark and yet more commotion outside. Peter returns once more, this time with Paul in tow. Without asking, they cross the threshold into the house to inform Anna that her dog barked at them, causing Peter to drop the replacement eggs. Anna shrugs. Her patience is exhausted. Peter insists, again, that Anna earlier bragged about having eggs aplenty, so, "*please*," he urges, get some more. She simply stares at him, not quite believing the temerity. Something in Peter's polite manner now rings horribly false. Anna refuses, and as Peter entreats her again on the number of eggs she can spare, Paul steps in to accuse Anna's dog of causing the second breakage—it is thus her fault. She does, in fact, *owe* them the eggs. Anna hoots in disbelief and orders them to leave (see Figure 2.2).

But they will not leave. Another awkward silence follows as Anna stands her ground, insisting they go. They remain. Georg arrives and quickly looks bemused at this bizarre impasse, uncertain what to do. While Anna has experienced the slow transformation of Peter's obsequious manner into something insidious and threatening, Georg

Figure 2.2. Testing Thresholds in *Funny Games*. Michael Haneke, Concorde-Castle, Rock/Turner, 1997. Digital frame enlargement.

just sees two innocent-looking, polite, and deferential chaps being confronted by his exasperated-looking and panicked wife. Lacking all context, Georg tries to defuse the situation, asking Anna her reasons for throwing them out. "Just give them the eggs," he says. But she knows something is not right. Now, visibly distressed, Anna simply states, "Maybe I have my reasons." She storms off, leaving the decision to Georg. He apologizes for his wife's behavior and tells the boys that she's clearly not feeling well. He gently ushers Paul and Peter to the door. But Paul holds out his hand. They will leave only on one condition: that Georg fetch their eggs. Now Georg senses that something is awry. He demands that they leave, at which Paul jokes that he will break *Georg's* eggs if he's not careful. Georg instinctively slaps Paul, who responds by picking up one of Georg's golf clubs and breaking one of Georg's legs (eggs).

David Sorfa writes that this scene pushes Derrida's logic on hospitality to the end. Not only must I extend hospitality to the stranger, the "visitor" who arrives unannounced and can demand of me whatever his heart desires, but I must give freely "even to the guest," Sorfa writes, "who will destroy and murder you." The ultimate gesture of hospitality is, then, to knowingly "invite in [to one's home] one's own murderer" (177). Haneke "tortures" this idea by having his villains insist on being courteous throughout the film, even when they are playing their euphemistic "games." After her initial shock and disbelief, the full horror of what is happening to her family dawns on Anna. She asks Peter and Paul to "please stop this." Her use of the word "please" delights Paul, who points out that "it's easier when things are polite." He then apologizes for "before" (breaking Georg's leg) but reasons that "you have to admit Georg, the slap in the face—it really wasn't the most appropriate reaction," to which he adds that "the point of begging for the eggs was degrading." Indicating that they should start afresh, Paul thrusts out his hand to formally introduce himself (Georg declines the offer), and when Anna subsequently breaks one of his "rules," for which they are punished by Peter with a vicious beating (offscreen), Paul sighs: "So much stress for politeness' sake."

That all the violence takes place offscreen in the film is an example of what Catherine Wheatley describes as Haneke's "unseen obscene." The "cinematic unpleasure" in *Funny Games* not only frustrates our pleasure in watching a film like this but mobilizes "a range of 'negative' emotions on the spectator's part, among them discomfort, embarrassment, anger and guilt." Why didn't Anna just say "no"? Why wasn't Georg more heroic (in particular, why did he not trust his wife's distress, even going so far as to apologize on her behalf)? Such displeasure, Wheatley concludes, "calls attention to itself in a way that pleasure does not" because of the "tension between reason and emotion, creating a moment of 'impact' for the viewer" (78). When Anna finds their pet dog dead during a game of "hot or cold," Paul turns to the camera and winks at us, the viewers of Haneke's film, in an inviting gesture that seems to include us in his game, invites us to be "in" on his sick joke—like the sadist whose conversation with his victims is intended not to convince or persuade (and much less to educate) them. Such gestures "demonstrate that reasoning itself is a form of violence," as Deleuze wrote in *Coldness and Cruelty* (18). Paul's "games," as with those of any sadist, demonstrate only the solitude and exceptionality of their author. "The sadistic 'instructor'" is one who makes "quantitative reiterations"—demands—of their victims, wrote Deleuze. Such a figure "stands in contrast to the masochistic 'educator'" (19), whose "qualitative suspense" always puts us on the side of the victim. In Haneke's film, we have the "gathering momentum of repetition," placing us on the side of the torturer and forcing us to "identify with the sadistic hero" (34). The film is unpleasant because it annihilates any desire other than to "see the worst." And rather than switch from one side (the host) to the other (the hostage taker), it forces us to experience the tension in both positions at once.

V. F. Perkins memorably described our experience of watching film as one of sitting in the "self-forgetting darkness" of the cinema, a darkness in which "we attain faceless anonymity, a sort of public privacy, which effectively distances the real world and our actual circumstances" (*Film as Film* 134). The darkened cinema is the "precondition of involvement," he added, of our identification with a subject onscreen. We are "shielded" in that dark space from being too exposed to the disturbing effect of shame at the pleasures film yields. Haneke famously said that those who don't make it through his film—who walked out of screenings in disgust—didn't need it. But for those who stayed to the end—and especially those who got angry at him for letting Peter and Paul butcher this family without being punished for it—Haneke was scathing. Their displeasure was rooted in a disavowed desire—a disavowal Haneke wants us to avow. It is, as Nigel Rees puts it, the "audience member who is drawn out of the anonymity of a darkened auditorium," and who is thus "not being treated considerately." Consideration for the viewer is, Rees adds, "the basis of manners" (160–61). But what *Funny Games* forces us to confront is that which we ordinarily thrust aside to go on watching "home invasion" films: to derive pleasure from suffering. By putting us into the position of Peter and Paul, whose perspectives (one hopes) cannot align with our own moral code, Haneke traduces us. We can only ask, like Anna, "Could you please stop this?" And like Paul, Haneke's response is to ironically point to our manners as viewers, as we go on sitting in the auditorium in hypocritical silence rather than interrupt the film by (rudely) leaving it. This is an example of what Foucault referred to as a "politics of discomfort." Haneke is the sadistic host, and we are his polite guests. As with the paradox of hospitality, Haneke fails in succeeding, fails in such a way that he remade the film, shot-for-shot, in English (2007)—which also failed. Haneke wrote that the only way to make the horror of a torture situation "palpable" is through intensifying repetition and unrelenting duration. "The question is: how do I reach the moment when it starts to hurt?" (qtd. in Grissemann 53)—to hurt *me*?

Frontiers of Shame: *The Girl with the Dragon Tattoo*

> Hospitality, hostility, hostpitality.
>
> —Derrida, *Of Hospitality*

Derrida opens his work on hospitality by pointing out that the guest/stranger/foreigner brings up the "unbearable question," the parricide question. What he calls "absolute hospitality" is the requirement that I open my home up not only to one I recognize but to the "unknown, anonymous other, and that I *give place* to them, that I let them come, that I let them arrive, and take place in the place I offer them, without asking of them either reciprocity (entering into a pact) or even their names" (*Of Hospitality* 25). But the entire point of Derrida's work on hospitality is to show us the limits we place on hospitality and the extent to which "absolute hospitality" is impossible. This is not to say that it should be simply discarded, however. Judith Still criticizes Richard Kearney for arguing that Derrida's "undecidables" paralyze our thinking. For Kearney, an "undecidable" appertains to our incapacity to "differentiate between good and evil aliens, between benign and malign strangers, between saints and psychopaths," hence the stranger must remain "unidentifiable and undecidable" (qtd. in Still 10–11). But Still argues oppositely. Quoting Derrida, she points out that "there would be no decision, in the strong sense of the word, in ethics, in politics, no decision, and thus no responsibility, without the experience of some undecidability." If we aren't wracked with uncertainty over hospitality, any decisions could be simply made by the "application of a programme, the consequence of a premiss or of a matrix" (Derrida, qtd. in Still 11). The same holds true, of course, with any "mechanical" adherence to the rules of etiquette. As with any undecidable, a decision forces a loss.

The point is made in David Fincher's remake of *The Girl with the Dragon Tattoo* (2011). Toward the end of the film, a journalist turned private investigator, Mikael (Daniel Craig), on the trail of a sadistic killer gets a breakthrough in the case. A new prime suspect, Martin Vanger (Stellan Skarsgård), has emerged, but Mikael needs proof. Having dined with Martin several nights earlier at his luxurious hillside property, Mikael decides to snoop around. But when Martin returns home suddenly, the investigator must quickly flee. He grabs a kitchen knife and attempts to hide in the bushes outside. However, he gives himself away by slipping on the steep incline. Recognizing his intruder Martin hails him. "Mikael?" he asks, quite chummily. When Mikael awkwardly presents himself and stutters through an inadequate explanation, Martin responds by warmly inviting him in for tea. Mikael hesitates. His instincts clearly tell him to run. Instead, he accepts the offer. Inside, Martin pours Mikael a scotch and calmly asks for his knife to be returned. The investigator freezes. His options narrow to zero when he spots that Martin has a gun. With no other choice, Mikael is led at gunpoint to a well-secured secret chamber. With his quarry cornered, Martin gasses Mikael into unconsciousness, and when he awakes he finds himself strung up in a sterile, brightly lit room—a cross between a science lab and an abattoir. Completely prone, Mikael resigns himself to the fact that he is to be tortured to death by the sadistic killer he has been pursuing and had (he rues), correctly identified.

But before torturing Mikael, Martin sits comfortably in a chair and points out that he likes to talk to his victims before he hurts them.

He asks Mikael why he didn't trust his instinct to flee: "You knew something was wrong, but you came back into the house. Did I force you? Did I drag you in? No. All I had to do was offer you a drink. It's hard to believe that fear of offending can be stronger than the fear of pain, but you know what, it is." Norbert Elias considered the fear of giving offense one of the crucial developments in the "civilising process." This fear, Elias wrote, arises when "socially undesirable expressions of drives and pleasure are threatened and punished with measures that generate displeasure and anxiety." Such mechanisms set in motion the "frontiers of shame," a "threshold of repugnance," and "standards of affect" (172). Over time, these have resulted in the gradual modification of human behavior—even overriding our basic instinct for self-preservation.

Martin continues to ironize his role as the perfect host by mocking the very "ceremonial behaviors" Mikael was fearful of offending. He admits to being the killer and notes that he picked up where his abusive father left off. But Martin notes a crucial difference: while his father was a "loud and garish man," he is mannered and polite, making it not only easier to evade detection but easier to *conduct* his torturous proclivities. "You can't be a sloppy technician," he confides with some pride. "This takes discipline," he adds while pumping alcohol cleansing gel from a dispenser to sterilize his hands (recalling Laurence Olivier's careful handwashing just prior to torturing Dustin Hoffman in *Marathon Man*). Unlike his father's brutishness, Martin reasons, *his* victims "always come willingly." Then Martin considers the point of view of his victims. "They know it's all over, just like you do. But somehow, they still think they have a chance: 'Maybe if I say the right thing? Maybe if I'm polite? If I cry? If I beg?'" Finally, he places a plastic bag over Mikael's head, constricting his breathing. He asks if it is "too tight to talk," as though concerned about his guest's comfort. When Mikael indicates that it is too tight to breathe, his captor coldly replies, "Good—I'm tired of talking to you." Martin leaves Mikael to suffocate while playing Enya's "Orinoco Flow" over the sound system. The song is a New Age, easy-listening record with vacuous lyrics about "sailing away"—an additional "sonic" torture for Mikael's ears.

Unlike Martin, I don't have any trouble believing that fear of offending can be stronger than the fear of pain. Perhaps it has to do with the fact that I am English (as is Daniel Craig), for, as Ralph

Waldo Emerson once noted, "'Tis in bad taste' is the most formidable word an Englishman can pronounce" (521). Perhaps. But this only takes care of the fear-of-offending side of things. When it comes to the word "pain," Stanley Cavell noted Ludwig Wittgenstein's conjecture that "I cannot know that another man is in pain because I cannot have his pain" (*Must We Mean* 222). On this, Cavell wrote that "the fundamental importance of someone's having pain is *that* he has it" (226), that in looking at his face I see it exhibited. The turn in Cavell's logic pivots on the shift from "knowledge" to "acknowledgement," from which he memorably concluded: "To know you are in pain is to acknowledge it, or to withhold acknowledgement. —I know your pain the way you do." If there is any uncertainty, any "undecidability" in my knowing another's pain (or what they want, for that matter), then proceeding based on that uncertainty is the most human way of proceeding with hospitality. And this, in the most blackly ironic way, is why Martin has enjoyed such success with his abuse of hospitality as a lure for his victims. A psychopath like Martin doesn't experience the uncertainty of not knowing whether another person is in pain. It is not that the psychopath doesn't feel such emotion (as is commonly misconceived), but that he lacks the intuitive capacity to respond feelingly to the exhibition of emotion in others (when they scramble to say the right thing, speak politely, cry, beg, and so on). He is expert at manipulating others' emotional states on account of his aloofness from them, because he sees language itself as instrumental.[4] But this is not really my point. What this little moment demonstrates is that a man like Martin *would* find it surprising that fear of offense outweighs fear of pain. For most of us, however, it is the most normal thing in the world.

Acknowledging Harry: *A Bigger Splash*

Derrida's suggestion that the ultimate guest is the migrant offers a way of reading the torturous hospitality in Luca Guadagnino's *A Bigger Splash* (2015). The film begins when an effusive and garish music promoter, Harry Hawkes (Ralph Fiennes), turns up unannounced at the Italian villa of his old friend (and former flame), Marianne Lane (Tilda Swinton)—an internationally famous British rock star. Marianne is recovering from throat surgery and so cannot speak and had intended to convalesce in the peace and tranquility of her idyllic holiday retreat alongside her reserved and considerate (and much younger) lover, Paul (Matthias Schoenaerts). The arrival (more like a visitation!) of brash Harry demolishes their calm, however, as he crashes in on the couple—dragging with him his reluctant daughter, Penelope (Dakota Johnson)—to make himself at home at their villa. Harry leaves a trail of destruction in his wake. He makes everyone breakfast but leaves the kitchen in a mess. Marianne strains her voice responding to his teasing about her not speaking. He invites guests of his own to their villa without asking permission, and, to top it all, his daughter proves herself arrogant and aloof (albeit in the way most teenagers are). Harry particularly antagonizes Paul. He still desires Marianne, with whom he had enjoyed a passionate and cocaine-fueled relationship ended (the film implies) by his rapacious and overbearing character. Unable to sustain their stormy fling, Harry had introduced Marianne to Paul but now he wants her back. He resents Paul, and so taunts him by filling the fridge with booze (knowing Paul is an alcoholic in recovery) and reminding him often of his and Marianne's former intimacy.

However, unlike the torturous guests and hosts featured in the other examples in this chapter, Harry essentially has a good heart and seems to mean well. But despite this, Paul's blood boils with every imposition. Sensing this frustration, Harry jokingly confronts Paul. "You wish we'd stayed in a hotel," he says. Paul half-heartedly convinces him he is welcome, at which Harry self-deprecatingly speaks the truth: "You *tolerate* me," he says, and Paul struggles to convince him otherwise. Harry won't leave, however, and as he and Paul continue to wind one another up their false bonhomie turns increasingly hostile. Paul allows Penelope to seduce him and Harry attempts to seduce Marianne. Then, when Harry returns blind drunk one night, he picks a fight with Paul beside the swimming pool. As their argument gets heated, they fall in, and in a fit of rage Paul unintentionally drowns Harry. Horrified, he tries resuscitation before leaving Harry floating in the pool for the maid to discover him in the morning. After initially declaring Harry's death an accident on account of his intoxication, the police begin to suspect foul play. Marianne quickly deduces the truth but covers for Paul. The film ends with them being hauled in for questioning but relieved to discover that the police want to pin the blame on the African migrants camped on the outskirts of town.

It is unclear if they believe the migrants to be really responsible or just want a pretext to get rid of people they call "human beings, theoretically."

A Bigger Splash (its title taken from the David Hockney painting of the same name [1967], and its story loosely based on Jacques Deray's *La piscine* [1969]) was greeted with some uncertainty by many critics who struggled to make sense of what it was about. But I think the key to the film lies in the liminal presence of the migrants, who appear at the margins both of this (essentially privileged) community and of the film itself. They appear in four key scenes. First, when Paul and Penelope go on a long walk and contemplate having sex, they are surprised to bump into a crowd of startled migrants who look half-intimidating, half-intimidated by their presence (despite dressing skimpily throughout her stay with Marianne and Paul, Penelope self-consciously covers her bikini under the gaze of the migrants). Second, during a scene at the villa the radio announces the arrival of the migrants and urges locals to be welcoming and understanding. Third, we have the detective's comment about them being "human beings, theoretically," and making it clear he intends to arrest them for Harry's murder—despite having no evidence of their guilt. And fourth, in response to the detective's suggestion, Marianne and Paul both agree that this is the most likely explanation for Harry's demise. "Whenever the 'home' is violated," wrote Derrida, "wherever at any rate *a violation is felt as such*, you can foresee a privatizing and even familialist, by widening the ethnocentric and nationalist, and thus xenophobic circle" (*Of Hospitality* 53, emphasis mine). Hospitality threatens the law, and to protect that law one must kill the stranger. "Anyone who encroaches on my 'at home,'" he continued, "on my power of hospitality, on my sovereignty as host, I start to regard as an undesirable foreigner, and virtually as an enemy. This other becomes a hostile subject and I risk becoming their hostage" (*Of Hospitality* 53–54). In all four of the migrant scenes, their presence in this Italian town (popular with rich tourists) stands metonymically for Harry's uninvited intrusion at Marianne and Paul's villa. Likewise, the strain Harry places on his hosts' hospitality gives the same lie to their pretense of unconditional welcome that the police sergeant's racist blaming of the migrants for Harry's death gives to the official radio announcement urging locals to integrate them into their community. The migrants, like Harry, appear in need of support—support the law is quick to withdraw (subtly, the film appears to suggest the migrants might in fact be refugees).

Perhaps the most memorable scene in *A Bigger Splash* is the moment Ralph Fiennes puts on a Rolling Stones record, *Emotional Rescue* (1980). As the others mope and loll about, Harry searches frantically (as though his life depended on it) through Marianne and Paul's record collection before finding the record. He seizes it and gives a short spiel about one of the Stones' recording sessions to which he contributed percussion. As the needle drops, however, Harry is possessed by the beat—to which he now dances. He is sensual and moves according to his carnal instincts. As he dances alone around the room and sings along to the track, he gradually, one by one, lights up the face of everyone in the room (see Figure 2.3). He moves outside the villa to find his daughter at the pool and brings a smile to her face, too. Finally, Harry stands looking out at the horizon. He flings his arms open and embraces the view, eyes closed, shirt billowing in the wind. It is almost impossible not to love him.

It is also impossible not to find him boorish and irritating. I like the scene because as often as I find myself sympathizing with Paul (who just wants some peace), Harry's graceful movement to this song is elevated. Against the destructiveness of his other carnal passions (for food and drink, for Marianne), and seeming indifference to those

Figure 2.3. Emotional Rescue: Ralph Fiennes in *A Bigger Splash*. Luca Guadagnino, Studio Canal, 2015. Digital frame enlargement.

who suffer for his indulgence in those passions, Harry momentarily exudes "good grace." The scene recalls Karmen MacKendrick's idea that social grace helps us extend our bodies in space, and without it we would struggle to move: "Social grace is a dance with other persons; one sees and one takes the chance to add small pleasures, small beauties to the interpersonal space between. In making the other at ease, perhaps even happy, one draws her toward oneself; one is drawn to her as in invitation to these small graces, these ornaments on what is necessary in interaction" (201). Such a view of grace, notes MacKendrick, makes it not only difficult to know but unknowable (unlike laws, for example, which are finite, despite being voluminous enough to make knowing them all seem impossible). Social grace is unknowable because, unlike the law, it expands and contracts depending on the situation, the persons, and the spaces in which it is performed.

Contrastingly, Harry's general ingratitude—his lack of social grace—marks a kind of impotence in social encounters. His general comportment, as Kevin MacDonald put it in another context, demonstrates that "the vulnerability of the thankless is revealed. For those without grace, nothing is guaranteed, not even a place in the sun—precisely because it is the ungrateful and thankless who demand a guarantee of the absolute right" (166–67). Harry is the living test of Marianne and (especially) Paul's graciousness, of their gratitude to life. Harry represents "the outcome, the last conclusion, of the ungrateful" and "that which does not please us must die, even though we may be very polite as we kill" (169). In other words, had Paul simply told Harry to fuck off, Harry would not have drowned (likewise in *Funny Games*, had Anne simply been rude to Peter and Paul). MacDonald warns that the sacrificial guest is well within his right to turn around to such hostile hosts and declare, "So kill us if you must, if we have offended you, if we stand in your way, if our manners are bad enough to warrant our execution. . . . At least we are resolved to die graciously" (169). The problem is that you, my host, extended to me a freedom I was not supposed to exercise in any way I chose. The freedom of your hospitality was illusory, false, cut through by invisible thresholds never set out, which could not have been set out (lest the illusion burst), but thresholds that nonetheless limited what I could and could not say, should and should not have done. Moreover, these lines are capricious and mutable, and depend on who we are, on what kind of a person I—your guest—am. For a man like Paul, the thresholds of hospitality inhibit his capacity to extend and flex (and dance) his way through the world. For Harry (and for the migrants he synecdochally represents), it means living in a world in which you are abject to those around you without ever quite knowing why. To quote Kristeva, such a world is marked by sinister scheming, and "a terror that dissembles, a hatred that smiles . . . a friend who stabs you" (*Powers of Horror* 4). To extend unconditional welcome to a stranger opens me (and my guest) to the possibility of torture. But to deny that gesture of hospitality is to deny what the ancient Greeks called *xenia* ("guest-friendship")—that which confers on us our dignity and civility, that which makes us truly human in the eyes of others.

3

Crossing the Line

Embarrassment

> Adapt or perish, now as ever, is nature's inexorable imperative.
> —H. G. Wells

∽

WHILE THE HIGH ETIQUETTE of the upper classes can be easy to get wrong, either because the requisite motor skills have yet to be acquired (delicately filleting a fish) or because the etiquette is simply not known (what is the correct means of conveying asparagus to the mouth . . . with fingers or fork?), showing a rudimentary regard for others by acknowledging "basic etiquette" constitutes the essential unit of social conduct. However, to spend even a few minutes of time in the company of others is to see how quickly even general etiquette can become stiflingly formal, precluding rather than facilitating deeper connections with one's companions. It is often more in the breach than the observance of etiquette that a "risky" remark "breaks the ice." This is not to say that such breaches are indecorous, per se; but to avoid causing offense, joshing and banter must be approached in the right way. If not, it can be no less socially fatal than outright rudeness, intended as such.

The mark of true friendship is often tacitly confirmed (and somewhat counterintuitively so) by the ease with which individuals pointedly, and frequently, violate etiquette. The "joking relationship," writes Alfred Radcliffe-Brown, "is by custom permitted, and in some instances required, to tease or make fun of the other, who in turn is required to take no offence." Such relationships feature the "peculiar combination of friendliness and antagonism" and rely on both parties understanding the boundaries within which such remarks must stay (qtd. in Locke 37). There is a time and a place for banter. Certain subjects (including body features or character quirks) might be "on the table," while others are "off limits." One must know how far one can go, and with whom. Though "dogs seem to sense just how hard they can bite," writes John L. Locke, "how do men know that their lexical bites will not draw blood?" (37). Do they notice subtle reactions from the "bitee," prepared to swiftly withdraw at the first sign of distress? A well-known feature of the joking relationship is, by turns, to play up to a remark that has seemingly transgressed the boundary and gone "too far," precisely by *feigning* that offense has been taken. Just as one must be careful about where, when, and how hard one "bites," so too does the bitee risk overstepping the (invisible) line by leaning too far into his or her performance as the "victim" (in both cases, the best solution is to break character, that is to grin, wink, or gesture—indicating that one is still "at play"). Much depends on sensitivity, personality, and social circumstances.

At the heart of this chapter, then, is the vexing question of how and when it is right and proper to briefly drop "airs and graces" to facilitate a closeness usually foreclosed by high etiquette (which keeps us at a distance). The examples in this chapter illustrate the potential successfulness as well as disastrousness of dropping etiquette with a stinging remark intended to momentarily drop the cloak of decorum. In each case, the reader might notice that the examples eventually lead to an education of sorts, a social pedagogy feeding back into etiquette.

Risky Banter in *Gran Torino*

Let us . . . be insulted, whilst we are insultable.

—Ralph Waldo Emerson, "Conduct of Life"

A signal case can be found in Owen Wister's *The Virginian* (1902), which begins with a man from "back East" reflecting on his arrival at a provincial town in Wyoming sometime in the 1880s. As the traveler tremulously disembarks the train, he is quickly captivated by a gang of cowhands struggling (and failing) to rope a stubborn pony in a corral. The colt is suddenly and effortlessly lassoed by a tall man, prompting an awestruck fellow passenger to remark that "that man knows his business" (n.p.). With his luggage lost, stomach rumbling, and senses disorientated, "the Tenderfoot" (as he is later dubbed) is soon distracted by the Tall Man (shortly named "the Virginian") trading facetious verbal blows with an older gentleman. As the Virginian playfully ribs the older man in his "Southern and gentle and drawling" voice, his droll performance elicits surprise in the Tenderfoot—surprise that such a rugged man (described as moving with the "undulations of a tiger, smooth and easy, as if his muscles flowed beneath his skin") could possess such sharp wit. The experience puts the Tenderfoot at ease when he discovers that this Virginian (whom he has been assured is a "trustworthy man") has been hired to accompany him to his destination in the neighboring town.

The Tenderfoot attempts to engage the Virginian in some light banter himself, using the older gentleman (since departed) as a target. But his comment draws a caustic reply. Daunted, the Tenderfoot drops his "method of easiness" and attempts (safer) observational small talk, remarking on the inconvenience of his lost luggage, to which the Virginian gives only short perfunctory replies. He is finally stunned to silence when the Virginian informs him that the nearest town is two hundred and sixty-three miles away and that they must stay the night. Exasperated that this awkward relationship must continue, the Tenderfoot reflects on his faux pas in this strange country (some distance from what he calls the "far shores of civilization") and wonders what caused the Virginian's sudden surliness:

> My questions had not fared excessively well. He did not propose making me dance, to be sure: that would scarcely be trustworthy. But neither did he propose to have me familiar with him. Why was this? What had I done to elicit that veiled and skilful sarcasm about oddities coming in on every train? Having been sent to look after me, he would do so, even carry my valise; but I could not be jocular

> with him. This handsome, ungrammatical son of the soil had set between us the bar of his cold and perfect civility. No polished person could have done it better. What was the matter? (n.p.)

It does not take much understanding of etiquette to identify the "matter" here. For one thing, the Tenderfoot prejudged the Virginian as a man of violence, a man who might make him "dance"—that is, subject him to cruel ridicule by shooting at his feet (something the Tenderfoot undoubtedly would have picked up from popular dime novels sensationalizing the "wild west"). For another, the Virginian's "skilful sarcasm" when responding to the Tenderfoot's attempted lampooning of the older gentleman is a like response to a presumption of familiarity with the latter, to whom he has not yet been introduced (nor could be, since the gentleman had departed). Hence the Virginian's "cold and perfect civility" sets a social bar no "polished" (that is, grammatical!) person could have bettered.

The Tenderfoot realizes his error, and he soon offers a more penetrating (and generous) insight of the Virginian:

> I looked at him, and suddenly it came to me. If he had tried familiarity with me the first two minutes of our acquaintance, I should have resented it; by what right, then, had I tried it with him? It smacked of patronizing: on this occasion he had come off the better gentleman of the two. Here in flesh and blood was a truth which I had long believed in words, but never met before. The creature we call a *gentleman* lies deep in the hearts of thousands that are born without chance to master the outward graces of the type. (n.p.)

What is interesting about this passage is not just how shocked the Tenderfoot is to discover a gentlemanly nature in one he thought "ungrammatical" (that is, unmannered), but, rather, it is the shock of thinking of such a nature as innate—not taught. If the Virginian has any natural skill with manners ("manus"—hands, handling) it is with a lasso and wild ponies, not with people like the Tenderfoot (from the "East"—that is cultured, practically European). How could a man "of the soil" have such civility?

Having blundered in his first impression, the Tenderfoot begins to ingratiate himself by keeping mum and observing the Virginian in his interactions with the locals. First, he is astonished when an innkeeper friendly with the Virginian ends their conversation by calling him a "son of a— [bitch]." The Virginian merely chuckles, prompting the Tenderfoot to suppose that "this wild country spoke a language other than mine—the word here was a term of endearment." However, later that evening he modifies this assessment. A cowpuncher, Trampus, is losing money to the Virginian at cards and so resorts to assuming a past acquaintance (that they don't share). When Trampus suffers yet another costly defeat, he makes a snide comment about "amateurs" before also calling the Virginian a "son of a—." This time, however, the Virginian draws his pistol and calmly lays it on the table. Then, "with a voice as gentle as ever, the voice that sounded almost like a caress," he says: " 'When you call me that, *smile*." Trampus quickly backs down to the relief of all, leaving the Tenderfoot to observe "a new example of the old truth, that the letter means nothing until the spirit gives it life."

The point is perfectly rendered in a scene from *Gran Torino* (2008)—a film that has the DNA of Wister's novel running right through it. The equivalent to the "Virginian" in this film is an elderly war veteran, Walt Kowalski (Clint Eastwood), who against his cantankerous nature decides to take his troubled young neighbor, Thao (Bee Vang)—a Korean American—under his wing. To teach him a lesson about how "guys talk," Walt takes Thao to his local barbershop to observe the way he and his Italian American barber pal, Martin (John Carroll Lynch), trade insults as banter. The extent to which such "talk" is about more than passing the time while the barber cuts hair is made explicit here (no hair is cut in the scene), as is the extent to which their highly specialized talk treads a razor thin line between "play" and "offense."

"Just listen," Walt instructs his tenderfoot before they walk in, to the way "Martin and I batter it back and forth." They enter the shop and Martin sarcastically greets them with offensive racial epithets to which Walt volleys back: "How you doin' Martin, you crazy Italian prick?" "Well, you cheap bastard . . . ," the barber replies, and so on. Eventually, they break off and Walt turns to Thao. "You see, kid? Now *that's* how guys talk to one another." Walt instructs Thao to go on out and reenter, but this time "talk to him [Martin] like a man, like a *real* man." Thao leaves, returns, and with affected bluster says, "What's up, you old Italian prick?" In (mock) anger, Martin aims his shotgun at Thao and irritably warns him to get out of his shop. Walt similarly turns on Thao. "What the hell are you doing, have you lost your mind?!" Confused, Thao bumbles, "but . . . but that's what *you* said! That's what you said men say!" Walt counters. "You don't just come in and insult the man in his own shop. You just don't do that." Thoroughly confused, Thao asks what he should have said, to which Martin and Walt deliver the following instructions, rapid fire:

MARTIN: Why don't you start with 'hi' or 'hello'?

WALT: Yeah, just come in and say, 'Sir, I'd like a haircut if you have the time.'

MARTIN: Yeah, be polite—but don't kiss ass.

WALT: In fact, you could talk about a construction job you just came from, and bitch about your girlfriend and your car.

MARTIN: Erm, 'Son-of-a-bitch, I just got my brakes fixed, and those sons-of-bitches *really* nailed me—they screwed me *right in the ass!*'

WALT: Yeah, don't swear *at* the guy, just talk about people who are not in the room. See, now go out, come back, and talk to him—it ain't rocket science, for Christ's sake!

"Yeah, but I don't have a job, a car, or a girlfriend!" complains Thao, to which Walt frostily responds: "O-kay. I want you to turn around and go outside and come back, and don't talk about having no job, no car, no girlfriend, no future, no dick! Okay?" Thao leaves and returns, this time with brio: "Excuse me sir, I need a haircut if you ain't too busy—you old Italian son-of-a-bitch-prick-barber," to which he adds (with perfect withering sarcasm): "Boy, does my ass hurt from all the guys in my construction job!"

Thao's response constitutes perfect banter for two reasons. First, because he deploys skilfull sarcasm to ironically reflect the ineffability, even the paradoxical nature of barbershop talk from the point of view of the outsider. By volleying back at Walt and Martin a mashup from their own lengthy (and self-contradictory) instructions on "guy talk," he reflects on its exclusionary intentions. But also, Thao has (astutely) grasped that having first entered the shop "cold," and then disastrously reentered it "hot," his relationship with Martin has evolved (just as each encounter with the curmudgeonly Walt has gradually drawn the latter to fill the vacant paternal role in his life). Having been threatened (however mockingly) by Martin for calling him an Italian prick, his recapitulation of the ethnic slur becomes a joke on account of its knowing repetition as such. Faux pas, in this case, marks the gateway to a rite of passage. The scene ends with Walt and Martin roaring with laughter.

In this example from *Gran Torino*, we see reflected the Virginian's warning, "when you call me that, *smile*." They demonstrate a complex truth about etiquette and humor. For if the "cold and perfect civility" of etiquette establishes a bar protecting us from giving and receiving offense to and from others, how then is such a bar to be transgressed? At what point can we risk a formal relationship by evolving it into a bantering one? If true friendship requires a little antagonism, it necessitates a breach in decorum. For those who refrain from risking such a breach, their relationship will retain a degree of obstructive formality. Such a recognition or discovery cannot (as Martin and Walt amply demonstrate) be taught. To borrow E. M. Dadlez's words (written apropos of a different context), Thao's is a "revelation of the causal process that made the outcome inevitable," not in the sense of irony—in which what is said is opposite to what is meant—but in the "realization of the intended rather than the literal meaning" (21). As Wister's Tenderfoot put it, the "letter" of etiquette is nothing without the antithetical joshing "spirit" that gives it life.

Badly Done in *Emma*

> She had the comfort of appearing very polite, while feeling very cross.
>
> —Jane Austen, *Emma*

The notion that virtue must be taught and learned, that it can be easily attained by the young provided they are "well-born" and in possession of a "good nature," has been at the heart of philosophical thinking on manners since Aristotle's *Nicomachean Ethics*. Cynthia Freeland notes the young are especially prone to blunders as they strive to learn and recognize "how to act just so, in the correct situation toward the right person, and for the right reason, in the right way, and so on" (56–57). For her, mistakes are not only inevitable on the path to virtuousness; they are necessary since shame alone can fully inculcate a virtuous disposition (hence, the most devastating parental assessment: "I'm not angry, just disappointed"). Far from indicating a moral failure, the sting of shame in fact demonstrates its educational effect—just as the full habit of virtue comes from discovering the pleasure of virtuousness, so too does shame at one's action imply contrition.[1] The pleasure of doing good is less compelling than fear of disgrace (that is, negative reinforcement). Few adolescents learn to love virtue for its own sake (59). That may be true, writes Freeland, but the Aristotelian lesson is that fear of failure habituates a well-raised youth to develop a *taste* for acting decently in adulthood. Such habits inculcate values, whereas for the adolescent, the pain of humiliation is still required in those unapt to resist the instant gratification of instinctual flashes of narcissistic aggression.

Jane Austen was aware of the role such "internal" learning played in nurturing moral perception. Perhaps the most famous example of the educational effect of shame is experienced by Miss Emma Woodhouse in *Emma* (1815), who, having made a cruel joke at the expense of Miss Bates, is given a dressing down by Mr. Knightley. In Austen's novel, Emma is a whip-smart adolescent in high society, whose qualities (caring, witty, discerning) are counterbalanced by flaws (spoilt, conceited, meddling), leaving her susceptible to moral failure. For instance, Emma's misguided tutelage of an inexperienced friend, Harriet Smith, on the finer points of upper-class manners threatens to spoil the young woman's chance at true love. In vain Emma's old friend, Mr. Knightley, attempts to steer her toward a more virtuous deployment of her considerable talents, but his paternalism inspires her disdain, strengthening her resolve. Most tiresome of all to Emma is Miss Bates—a déclassé widow whose declining social position has not inhibited her capacity to blather on about the beauty and accomplishments of her niece, Jane Fairfax (Emma's rival).

While Emma maintains a polite countenance as she suffers Miss Bates's incessant talk, her inner contempt is publicly vented at Box

Hill—a bucolic beauty spot at which Emma and her companions have gathered on a summer's afternoon to picnic. As the heat saps the mood and threatens to spoil this much-anticipated event, Mr. Churchill (with whom Emma has been flirting) suddenly declares that he is "ordered by Miss Woodhouse" that each person say "either one thing very clever, be it prose or verse, original or repeated—or two things moderately clever—or three things very dull indeed" (255). Miss Bates immediately responds that she ought not to be uneasy about "three things very dull indeed," for "I shall be sure to say three dull things as soon as ever I open my mouth, shan't I?" It is at this moment that Emma "could not resist" a witty barb: "Ah! ma'am, but there may be a difficulty. Pardon me—but you will be limited as to number—only three at once." The moment is devastating for Miss Bates, who, initially "deceived by the mock ceremony" with which the barb had been issued (Emma does say "Pardon me," after all), suddenly registers its hurtful intent. Miss Bates does not show anger at Emma's remark, but "a slight blush showed that it could pain her." Humiliated, she turns to Mr. Knightley: "I will try to hold my tongue," she remarks, somewhat self-pitying. "I must make myself very disagreeable, or she would not have said such a thing to an old friend" (256). As the picnickers depart, Mr. Knightley (taking great care to ensure he is not overheard) scolds Emma for being so unfeeling toward Miss Bates. Emma, too, blushes. Then she apologizes. Then she attempts to laugh it off. Finally, she claims no offense was given since none was received ("I dare say she did not understand me"), before huffily excusing her lapse ("what is good and what is ridiculous are most unfortunately blended in her"). Undeterred, Mr. Knightley insists on highlighting the egregiousness of her remark—

> [Miss Bates] is poor; she has sunk from the comforts she was born to; and, if she live[s] to old age, must probably sink more. Her situation should secure your compassion. It was badly done indeed!—You, whom she had known from an infant, whom she had seen grow up from a period when her notice was an honour, to have you now, in thoughtless spirits, and the pride of the moment, laugh at her, humble her—and before her niece, too—and before others, many of whom (certainly *some*), would be entirely guided by *your* treatment of her. (259)

Mr. Knightley's hard rebuke, writes Mary Poovey, "reminds Emma not only of her current place in the social hierarchy but also of that moment when the notice of any adult—even Miss Bates—was an 'honour' for a child" (403). It is a reminder that positions Emma in two relations to Miss Bates, "first as chronological inferior, then as social superior." It reminds her both of her dependence on and responsibility for other people. As Mr. Knightley storms away, Emma is speechless to respond. "Never had she felt so agitated, mortified, grieved . . . She felt it at her heart. How could she have been so brutal, so cruel to Miss Bates!" (259). The chapter ends with her riding home with tears streaming down her face—tears she does not wipe, "extraordinary as they were" (260).

David Southward writes that with *Emma*, Jane Austen introduced a literary innovation: "a refined technique for describing impression management as it occurs moment by moment . . . in Emma's constant reappraisal of a given situation and her calculated prediction of what effect her words and gestures will have on people" (780). Emma's Box Hill gaffe thus constitutes a considerable lapse in her impression management, whereupon she suffers what Southward considers to be a complex form of embarrassment, resulting in "the confused halting of the social machinery, an awkward lack of direction in speech and behavior, the contagious darting from person to person, in short, the 'little zigzags' of mind looking inward in its sudden self-consciousness and outward as it scurries to rectify the situation" (764–65). This zigzagging has given adapters of the novel much to consider when rendering Emma's blunder onscreen—with varying outcomes.

Prior to the 1990s, David Monaghan accuses Jane Austen's screen adaptors of conforming to the conventions of the "BBC classic drama house style . . . characterized by textual fidelity, solid acting, and use of historically accurate settings and costumes," resulting in "unobtrusive and conservative camera and editing techniques that reflect their creators' unwillingness to rethink Austen's novels in visual terms" (449–50). Such approaches flattened Austen's style, Monaghan complains, shifting between sparseness in emotional description (emphasis on dialogue and superficial expressivity) to more psychological "free indirect style" (focus on Emma's interiority).[2] More recently, however, Austen adaptations have exploited cinema's technological (camera positioning and movement; editing and sound) and performative (body posture and movement; gesture and vocal expression) facilities to render Austen onscreen. As such, subtle variations in the way Emma's Box Hill blunder have been filmed yield differences in how her breach of decorum leaves us to reflect on her, often enigmatic, character. I want to focus on the scene in three versions. First, as it appears in Jim O'Hanlon's comprehensive but inconsistent television miniseries (2009) starring Romola Garai as Emma. Second, in Douglas McGrath's syrupy adaptation (1996) starring Gwyneth Paltrow as Miss Woodhouse. And finally, in Autumn De Wilde's concise but sharp version (2020) with Anya Taylor-Joy in the title role.

O'Hanlon's version (adapted by Sandy Welch) foregrounds Emma's thoughtless immaturity over sneering condescension, emphasized by Garai's gushing delivery of the insult to Miss Bates (Tamsin Greig). Her remark remains witty, of course, but it is spoken with less bite and callousness from Garai's lips—more a breathless reflex or instinctual rejoinder to Miss Bates's claim (to which, in this version, no one so much as chuckles). Having delivered the barb, O'Hanlon does not cut away from Emma, who screws her face up (notably closing her eyes) as she and Mr. Churchill (Rupert Evans) literally fall about laughing. O'Hanlon briefly cuts to Miss Bates struggling to fathom Emma's meaning, then to Mr. Knightley (Jonny Lee Miller) whose curling lip makes evident his distaste. O'Hanlon cuts back to Miss Bates to show the "burst" of humiliation on her face before returning to Emma, whose own face falls as she (finally) registers the frigid atmosphere. While Miss Bates promises to "hold [her] tongue," Emma searches the faces of her companions to fathom why she has blundered. She remains none the wiser as Mrs. Elton (Christina Cole) coldly excuses herself and her husband, to Emma's evident dismay.

In McGrath's version (adapted by McGrath himself), a key shift alters the structure and hence the dynamic of the scene. Whereas O'Hanlon follows Austen in having the sanctimonious Eltons leave after Emma's barb, McGrath has Mrs. Elton (Juliet Stevenson) brusquely announce their departure *prior*—that is, immediately following the suggestion by Mr. Churchill (Ewan McGregor) that they play the game.[3] When Mrs. Elton—who has already proven herself a vulgarian by impolitely referring to Mr. Knightley as, simply, "Knightley"(!)—announces her withdrawal, Paltrow pulls a sour, mocking expression. However, she is rather more insulted when Mr. Elton (Alan Cumming) declares himself too old for such games, adding that "I have nothing to say that could please Miss Woodhouse"—a jibe aimed at Emma's immaturity (Paltrow's expression conveys that Emma is hurt by this remark). Thus, when Miss Bates (Sophie Thompson) speaks up to claim that she will be sure to say three dull things, she breaks an awkward silence in which Emma is distractedly nursing her wounded ego following the Eltons' insults. When she catches Miss Bates mid-prattle, however, Emma's head whips around—her eyes narrow on her prey. As the group warmly chuckle at Miss Bates's self-deprecation, Emma breezily points out that "there may be a difficulty," to which Miss Bates (taking the bait) replies, "Oh, I doubt that. I'm sure I never fail to say things very dull!" The warmth evaporates from Paltrow's face as she coldly retorts, "Yes dear, but you will be limited to number—only *three*." Miss Bates founders as Emma glances at her companions for approval, but her face falls as she (much more quickly than Garai's Emma) grasps that she has erred. McGrath briefly cuts away from Paltrow before cutting to Miss Bates, who slowly processes Emma's meaning.

In these adaptations, Knightley's rebuke that Emma has not acted decently—punctuated by his crushing verdict ("Badly done, Emma!")—is partly ameliorated. Like the child who knows only *that* her remark was cruel but not why (because she has the rules of etiquette memorized by rote only—not yet internalized), Garai's Emma faces Mr. Knightley's rebuke as if recovering from being led astray (Evans's portrayal of Mr. Churchill emphasizes his corrupting influence).[4] Paltrow's Emma, by contrast, turns her face away from Mr. Knightley as he scolds her. The scene seems to turn on Emma's attempt to maintain "face," that is her dignity, before this man she has not yet recognized as her true love. (Correspondingly, while Miller's rebuke in the former is more scathing and paternalistic, Jeremy Northam plays more on Knightley's gentler, romantic frustrations.)

Regarding the role of shame in both scenes, it is worth recalling L. B. Campbell, who wrote that "pride or self-esteem is the condition in which anger takes its rise, vengeance becomes its immediate object, and some slight, real or imagined, is its cause. Anger is folly; anger brings shame in its train. The sequence of passions is pride, anger, revenge, and unless madness clouds the reason altogether, shame" (qtd. in Cavell, *Must We Mean* 264). While Garai's Emma is clearly shallow and prideful, her witticism carries little of the spite of Paltrow's Emma (who substitutes Austen's "pardon me" for the more patronizing "yes dear . . .") and Garai conveys almost no vindictiveness. But if Paltrow's Emma is vengeful, its source is at least partly (arguably largely) aroused by the Eltons. In both versions, Miss Bates is a "soft" target, and Emma's "retaliation" is clearly disproportionate to her garrulousness (irritating though Miss Bates undoubtedly is). Both adaptations seek to mitigate Emma's actions by offering external instigators (Mr. Churchill's perverting agency in the former, the Eltons' sneering smugness in the latter). But in doing so, they arguably diminish the weight of shame Emma experiences at Mr. Knightley's scold. Monaghan might be a little unfair to dismiss Paltrow's Emma as little more than a "spoilt and silly young woman" in a production that prioritizes its "elegant and vital visual surface rather than thematic complexity" (450), but the tears Paltrow's Emma sheds at the end of the scene, while not without provocation, seem correspondingly less "extraordinary" than those described in Austen's novel.

Contrast a third version of the same scene, this time from Autumn De Wilde's *Emma* (adapted by Eleanor Catton), in which Anya Taylor-Joy offers a much less sympathetic protagonist.[5] Taylor-Joy's Emma is dissembling without being superficial; canny without appearing aloof. Her blunder at Box Hill is less calculated than Paltrow's (like Garai's, she responds almost instinctively), but Taylor-Joy's Emma more swiftly registers her error. Catton also retains the structure of Austen's plotting of the scene—that is, the Eltons leave after (and in response to) Emma's humiliation of Miss Bates (Miranda Hart), not before. Hence there is no "external" provocation (invented by McGrath). Taylor-Joy's Emma also seems uneasy at the picnic from the off—distracted, fidgety, even while Mr. Churchill (Callum Turner) flirtatiously sings her praises. Moreover, almost as soon as Emma's witty repartee has left her lips her face seems to crumple—as if her sudden, unprovoked cruelty has shocked even her. It is as if some truth has been "revealed," her mask of civility "slipped." Unlike the unthinking childishness of Garai's Emma, or the misdirected retaliation of Paltrow's, Taylor-Joy's Emma has, in a moment of unintended disinhibition, voiced a deeply held prejudice. That Mr. Weston (Rupert Graves) interrupts the awkward silence that follows her remark to extoll Emma's "perfection" only exacerbates the pain of having her conceited snobbishness exposed.

It is a moment that reminds me of D. W. Harding's famous 1939 essay on Austen's fiction, in which he complained that he had been put off reading the author by the general assessment of her novels as "expressing the gentler virtues of a civilized social order" (378). When he did read them, however, Harding recalled his surprise at finding protagonists like Emma whose contempt for the rising middle classes reflected Austen's own hatred for the people comprising her main readership. Unlike the satirist, Harding claimed—whose exaggeration and distortion of characters like Miss Bates offer up caricatures for didactic purposes—Austen offers no such moralizing. "Her object is not missionary," Harding claimed, "it is the more desperate one of merely finding some mode of existence for her critical attitudes" (380). Figures like Miss Bates might be exaggerated for fun, Harding supposed, but they were in fact the sort of people Austen really detested and feared. Likewise, in a more subtle form, "Emma's personality includes some of the tendencies and qualities that Jane Austen most disliked" (380).[6] One might turn to Austen, Harding concluded, "not for relief and escape but as a formidable ally against things and people which were to her, and still are, hateful" (381).

It is far from my intention in highlighting the differences between these versions of *Emma* to declare De Wilde's the "most faithful" or "accurate" to Austen's novel and character. It is, however, in De Wilde and Catton's version—bolstered by Taylor-Joy's restive performance—that I find an adaptation of *Emma* closest to what Harding memorably described as Austen's "regulated hatred." In terms of etiquette, the differences between the three versions are telling. Garai's Emma is clearly on the path to virtuousness: she appears to be "naturally" decent (because well raised) and knows how to act virtuously. It is for her nascence that she is gaffe prone. Paltrow's Emma is the more "finished" gentlewoman. She understands not just how but also why she must act with virtue. Here, it is her pride that leads to misjudgment: wounded first (by the Eltons), her actions are not without provocation (however misdirected).

Taylor-Joy, however, adds to this Emma something missing from the other two, something George Justice draws attention to apropos of the remark in Austen's novel—given a line of its own: "Emma could not resist." The word "resist," Justice writes, is a transitive verb, hence usually takes a direct object, but "Austen lets it remain unclear what, exactly, in her own mind Emma cannot resist. What else might she not have been able to resist? A penchant for cruelty? Her assertion of youthful spirits? Her frustration with the entire day? Her psychological mastery?" (xxvi). Compare this open question about Emma's unconscious drives with George Toles's writing about the role of humiliation in scenes (abundant in cinema) that open windows onto complex characterization:

> Their structure commonly traces a movement from a scalding exposure (that seems to mark a point of no return) to a partial replenishment of dignity. The hole that has burned open in a character's self-image is usually closed up by a surge of spectator sympathy/identification that has been orchestrated by the director. The camera takes us to the edge of what we can bear to witness of another's writhing in shame, then answers our need for a reprieve, providing some sort of image protection or veiling which we are tempted to regard as our own doing. It is as though our compassion proved the antidote to a character's misery and reclaimed her humanity by warming it in the light of our own. (237–38)

This is the image of shame we get in the final moments of the Box Hill scene in the first two adaptations. Having rebuked Emma, McGrath gently pulls the camera away from Paltrow as Mr. Knightley storms off into the background. The same moment is presented differently by O'Hanlon, who cuts to a gorgeous framing of Garai in long shot to emphasize how alone Emma is in this clearing, suddenly devoid of her companions (O'Hanlon is easily the more painterly of these adaptors). In both, the camera's reestablishment of some distance from Emma permits us, to return to Toles (writing in a different context), "to exchange the accelerated perceptual involvement born of tightening identification or thrilling trespass for a more abstract, arguably freer, activity of contemplation" (239). As McGrath's camera pulls away and O'Hanlon cuts to view Emma at extreme long distance, the effect "widens the field of vision, restores a sense of larger context, and releases the spectator from the moment-to-moment push of keyed-up, hyperbolized details" (239).

By contrast, De Wilde closes in on Emma. She intensifies Mr. Knightley's concentrated glare long after he has departed. In this version, Emma begins to delicately dab her teary face with a handkerchief but is soon overwhelmed by her embarrassment, which has turned to shame. Barely able to breathe, she blurts, "Go!" at her driver before collapsing in her seat. Now, framed by a front-facing close-up, Emma's delicate tears come in heaving, uncontrollable, sobs (her hankie forgotten), her head bowed. The carriage shakes and jolts her away from Box Hill and we go with her, tumbling down the hill (see Figure 3.1).

Here, we have the kind of "transparency" of humiliation Toles described as

> terrifying when one is rendered 'obvious' to others in the wrong way. Filmed images are able to register, with the force of a drill, this kind of transparency, born of the childhood anxiety that nothing is sufficiently yours to keep hidden from a strong, adult gaze. Film regularly retags moments when someone is effectively reduced to a stammer, to dirty, guilt-stained hands, or to a spreading, visible wetness on one's pants or dress. At such times there appears to be no way to stave off any form of censorious scrutiny. Anyone with eyes can see to the bottom of one's soul, and it is a bottom lined with sores, immutably abject. (238)

Emma's lapse in etiquette distances her from Mr. Knightley, but by refusing to withdraw to a contemplative distance at which Emma

Figure 3.1. Anya Taylor-Joy in *Emma*. Autumn de Wilde, Focus Features, 2020. Digital frame enlargement.

might recompose herself, De Wilde distances her from us, too. Julian Hanich writes that "in shame one feels singled out, cut off from but also exposed in front of a—real or imagined—group. As a result, the individual tries to escape the piercing gaze of others by attempting to vanish or to gain renewed access to the group" (195), as in the desire to be "swallowed up by the earth" (a natural extension of humiliation—to be humbled, laid low). In shame one tries to disappear from the castigating gaze of others, beg readmittance to the group, or furiously reject the group altogether. In psychiatry, this is called "splitting" and "projection."

However, Emma remains exposed, her privacy punctured. She can do no more than Mrs. Ramsey does in Virginia Woolf's modernist masterpiece *To the Lighthouse* when her husband makes a hurtful comment. "To rend the thin veils of civilisation so wantonly, so brutally," Mrs. Ramsey reflects, is so "horrible an outrage of human decency that, without replying, dazed and blinded, she bent her head as if to let the pelt of jagged hail, the drench of dirty water, bespatter her unrebuked. There was nothing to be said" (51). In De Wilde's adaptation, Emma meets the full force of Mr. Knightley's accusation—the major turning point in the novel following which Emma undertakes to do and be better. The moment is neither diminished nor excused. We fully experience that shame with her.

Part II

Exchange

4

No Joke

Humor

Laughter naturally results only when consciousness is unawares transferred from great things to small—only when there is what we may call a *descending* incongruity.

—Herbert Spencer, "The Physiology of Laughter"

The only truly safe and proper subject for a joke is oneself.

—Judith Martin, *Miss Manners' Guide to Excruciatingly Correct Behavior*

∼

WHILE THE SUBJECT OF joking was scarcely found in etiquette guides of the Victorian era, their wires crossed often enough to let fly the sparks of indecorousness. Shortly after the appearance in 1842 of Charles William Day's *Hints on Etiquette*, Lewis Carroll published his own *Hints for Etiquette; or, Dining Out Made Easy* (1849), which skewered Day's guide with an impeccable caricature of its form and style (notice Carroll's subtle alteration of the preposition in Day's title). A typical observation from Day's guide instructs us to "eat PEAS with a dessert spoon; and curry also. Tarts and puddings are to be eaten with a *spoon*" (28). With which we can compare Carroll's, rather more understated, version: "We do not recommend the practice of eating cheese with a knife and fork in one hand, and a spoon and wine-glass in the other; there is a kind of awkwardness in the action which no amount of practice can entirely dispel" (91). Carroll's absurdist spearing of etiquette "lands" (as it does in his *Alice* books) because the imitation, as with all good satirical writing, closely apes its target. Carroll needed only (in some cases *very* slightly) to exaggerate the language and expression of the serious guide to parody the form. Moreover, having read Carroll's lampooning (of) etiquette— which also included such observations as "to use a fork with your soup, intimating at the same time to your hostess that you are reserving the spoon for the beefsteaks, is a practice wholly exploded" (90)—it is subsequently difficult to return to Day's solemn observations (the custom of "asking ladies to take wine is now quite exploded" [26]) without finding the latter somewhat "Carrollian." The "rude" satire infects, as it were, the style of its polite target.

In the twentieth century, etiquette manuals loosened up considerably. The famous doyennes of decorum, from Emily Post (1872–1960) to Judith Martin (1938–), are as celebrated for their sharp wit as for their navigation of social form.[1] However, while Post's guide extolled the virtues of the "ready wit" over the boor and the buffoon, nowhere in her book is the subject of "joking" indexed. Nor does it appear in many of the more recent guides, including the latest edition of Debrett's. And while Martin's razor-sharp contributions in *Miss Manners* comprise some of the wittiest statements on present day etiquette, "joking" is indexed only to cover bigoted humor. To put it one way: while etiquette has always been subject to ridicule and is today perhaps best communicated in the form of the ironic riposte, it has astonishingly little to say about the subject of joking itself in social life.

This should surprise us because joking is integral to social form. There are myriad ways to "save the blush" or "smooth the path into 'society'" (as was Day's stated purpose in publishing a book on etiquette in the first place [8]), but few can match the well-executed joke in achieving, sustaining, and indeed sometimes saving social grace. Told in the right context and company (and at the appropriate moment), a joke can shake off social dis-ease, as well as break the ice of cold formality. Comedy can come to the aid of a guest suffering a social faux pas, just as it can rescue a host whose evening threatens to be spoiled by some disaster with the dinner service. At its most fundamental, the joking process is itself social. While something comic can be appreciated alone, noted Freud, a joke must be told to someone else (143).

It turns out that etiquette (politeness) must not only tolerate joking (rudeness) but embrace as central to the social situation that which appears formally to break with it. Nikolas Pappas raises the challenge joking poses for etiquette when it appears in comedic fiction. "If what is laughable turns out to be what violates etiquette, then comedy's subject is and only ought to be rudeness." But "how can judgements grounded in etiquette tolerate systemic rudeness" (13)? Pappas offers a (somewhat satisfying) answer: that "the audience laughs from an elevated position (the laughter is exclusively laughter of ridicule) and thereby puts the rudeness in its place. Comic catharsis calibrates ridicule as tragic catharsis calibrates pity and fear. The norms of social intercourse are saved" (13). As with etiquette, joking (however playful) ultimately involves judgment. By ridiculing the buffoon, audiences are reassured of their own exalted position, thereby reaffirming the social compact. Moreover, their reaction need not be contemptuous—they are as likely to delight in the buffoon's victories as revel in his failures (14). It is a reassurance not limited to comedies. Let us take a rare moment of levity in David's Fincher's otherwise grisly psychological horror film *Seven* (1995)—a moment demonstrating how the comic breach of etiquette can resolve an impasse in social relations.

The film begins with David Mills (Brad Pitt), a homicide detective transferring to a new unit to take over from William Somerset (Morgan Freeman), who is due to retire. Initially, the two men struggle to see eye to eye as each accuses the other of etiquette breaches. For Mills, Somerset's disenchantment with an increasingly immoral society has made him taciturn and uncooperative. For Somerset, Mills's brash idealism is doubly irritating. First, because his heavy-handedness risks exposing them both to a potentially fatal gaffe in the field. Second, because the younger man's hungry idealism highlights Somerset's jaded cynicism.

The deadlock between the two is finally broken when Mills's wife, Tracy (Gwyneth Paltrow), unexpectedly invites Somerset to dinner without her husband's knowledge or consent. Having run out of platitudes and pleasantries, the trio sit in an uncomfortable postprandial silence softened (only slightly) by a jazz record playing in the background. Somerset distractedly folds and refolds his napkin while Mills cradles his chin in his hand as he stares into space, making zero effort to hide his boredom. Tracy, who emanates warm ebullience, seizes on this silence to casually ask Somerset why he isn't married. "Oh, Trace, what the hell . . . ," Mills chides; but Somerset answers—giving no indication that he has taken offense (the impertinence of asking such a question is cushioned by Tracy's doe-eyed sincerity). In the middle of dourly explaining his personality flaws, Somerset abruptly stops talking as a distant rumble intensifies to a violent roar and the entire apartment begins to shake—the needle slips off the vinyl and cutlery slide off the empty plates. Somerset is somewhat reassured that his hosts share neither his concern nor his surprise but simply move to secure their wine glasses on the shuddering table. After exasperatedly explaining that the source of the disturbance is the nearby subway, Mills then proceeds to curse the real estate agent who neglected to mention it when showing them around the place. It is here that Somerset cannot resist making a joke. As the noisy tremors finally cease, Mills and Tracy look embarrassed as their guest wryly comments that this is "the soothing, relaxing, vibrating home, huh?" Fincher cuts to Tracy and Mills awkwardly smiling at the remark before cutting back to Somerset, whose face now struggles to contain an impulse to giggle. "I'm sorry," he gasps, before bursting with laughter (see Figure 4.1). Tracy soon joins in, leaving Mills to sardonically quip that they should both "laugh it up."

Figure 4.1. Morgan Freeman bursts during an awkward evening at the Millses in *Seven*. David Fincher, New Line Cinema, 1995. Digital frame enlargement.

Fincher ends the scene by cutting to a long shot framing all three at the table, the jazz music now accompanying a meal with very real conviviality, contrasting the earlier contrived pretense of it.

This scene proves pivotal in developing Mills's and Somerset's relationship in the film. Much will hinge on these reluctant partners opening up to one another and setting aside their differences, as demonstrated in the next scene (sometime later that same evening) when the detectives collegially discuss their case while drinking beer (this time, when the bothersome train passes by again, neither pays much heed beyond casually grabbing their bottles to avoid spillage). Somerset's joke constitutes a complex violation of etiquette. The train clearly embarrasses Mills and his wife by exposing their naivete at having been fooled by the estate agent's ruse (who never showed them the apartment for more than five minutes at a time). The train has also disturbed Tracy's well-orchestrated evening, emphasized in the soundtrack (the dogs begin barking, the needle slips audibly on the record, the cutlery clatters noisily from the plates of carefully prepared food). Read this way, Somerset's joke can be read as a simple breach of etiquette (indeed, *he* reads it this way, apologizing for the remark and the belly laugh he knows he cannot contain). But the scene doesn't play that way at all. In answer to Tracy's earlier question about his being unmarried, Somerset had (somewhat Eeyorishly) observed that "anyone who spends a significant amount of time with me finds me disagreeable," to which Mills responded, "Very true. Very, very true." But this was not the kind of casual banter expressing intimacy and joshing camaraderie. Somerset's remark expressed a painful truth, even a warning not to get too close, and Mills's retort was all too honest—since he cannot, in fact, wait for Somerset to finally retire and leave him to do the job his own way. Mills's "bantering" comeback confirms Somerset's disagreeableness, breaking the protective irony usually shielding those who engage in such discourse.[2] Mills's refusal to ask questions of Somerset is framed as politeness, when in fact he wields it like a stick to maintain his distance, not to say his aloofness.

By contrast, Somerset's joke (somewhat involuntarily) suspends this dis-abling etiquette. That same Eeyorish voice (well known to audiences from Freeman's famous voiceover work) is now stripped of self-pity. His teasing constitutes real banter. After all, the actual target of his mockery is the situation, not them. The form of the joshing comment mimics the disingenuousness of the real estate agent, spinning what is a fatal flaw in the apartment into a unique selling point ("the soothing, relaxing, vibrating home"). And, in addition to providing the (perfect) cover for their embarrassment, Somerset's laughter finally bonds him to Tracy—who never really takes herself (or the situation) too seriously. (As the film progresses, Somerset will come to be a crucial confidante for Tracy in this unfriendly and alienating city, just as he will prove instrumental to Mills in their investigation of a dangerous serial killer.) So, finally, while Mills puts on a show of having been wounded by the barbed comment, he is, in fact, now playing a social role in the pantomime organized around this breakdown in the frigid decorum. Mills's mocking of Tracy ("I don't know why *you're* laughing") demonstrates his gameness in accepting Somerset's remark, shows no offense was taken, and breaks down the "us-him" dynamic. Moreover, Somerset's mocking of Mills is a mark of acceptance (as a rule, we mock only those we like), and this after all is what Mills craved from the beginning: the recognition and approval of his more experienced colleague.

If Somerset's explosive laughter is the social equivalent of releasing tension in a form that has become stifling, what follows along the tracks is not indecorousness, but a new formalism based on mutual respect occasioned (perhaps only) by a social lapse (in this case, a sort of joke). Hence, joking doesn't necessarily break with etiquette so much as recast it, just as Carroll's "hints for etiquette" reframed Day's "hints on etiquette," arguably leading to the sharper, wittier contemporary form of etiquette writing we see in Post and Martin. To risk a philosophical formulation, one might say that the formal occasion is initially wrapped in its own stifling stricture (that is, it appears "in-itself")—a set of rules one must learn and then apply. From this, however, the trio are freed via a circuit break affording a little ironic reflexivity (the form appears "for-itself," enabling informal play). With a little pliability now introduced into the form of etiquette, formality no longer appears so unaccommodating of the antagonistic personalities of Mills and Somerset. It is on this basis alone that they can proceed with something approaching *savoir faire*.

This chapter is about the use and (increasing) misuse of joking to "soften" the form of etiquette. It focuses on etiquette in the workplace (and working relationships) partly to build on some of the work completed in Chapter 3 on banter and relationships, and partly because professional environments present finely balanced situations for interpersonal relationships. On the one hand, officiousness in business smothers collegiality—it stifles creativity and, ultimately, productivity.³ On the other hand, too much laxity in the workplace can expose workers in ways that damage professional conduct. Clearly, this scene from *Seven* belongs to the former, and, at the risk of oversimplifying matters at this early stage, much can be said to depend on the intentions of the joker. In the examples that follow, I focus on increasingly aggressive forms of hostile joking. Each successive example takes us further and further away from the bonding role that joking can play in the social situation, demonstrating how the "softening up" of the "hard" workplace etiquette can have quite painful—even fatal—costs (although viewers familiar with *Seven* will doubtless recall its ruthlessly macabre ending).

Mistiming in *I Love You Phillip Morris*

The ungracious man is like a story told at the wrong time.

—Ben Sira 20:19 (Revised Standard Version)

As the remark commonly attributed to Mark Twain has it, "Comedy is tragedy plus time" (qtd. in Fox 83). Yet mistiming a joke can quickly turn comedy into torture. Take a scene in *I Love You Phillip Morris* (2009), in which a newly hired office worker, Steven Jay Russell (Jim Carrey), casually sets up a joke for an unwitting colleague, Vera (Maureen Brennan), just as though he were earnestly reporting on his morning's endeavors: "Just got back from my lawyer's office, I asked him 'What's your fee?' He says he charges fifty dollars for three questions, so I asked him, 'Don't you think that's a little expensive?' He said, 'Yes, it is—*now what's your final question?*'" Initially sucked into Steven's casual conveyance of the joke, Vera's concentrating face suddenly brightens as the penny drops—she laughs, offers an appreciative remark ("Oh . . . *lawyers!*"), before turning to a different colleague to share the joke ("Oh, Annie, you gotta hear this . . ."). Steven smiles to himself, then silently withdraws. It is a smile of satisfaction since his joke was intended as an icebreaker, a social offering briefly suspending workplace etiquettes that, by demanding concentration and professionalism, proscribe the "play" Steven's joke invites.

With its benign intention, Steven's joke is an innocent version of what Freud called "tendentious joking," which requires at least three people. The "first person" makes the joke (in this example, Steven), a "second person" serves as the joke's target (the fictitious lawyer), and a "third person" constitutes an audience (here, Vera) (see *Jokes* 100). When the aim of the joke is no longer self-contained—that is, when the object provoking laughter ceases to be the form of the joke itself—it becomes, wrote Freud, "tendentious" (or hostile). Steven's joke is clearly only mildly, if not borderline, "tendentious." After all, any real hostility is ameliorated by the absent (because fabricated) target, the lawyer. Vera's delighted exclamation, "Oh . . . lawyers!" gestures at the joke's real target—the lawyerly means used to extract exorbitant fees, expressed through the (initially concealed) tripartite structure, revealed and registered only at the punchline. As these workers here in this office job clearly have no such means to command such high wages, the joke unites them in their common role as ordinary workers. Quite unselfishly, Steven delights in the way Vera eagerly seeks to pass the joke on, potentially deepening this unity.

However, while he withdraws in satisfaction, we catch the beginning of Vera's retelling of Steven's joke. She evidently lacks Steven's timing and delivery (which is, of course, Carrey's timing and delivery) and, what is worse, begins with the punchline ("There's this lawyer . . . with three questions . . .") compromising the integrity of the joke's structure. While Steven is merely satisfied to have made a connection, Vera's inferior delivery augurs badly for the way this joke will evolve as it passes around the office. Indeed, Steven is subjected in successive scenes to increasingly botched retellings of his joke. The next teller (Jessica Heap) screws up the punchline during a coffee break and must resort to explaining it (and, as any joker knows, if you need to explain a joke . . .). Then, at a company event, yet another employee (Antoni Corone) clutters the joke with trivial details. It falls dead. Worse still, during a round of golf sometime later, a client (Tony Bentley) incorporates racist slurs (the lawyer is now a "Jew lawyer"), stopping Steven in his tracks. Disgusted, he mutters, "Fucking moron" as the client walks away chuckling to himself. This is a classic instance of diminishing returns. Central to the issue here is not just the timing of the joke telling, but the time between retellings: the joke degrades, as if each subsequent version impoverishes the last.

If we look at the joke as a breach of etiquette, however, another dimension to the scene emerges, one underscored by John Requa and Glenn Ficarra's direction (and Thomas J. Nordberg's editing), as well as Jim Carrey's performance. In Vera's first retelling, Carrey smiles as he withdraws despite her botched opening, but in the second retelling in the coffee room, Carrey (central in the frame) begins to show his irritation as he turns to see the witless joker flash a toothy grin (a signal to laugh—which, out of politeness, her colleague does). In the third retelling, Steven is now positioned as the "audience" along with another. As the joker kills the delivery with needless embellishment, Steven turns to give the other receiver an ironic look . . . but finds him eagerly and (apparently earnestly) engrossed. At the punchline, Steven exaggeratedly throws his head back in mock appreciation (a classic Carrey caricature). In the final version, Steven is literally left alone in the shot as the racist joker waltzes offscreen, left unaware that Steven has taken offense. By now the joking structure has become irrelevant, a vehicle for the racist slurs (under cover of "it's only a joke"). The slur becomes the punchline.

As each iteration degrades the joke, Requa and Ficarra take us further and further from spaces governed by workplace etiquette (that is, from office to coffee room, office party to golf course), as if the joke is opening onto increasingly casual, increasingly "backstage" spaces nonetheless still regarded as "workspaces," and thus covered by workplace etiquettes. Correspondingly, but not necessarily consequently, the joke becomes increasingly offensive at each remove, further alienating Steven from rather than bonding him to his new colleagues. The degrading joke also turns increasingly tendentious (that is, in Freud's language, hostile). The suspension of etiquette facilitates and exacerbates its offensiveness. Designed to foster collegial relations, Steven's joke has soured them. His minor etiquette violation has snowballed (beyond his control) into a major one. Suffice it to say, when Steven returns to the official space of the office, he can no longer bear it. Shortly after, he quits and becomes a fraudster.

But looked at another way, might we question Steven's reaction to these witless bunglers? From Shakespeare (*Love's Labour's Lost*):

> A jest's prosperity lies in the ear
> Of him that hears it, never in the tongue
> Of him that makes it. (5.2.849–851)

Why does the "prosperity" of Steven's joke die when he transitions from being the joke's "tongue" to its "ear"? An initial answer is that

Steven loathes bigotry, and this is where his joke ends up. But this would be to overdetermine the scene by the final, racist, iteration (the other jokers are mostly just incompetent). Furthermore, Steven does not call the racist joker a "fucking bigot" but a "fucking moron," which might as easily be applied to his other bungling colleagues. A second answer might emphasize Steven's regret at ceding control of the telling in the first place—his desire to retain the role of the "tongue." A natural performer, he could have protected the sophisticated wordplay and structure, facilitating the joke's "prosperity." That is, his refined joke requires a competent "tongue" to tell it. But Steven seemed happy enough when Vera fumbled the joke early in the scene, and many of Steven's co-workers appeared to enjoy hearing it. No, for me the scene reveals Steven's snobbishness as a receiver, his refinement as an "ear." Having invited his colleagues to loosen up, to drop the formal frigidity of the office etiquette hitherto keeping them at a professional distance, he suddenly discovers his co-workers are irritatingly witless. It is their sudden proximity to him that invites his scorn. His joke is no longer a social gift but a litmus test of sophistication that none have passed.

My reading of Steven's irritation in this scene from *I Love You Phillip Morris*, then, is that it is only partly provoked by his colleagues' lack of facility in joke telling—that is, in telling it exactly as he, Steven, told it (a "failure of the tongue").[4] After all, only Vera heard Steven's virtuoso delivery. Such "natural wits" as Steven (and Carrey) are rare. What is perhaps more irksome to Steven is the dearth of reciprocity among those colleagues also subjected to the botched retellings. In addition to the "failure of the tongue," then, is a corresponding "failure of the ear," detectable both by negative inference in those who laughed (out of politeness or in earnest) at the versions of Steven's joke that were unfunny, and, by positive inference, in those who failed to acknowledge or reciprocate Steven's cues registering ironic detachment or patronizing distance from the bungling joker. Such ironic asides constitute, of course, another form of tendentious codeswitching whose aim is to reposition the joke teller as the new target of humor. Having failed to deliver the joke successfully, those positioning themselves as the "first person" (that is, as joker) cede to the "third persons" (their audience) control of the tendentious humor, exposing themselves as potential targets (that is, as "seconds"). Here, however, Steven's expressions—which again are Carrey's expressions (animated by his famous gurning plasticity)—only register with us, the viewers of the film. Having interrupted workplace etiquette with a joke designed to soften the outer shell of his colleagues' professionalism, Steven discovers no kindred spirits, only an intellectual (and sometimes moral) vacuity. It is unsurprising that none match his facility as a "tongue," but that none share his "ear" does not bode well for a man with Steven's wit surviving in this job. He soon turns his gift for manipulation (which joking, in a sense, is) to commit fraud. In jail, he will meet Phillip Morris (Ewen McGregor), who will become his soulmate. But here, in this early scene, there is no "third" community with whom Steven can bond. Hence, it is he who hardens. His withering retort to the racist, "fucking moron," passes a sneering judgment on the lot of them.

Mis-staging in *Chinatown*

As we have seen, hostile joking looks to establish a bond through shared aggression between joker and receiver at the expense of an imagined (or present) "second person." The other form of tendentious joking described by Freud is obscene joking. Its purpose is to expose this second person to the indecency of a sexual desire arising in the first and witnessed by the third. Smut begins, wrote Freud, when an individual (usually male) expresses a sexual thought directed at an object of desire (usually female), a proposition (he imagines) she will reject.[5] However, with the arrival of the third person (again, usually male), any expectation that the thwarted desire is now confronted by a further obstacle (his presence further precluding transition to the sexual act) is belied: by transforming the obscenity into smut, the obstacle to sexual conquest becomes amusing. This works because smut exposes something private, provoking shame or embarrassment in the desired *object*. The aim of the obscene remark is thus transformed. The (now public) humiliation of the woman satisfies a sadistic component in the male sex drive, bonding the "first" to the "third" person by making moot any refusal on her part (she can only say "no" to the act, she cannot refuse the public exposure brought about by the smut itself).[6]

The hostility of such talk being so evidently indecorous, Freud noted it is only among those he calls "country people or in inns of the humbler sort" that smut is uttered in the presence of its intended object. At "higher social levels," however, "the presence of a woman brings the smut to an end. . . . Only when we rise to a society of a more refined education do the formal conditions for jokes play a part. . . . The greater the discrepancy between what is given directly in the form of smut and what it necessarily calls up in the hearer, the more refined becomes the joke and the higher, too, it may venture to climb into good society" (99–100). Smut can enter high society, then, on one of two conditions. First, the joker can excuse from his audience anyone (especially women) who might feel embarrassed (because "exposed") via conflation with the sexual object of the joke. And second, the joking "envelope" (the form of the joke) can be sophisticated enough to encode the obscenity such that the sexual exposure "takes place," as it were, only inside the imaginations of the receivers (so that any obscenity, and thus any possible offense, can be effectively disavowed). What Freud calls "good society," then, admits the usefulness of obscenity and smut in channeling those frustrated sadistic impulses, only on the basis that any lingering tendentiousness is concealed, either by managing the audience in front of whom the joke is told, or by concealing the smut itself in the joking form.

In *Chinatown* (1974), a smutty joke is ruined by a misjudgment of its staging. In the scene, private detective Jake Gittes (Jack Nicholson) rushes into his office clamoring for his male colleagues (Bruce Glover and Joe Mantell) to hear an obscene joke he is almost bursting with the need to pass on. As well as being racist, it is also crude, so Jake excuses his female secretary (Nandu Hinds) to the "little girl's room" so it will be just him and the fellas (his "third men"). As Jake enthusiastically launches into the joke now, he brushes off his colleagues' urgent but too polite attempts to warn him that in the office behind his back a new, female, client (Faye Dunaway) is waiting. The situation worsens when the joke shifts into lewder territory, and, unbeknownst to Jake, this new client appears behind his back looking distinctly unamused. As the client patiently (and politely) waits for him to finish, Jake is alone in his excitement and seems ignorant of the irreverent mood. Perhaps because of his colleagues' lack of enthusiasm, he lingers over lurid details as if to reel them in (details like "his wife is getting sore as hell!"—at which the client turns her head in embarrassed disgust). As he delivers the punchline and Nicholson bursts into one of his hysterical trademark laughs (as from *Easy Rider*), Jake laughs alone (Figure 4.2).

Figure 4.2. Jack Nicholson misses his audience in *Chinatown*. Roman Polanski, Paramount Pictures, 1974. Digital frame enlargement.

The fact that the joke is now unfunny is irrelevant. The performer, having carefully selected what he judged to be an appreciative (and appropriate) audience—who would ordinarily have cackled anyway—quickly realizes he has misjudged this as a space suitable for smut. The appearance of a woman has transformed a "joke-safe space" into one that is not safe. That the others could see her—and that we could see them seeing her, and see her as they saw her—but not communicate this to Jake is what makes the scene so (excruciatingly) amusing for *us*. While his faux pas has deadened Jake's performance for his male audience, it has enriched Nicholson's performance for us.

The situation worsens as Jake attempts to switch into professional mode to address his new client who is ominously flanked by an officious looking associate. She asks him if they have ever met. He bemusedly responds that they haven't, still struggling with the abrupt switching of codes. Are you quite sure, she presses? Jake says he thinks he would have remembered (clearly attracted to her, Jake still struggles to dispel his smutty thoughts). When she reveals her name is Mrs. Evelyn Cross Mulwray, however, Jake's confidence evaporates. He knows the name well, having been hired by a woman (played by Diane Ladd) purporting to be "Mrs. Mulwray" to take photographs of her supposedly cheating husband. Confronted now by the real Mrs. Mulwray, Jake realizes he had been duped into facilitating a smear campaign against Mr. Mulwray by his business rivals. Evelyn bids the floundering private detective a good day before her lawyer serves him with legal papers. Jake can only turn back to scowl at his colleagues, who, grimacing, simply look down to inspect their shoes.

Jake's personal and professional dignity is stripped bare in successive moves by Evelyn (who is brilliantly played with an accentuated poise and dignity, brushed with haughty contempt, by Faye Dunaway). Recall that smutty jokes call for three people: one who makes the joke (Jake), the object of sexual aggressiveness (here, the imaginary wife in the joke), and the third person (Jake's colleagues). "Every exposure of which we are made the spectator (or the audience in the case of smut) by a third person," wrote Freud, "is equivalent to the exposed person being made comic" (222). Evelyn's appearance behind Jake has the effect of making Jake, himself, the "exposed person": "When we laugh at a refined obscene joke, we are laughing at the same thing that makes a peasant laugh at a coarse piece of smut. In both cases the pleasure springs from the same source. We, however, could never bring ourselves to laugh at the coarse smut; we should feel ashamed or it would seem to us disgusting" (101). Jake is a man who can laugh at coarse smut, but only on the condition that the audience is carefully judged.[7]

This exposure hurts Jake. In the previous scene he nearly came to blows with a rival in a barbershop who accused him of plying an immoral trade. It was from the barber that he heard the joke (to cool him down). Isn't this what humor is—a good punchline aimed at deflating pressure and releasing tension? Freud called it a defense against an ego that *suffers*. In his essay on the "territories of the self," Goffman described the importance to etiquette of "conversational preserve," which means "the right of an individual to exert some control over who can summon him into talk and when he can be summoned; and the right of a set of individuals once engaged in talk to have their circle protected from entrance and overhearing by others" (*Relations* 40). To cut Jake some slack, we might ask why Evelyn allows him to go on exposing himself like this, why she doesn't give him a subtle cue to cut the joke short. Perhaps she is expressing a sadistic impulse of her own, a desire to humiliate the offensive, low-class detective, whom she (at least initially) appears to despise. But we can give the reading one final twist. For Aristotle, what is laughable is the kind of ugliness that causes no pain, or as Pappas puts it, a "minor moral failure" (10). Through no fault of his own, the appearance of Evelyn renders the moral failing less minor. But it also causes Evelyn pain.

Jake's joke about a woman being screwed by a Chinaman is not just racist and sexist, but especially inappropriate because Evelyn (as we later learn in a crucial plot twist), a victim of incest, will be murdered in Chinatown. Like the classic film noir hero, Jake is doomed to fail. However hard he tries he cannot help falling into a vicious circle skewing his otherwise good judgment.

Misunderstanding in *Goodfellas*

The conversation of the ready wit who does not know how to exercise moderation—if not simply to stop—when entertaining others can quickly turn their audience against them simply by failing to gauge when their audience is fulfilled. Such individuals always take one more turn, one "encore" too many. The air of appreciation, as Emily Post put it, no longer rushes from the mouths of the audience but "becomes breath to the nostrils" (56) instead. One can hold too long onto an audience's attention, wearing out applause by returning too many times. Such "stalling" individuals not only induce their audience to hope that the performance they had been enjoying (perhaps a lot) will soon end; they risk turning that audience against the entire performance, corrupting whatever had been good about it. Captivation quickly becomes captivity (leave them "wanting more," as the saying goes). Pappas points out that in Aristotelian terms, mediation treads a fine line between extremes: to "friendliness" as the mean between "obsequiousness" and "churlishness," and "truthfulness" as the mean between "boastfulness" and "false modesty," he adds "the ready wit" as the mean between the "buffoon" and the "boor" (7–8).

The relative "height" of jokester and listener can be relevant. One case in which an audience's "elevated position" is itself exposed and then turned on its head, thereby testing (almost to the limit) Pappas's definition of comic catharsis (while simultaneously threatening to tip into—and indeed playing around with tipping in—a more "tragic" domain involving pity and fear), is Joe Pesci's "Funny Guy" schtick in Martin Scorsese's *Goodfellas* (1990). Pesci is an actor known for being short in stature.[8] He was ruthlessly teased for it in the 1989 sequel to *Lethal Weapon*, in which he played an irritating federal witness who idolizes the hero cops (Mel Gibson and Danny Glover). In *Goodfellas*, Pesci plays Tommy DeVito, a volatile gangster with a reputation for having a short temper often resulting in vicious violence. In one of the most memorable scenes from the film, Tommy turns on the charm to regale a table full of his gangster pals in a nightclub, who rapturously listen as he describes cracking wise with a tough police interrogator. Tommy's tale reinforces not only his tough guy credentials (his ability to keep mum under brutal interrogation) but his bullishness, since between the blows he "broke" his interrogator's "balls," literally adding insult to injury. A real performer, Tommy tells the story like a joke with a set-up ("What's really funny is . . .") and a "call back" (repeating an earlier phrase as a punchline). His anecdote goes like this: a police interrogator confidently predicted Tommy (a "tough guy") would spill the beans about a robbery, to which Tommy told the cop, "Go fuck ya mother," which earned him a beating. Tommy animates his story with cartoon sound effects ("Bing, pow . . ." etc.). He recalls coming to, his interrogator smugly confident the tough guy has been sufficiently "softened up." But Tommy doubled down. "What you doin' here?" he told the cop, "I thought I told you to go *fuck ya mother!*" The table erupts, and Tommy caps his performance off with a self-deprecating remark ("Gee, I wish I was big just once!").

As the laughter dies away, Tommy's good pal Henry Hill (Ray Liotta) wipes tears from his eyes and makes a throwaway comment, "Ahh, you're . . . really funny . . . really funny!" Tommy instantly sucks the mirth from the table, however, by switching codes from jester to interrogator.

TOMMY: What do you mean I'm 'funny'?

HENRY: Er . . . it's funny . . . y'know . . . the story. It's funny, you're a funny guy.

TOMMY: What do you mean? The way I talk? What?

HENRY: . . . It's just . . . you know . . . you're just funny, its . . . you know, the way you tell the story and everything.

TOMMY: Funny how? I mean, what's funny about it?

ANTHONY (another friend): Tommy, no, you got it all wrong . . .

TOMMY: Oh, whoa, Anthony—he's a big boy, he knows what he said. What'd you say? Funny how?

HENRY: . . . Jus' . . . just . . . you know . . . you're . . . funny.

TOMMY: You mean—wait—lemme understand this because, I dunno, maybe it's me and I'm a little fucked up maybe, but I'm funny how? I mean, funny like I'm a clown, I amuse you? I make you laugh? I'm here to fuckin' amuse you? What do you mean funny, funny how, *how* am I funny?

HENRY: . . . I dunno, just . . . you know how you tell the story . . . *what?*

TOMMY: No, no I don't know—*you* said it, *you* said I'm funny. How the *fuck* am I funny? What the *fuck* is so *funny* about *me?* Tell me! Tell me what's funny!

While Liotta stutters and stumbles his way through this exchange (his voice rising in pitch as he defends his good intentions), Pesci almost spits his lines in rapid volleys. His demeanor turns increasingly apoplectic as he shifts between three kinds of "turn" to which Henry can only answer with a stuttering variation on "I dunno, just funny." First, Tommy exaggeratedly feigns misunderstanding (*What do you mean? Maybe I'm fucked up?*). Second, he willfully misinterprets Henry's comment to infer malicious intent (*You mean the way I talk? Funny like I'm a clown*). And third, he elevates Henry's status to aggravate the offense (*I'm here to fuckin' amuse you? You said it!*). Just as Tommy seems on the verge of doing violence to Henry, the tension of the longest pause in the exchange is interrupted by Henry himself, who, finally catching on that Tommy is winding him up, collapses, gasping, "Get the fuck outta here, Tommy!" Tommy cracks a wide smile to confirm he was joking, and, with the tension cut, he returns to the man of wit ("You motherfucker! I almost had you!" he jostles). With palpable relief, the entire table bursts with more laughter and the bonhomie atmosphere is (at least on the surface) restored.

The key to this shtick is connected to Tommy's earlier joke about the police, particularly that final line, "Gee, I wish I was big just once." Such self-deprecation is on the one hand calculated to offset the braggadocio of his story, but on the other suggests Tommy suffers from an acute inferiority complex—confirmed when, later on in the film, Tommy violently murders a "Made" mafioso, Billy Batts (Frank Vincent), for "breaking his balls" in a bar. Moreover, when his pal Anthony attempts to pour oil on troubled waters, Tommy responds that Henry can speak for himself because he is a "*big boy*." Tommy, we suspect, can make but not take a joke. In another scene from later in the film, a well-respected young bartender (Michael Imperioli) is gunned down by Tommy for telling him to go fuck himself, which, as the above dialogue confirms, is a sentiment often expressed between these men. Respect is crucial for Tommy; but knowing when one can and cannot crack a joke at his expense is about more than timing (as in *I Love You*) or knowing one's audience (as in *Chinatown*). With Tommy, a joke might make him laugh or get you killed, just as refusing to engage in his banter can likewise place one at either end of these extremes. Tommy "tortures" the gangster code that, aside from being about who one can and cannot kill, is also about how, when, and to whom one can talk (and joke). Such rules demand that one never talks to the authorities (the subject of Tommy's original story to the table), but also that to earn respect one must play with language, manage one's image (the punchline to Tommy's story). One must "break balls," but without crossing the line. The problem with Tommy is that his line is impossible to see . . . until it is overstepped.

Comedy often ends, Pappas writes, "with a fatal violation of the dramatic illusion, that is, the conventions that determine what a play is; and being titillated by these violations amounts not to ridiculing them, not to seeing the comedy as a lesser being, but to guilty pleasure. You wish you had done that" (14). With Tommy, the humor at Henry's expense is contrived by him using his own (very real, and well understood by all at that table) insecurities to distort a throwaway comment into an insult. He artificially proposes Henry (who is already a committed member of Tommy's "audience," having laughed raucously at the first joke) as thinking himself superior.[9] As Pappas put it, the comedic subject is that which laughably violates etiquette. By demeaning himself (again, artificially), Tommy deflects the hubris of his interrogation story onto Henry, positioning himself as the object and target of Henry's amusement (as he was the object and target of the police interrogator's)—rather than its facilitator. He makes himself the punchline, as it were—and takes it as if he were being punched. Tommy codeswitches at an alarming rate, from being "in control" to being "confused," from raconteur to clown, bon vivant to social punchbag (see Figures 4.3 and 4.4).

The line separating jape from jibe has been erased. He is a funny guy in both senses, because he is both very good at holding court and, in fact, diminutive (does, in fact, speak a little funny). He is, in

Figures 4.3. and 4.4. Joe Pesci codeswitching in *Goodfellas*. Martin Scorsese, Warner Bros., 1990. Digital frame enlargement.

the Aristotelian sense, practically the definition of an "immoderate," in just about every way imaginable. He swings from buffoon to boor with no mediation. In the end, Henry has no option but to treat this whole situation as a joke itself, to reelevate Tommy's "footing" in the round by demeaning/diminishing himself. He really was taken in.

It is, to recall Pappas, a comic catharsis as the calibration of ridicule in which the "norms of [gangster] social intercourse are saved." After all, as Jorge Arditi puts it, "Manners becomes a language, a formal property through which a group takes shape" (qtd. in Hamann 63). To this, Trent H. Hamann adds that "to have a recognizable voice, to speak the proper behavioral language within a given genre of comportment, one must already belong to it, in which case one would probably not make the inappropriate demand that it legitimate itself in the first place" (63). Pappas insists we heed J. L. Austin's observation that "pretending to be rude could amount to being rude. 'I was just pretending' doesn't always neutralize the rudeness" (14). Tommy is a funny guy, but he is also impolitic by his very nature and we are never sure in the "funny guy" scene whether Tommy has in fact taken offense, or is simply pretending that he has.

It is perhaps not so surprising, then, that it is Tommy who becomes the final punchline to a rather dark joke toward the end of the film. As a native Sicilian, he is informed he is to become a "Made Man" himself—that is, inducted as a permanent member of the Mafia elite (a "Made Man" is made up, made big, made "untouchable"). He dresses in his best suit and arrives at the address at which the ceremony is to take place. However, Tommy enters to find an empty room. No reception committee, no celebration, no audience at all. "Oh no . . . ," he gasps before he is shot in the head. The reason? He killed a Made Man for teasing him about his place in the mafia hierarchy. By acting on his own authority, Tommy has behaved as though he already belonged to that club of Made Men, but it was an authority he did not (legitimately) possess.

~

Jokes cause us to squirm and even writhe with pain (as in the proverbial "splitting sides"). They require good timing and awareness of one's audience (a kind of spatial awareness of the performance area). They can misfire. While a good joke can draw us closer to and as a group, a bad one can estrange or in extreme situations ostracize. It is perhaps unsurprising, therefore, that joke telling can both uphold and violate etiquette in unpredictable ways, and perhaps this is the reason etiquette guides tend to steer clear of prescribing the dos and don'ts of humor. A joke can secure or resecure civility, just as it can render a social situation uncivil. Kenneth Burke wrote of the "comic corrective" by which the structure and mood of comedy instructs on how to conduct ourselves in society ("On Symbols" 261–67). A joke might cohere a group by forging or reaffirming a closeness that formal bureaucracies make distant. It might work through a person's being ejected from a group, their exclusion (as the joke's "butt") the object-cause of cohesion, which would of course (at least on the surface) go against etiquette's emphasis on inclusivity. In the *Goodfellas* example, however, the joke not only acts as a substitute for violence, but it also functions as (symbolic) violence, and as a precursor to actual violence.[10]

5

The Butler Did It

Service

> I've illuminated the blackness of my invisibility—and vice versa.
> —Ralph Ellison, *Invisible Man*

~

In classical Hollywood cinema, directors became increasingly adept at "pricking" film subjects out from the background, so much so that Jean-Paul Sartre noted that while drama in the theater proceeds from the actor, in the cinema it goes "from the décor to the man" (qtd. in Bazin 422). One thinks of Michael Curtiz's camera roving around Rick's Café Américain at the beginning of *Casablanca* (1942), searching out, and eventually finding, the world-wearied hero (Humphrey Bogart) toward whom the hushed and desperately urgent discussions taking place in the bar have been concerned. In British cinema, Orson Welles was introduced in Carol Reed's *The Third Man* (1949) by the sound of a mewing cat preening in a darkened doorway. The sound draws the camera to the feet of a man concealed among the shadows who, by the sudden light of a nearby window, is revealed to be the film's star: his smirking face is illuminated just long enough for Reed to slowly zoom in for a closeup. Such introductions carry political weight, as Mary Ann Doane demonstrated in the different ways Glenn Ford and Rita Hayworth were introduced in Charles Vidor's *Gilda* (1946). Here, the "pricking out" of the film subject is (if you can excuse the Shakespearean pun) gendered. As Doane demonstrates, while Vidor's camera draws up to Ford's face from his hands as he plays dice in a casino (that is, his face attracts the camera-gaze via his activity in the world), Hayworth famously bursts into the frame with her trademark flaming red hair (her face interrupts the world, bringing discord to the patriarchal equilibrium). Doane uses the difference between the two introductions to explore the structural contrasts by which male and female characters are framed in classical cinematography (100).

However, to give this screw another turn, consider the limited visibility afforded black bodies onscreen in Classical Hollywood. Robert Stam and Louise Spence write that it matters "which characters are afforded close-ups and which are relegated to the background," just as it matters if "a character [can] look and act, or merely appear, to be looked at and acted upon." It matters with whom the audience is "permitted intimacy" (889). Ralph Ellison opened his influential novel *Invisible Man* (1952) with an illustration of just how difficult it was for African Americans to "become visible" in contemporary society. "I am an invisible man," Ellison declared. Not in the way Claude Rains was in James Whale's film of the same name (1933) and nothing like Welles in *The Third Man* (audiences had to wait for well over half the film for its star to be revealed, and they waited). "I am a man of substance," Ellison complained, "of flesh and bone, fiber and liquids—and I might even be said to possess a mind. I am invisible, understand, simply because people refuse to see me." Instead of seeing, "when they approach me they see only my surroundings, themselves, or figments of their imagination—indeed, everything and anything except me" (3). Unlike Bogart's introduction in *Casablanca*, Dooley Wilson's club piano player, Sam, is "there," but as part of the "décor": performing Max Steiner's score in the background, first "for him (Bogart)" and then "for her (Ingrid Bergmann)"—never for himself (he also sits in the shadows as Bogart's sounding board).

"Going to the extreme," wrote the psychoanalyst Frantz Fanon in *Black Skin, White Masks* (also 1952), "we would say that the body of the black man hinders the closure of the white man's postural schema at the very moment when the black man emerges into the white man's phenomenal world" (138). I understand this statement in relation to Fanon's earlier point that "in the white world, the man of color encounters difficulties in elaborating his body schema. The image of one's body is solely negating. It's an image in the third person" (90). Third person: he, him, his—never I, me, mine. The extension of a body in the world, argued Fanon, is usually organized according to a set of self-determined spatiotemporal principles. Fanon's example is wanting to smoke, which might involve a smoker stretching his arm to reach for a pack of cigarettes, then moving his body to recover a box of matches, and so on. (Or, with Bogart and Bacall in *To Have an Have Not*, whistling for it!) Such "implicit" knowledge is not experienced by black subjects, Fanon argued. Their movements—to reach, to extend, to stretch, and so forth—belong in a schema framed by a white gaze: "beneath the body schema . . . a historical-racial schema" (91). In Chapter 1, I explored Goffman's problem of "territorial violation" in municipal spaces—the uncomfortable feeling I get when a stranger sits on the seat next to me on a train with vacant seats aplenty elsewhere, for example. Fanon remarks on a different kind of territorial violation for those regarded not only as a "third person," but, when on "the train, instead of one seat, they left me two or three . . . I existed in triple" (92). The stranger sits elsewhere not out of politeness (to give his fellow traveler some privacy), but to keep his distance.

Sometimes, one can start out as invisible and suddenly be exposed, de trop, on account of an ill-advised violation of etiquette. Take the moment at the end of George Stevens's *Giant* (1956), when "Bick" Benedict (Rock Hudson) takes his family to a diner. At the counter, a sign states, "We reserve the right to refuse service to anyone," meaning ethnic minorities. The owner (Mickey Simpson) of the diner insults Bick's daughter-in-law, who is Mexican, before rudely informing another Mexican family they are not welcome. Bick intervenes, insisting the owner let them stay. When he refuses, they fight. Bick loses. His tail between his legs, Bick laments failing to defend the family's legacy, but his wife, Leslie (Elizabeth Taylor), beams at him, declaring she has never been prouder of her husband—the "hero." A similar scene turns out differently in Alan Parker's *Mississippi Burning* (1988) in which Special Agent Alan Ward (Willem Dafoe), who is from the North, blunders in a segregated Mississippi diner while investigating the 1964 murder of three civil rights activists. When the waitress tells him he must wait for a table in the "white" section, Ward ignores the pleas of his partner, Special Agent Rupert Anderson (Gene Hackman)—who hails from the South—not to sit in the "colored" section. As Ward moves to the back, the bustling diner suddenly goes quiet. Undeterred, Ward not only sits but begins asking questions about the murdered campaigners of a young black man quietly eating his lunch. The man looks nervously at the white diners, whose collective gaze now bares down upon him and Ward, before answering, "I ain't got nothin' to say to you, Sir." Despite sitting in the correct section, this African American diner is now in the wrong simply because of the transgressing presence of Ward. The irony, of course, is that while it is Ward's offense against the racist etiquette of segregation, it is the black diner who is "exposed" to the hateful stares triggered by that offense. Ward finally recognizes his error and quietly withdraws.

Thomas Ross writes that just as "slavery became legally coherent when the subject was not human," "de jure segregation became legally coherent when whites supposed that blacks suffered no harm and experienced no stigma" (265). The problem, of course, was how to challenge these assumptions. The slave who gave evidence that he or she possessed a mind received a beating for willful disobedience; the diner who demonstrated the indignity of segregation was subjected to much the same. In response to such impossible double binds, Fanon and Ellison both flirted with violent resistance. Both quickly recognized that aggression feeds, and thereby reinforces, negative stereotypes—as in the white child's fearful, "Look, a Negro! *Maman*, a Negro!" which transforms into, "*Maman*, the Negro's going to eat me" (Fanon 93). "I am a slave not to the 'idea' others have of me," Fanon complained, "but to my appearance" (95). So, what is to be done? His blood rising, Fanon imagined (or recalled?) answering a more complimentary but no less insulting form of recognition: "Look how handsome that Negro is," a woman told him one day, to which he calmly but pointedly told her, "'Fuck you,' madame." Now, this response elicited a different reaction entirely: as the face of his admirer "colored with shame," Fanon recalled feeling "freed." "I realized two things at once," he wrote. "I had identified the enemy and created a scandal. Overjoyed. We could now have some fun" (94). The "enemy" Fanon identified here is the perfectly acceptable and politic statement (at least from the phenomenal worldview of whites). As for what he calls "fun," this is what I would like to call, "playing with *im*politics." Take the fun out, and you just have Ward's offense in *Mississippi Burning*. Such "fun"—one could also call it "play" or "subversion"—must be subtle and nominally polite (as in the addition of the respectful "madame" to Fanon's otherwise disrespectful " 'Fuck you' "). If the only "decent" world was a white one from which he was excluded, Fanon made it his mission to make himself seen, that is, to be "known." He would do this by challenging the inequity at the heart of so-called "decency" itself. He would, Fanon declared, make himself "appear" not by resisting, ignoring, or offending against white etiquette, but by having some fun with it; by torturing it. Likewise, Ellison imparted a similar lesson learned from his paternal grandfather ("an odd old guy . . . he who caused the trouble"), who on his deathbed instructed his son and grandson "to keep up the good fight. . . . Live with your head in the lion's mouth. I want you to overcome 'em with yeses, undermine 'em with grins, agree 'em to death and destruction, let 'em swoller you till they vomit or bust wide open" (16).

Three years after Ellison and Fanon wrote these books, Rosa Parks refused to give up her seat to a white man on a Montgomery, Alabama, bus (December 1, 1955). It took a courageous gesture of impropriety (although Parks's refusal was by no means the first such gesture) to bring about a change in the law. By forcing the question, at the right time and in the right place, Parks not only demonstrated that the apparent "legitimacy" of one side does not necessarily imply the illegitimacy on the other side; her "impolitic gesture" also illuminated (in every sense of the word) the "otherness" denied not only in but by social etiquette. Her refusal to give up her seat caused her to "appear," as it were, in the mind of the white man asking—however politely—that she move. Such a small gesture of defiance rendered visible the iniquity at the heart of the very etiquette drawn up to protect "civility." The gesture did not amount to a call for inclusion but drew attention to the very fact—rendered invisible by the system—that the exclusion of black people from etiquette guides had itself been excluded.

Jeff Weinstein notes that in their rush to keep up with the changing times, etiquette manuals in the 1970s began to include entries addressing the rising African American middle classes. They botched it, he complains: what we got was "advice about how to distinguish between and respond to intended versus unintended racism—an etiquette for 'us' " (35). It was for this same reason that *Mississippi Burning* has recently been viewed more critically as a "white savior narrative," and why Peter Farrelly's Oscar-winning *Green Book* (2018), also set in the early sixties, was as much maligned as celebrated for its portrayal of racism in the Deep South apropos of the "Negro Motorist Guide." When a society is organized around concealed prejudices, such blind spots are not only ignored in etiquette guides; they are perpetuated by them. In such circumstances, only an *impolitic gesture*, even a very minor one, will do.

As I turn to examine examples of impolitic gestures in cinema, let us keep in mind the response Fanon (rather scathingly) imagines from the white rationalists when faced with the irrationality of their codes of conduct being exposed to the charge of racism: "'You are so authentic in your life, so playful. Let us forget for a few moments our formal, polite civilization and bend down over those heads, those adorable expressive faces. In a sense, you reconcile us with ourselves'" (111). Such reasoning misses the point, Fanon argued. For a person armed solely with reason, "there is nothing more neurotic than contact with the irrational" (98). In one form or another, the following examples focus on service, on individuals bound to a system of etiquette, but who find (often imaginative) ways to challenge it, and in doing so challenge the white masters they serve. Each example examines the neurosis caused by racist etiquette, and the fun Fanon might have had disarming it.

Hand over the Table: *Jezebel*

> The action is the picture itself.
>
> —Murray Pomerance, "Three Small Gestures"

In 1961, James Baldwin lamented that "most American performers seem to find themselves trapped very soon in an 'iron maiden' of mannerisms." By way of example, Baldwin offered Henry Fonda, who, despite being "one of the most accomplished actors around," whose "*impulse* as an actor is very truthful . . . his physical attributes, and his quality of painful, halting honesty are usually at the mercy of some mediocre playwright's effort to justify the bankruptcy of the American male" ("Theater" 19). The effect, Baldwin complained, is an avoidance of a much-needed confrontation with our experience in favor of a justification and confirmation of our wishful fantasies regarding the world in which we in fact live. Worse: such justifications lock us in to those fantasies, obscuring truths a politically engaged actor like Fonda would presumably have wished to disclose in his performance. Cinema is awash in such limited characterizations, Baldwin wrote, reflecting not who we are but how we wish to see ourselves and be seen by others.

And if this is "unhealthy for the white actor," Baldwin continued, then it is "disastrous for the Negro" ("Theater" 20). The resentment of the black actor is compounded because "not only does the white world impose the most intolerable conditions on Negro life, they also presume to dictate the mode, manner, terms, and style of one's reaction against these conditions" ("Theater" 23). In *The World Viewed*, Stanley Cavell noted something similar of this period, pointing out that "types of black human beings were not created in film: black people were stereotypes—mammies, shiftless servants, loyal retainers, entertainers. We were not given, and were not in a position to be given, individualities that projected particular ways of inhabiting a social role; we recognized only the role. Occasionally, the humanity behind the role would manifest itself; and the result was a revelation not of a human individuality, but of an entire *realm of humanity becoming visible*" (33–34, emphasis mine). Cavell is discussing here a moment in Victor Fleming's *Gone With the Wind* (1939) in which a belle of the antebellum South, Scarlett O'Hara (Vivian Leigh), turns to her black (slave) maid, Prissy (Butterfly McQueen), for advice on what to do when her sister-in-law goes into labor and Prissy is unable to raise the doctor. Scarlett assumes Prissy will know how to deliver the baby, but her assumption, noted Cavell, "while apparently complimentary, is dehumanizing—with such creatures knowledge of the body comes from nowhere, and in general they are to be trusted absolutely or not at all, like lions in a cage, with whom you either do or do not know how to deal."[1] As much from terror as rage that her servant does not, in fact, possess this knowledge, Scarlett slaps Prissy, and after the slap we are left with "two young girls equally frightened in a humanly desperate situation" (*World* 34). Eventually, Scarlett delivers the baby herself, and all is (for the time being) well. But Cavell was left with the impression that the manner of the slap (as well, we might add, Scarlett's mutterings about taking the strap to Prissy for dawdling on her way to raise the doctor in the first place) marked an irreducible difference. While "equally frightened," these young naïfs differ in their respective positions—from the lethargy of one who can expect (but also forgets) that she is "to be bullied," to the energetic resourcefulness of the other who knows only how to bully. If the film can be celebrated, Cavell implies, it is for the general movement from the "type" in whom such expectations are flattened by assumptions and rooted in ignorance regarding race, to the way such individuals (and their bodies) are in fact treated onscreen. That is, in the film's "inherent tendency toward the democratic, or anyway the idea of human equality" (*World* 35). Contrariwise (and Cavell raises but resists resolving this dilemma), the film generally tends toward the fascistic and populist in its tendency to appeal to and attract a crowd in whom such a movement toward equality might not be recognized at all.

The racial politics in William Wyler's *Jezebel* (1938), however, have aged considerably better. While recent criticisms facing *Gone With the Wind* have led to its being censured, Richard Dyer writes that *Jezebel* is a film "related, through the sympathies of its stars, director and production studio, to progressive ideas on race," making it, notes he (quoting Jim Pines), "undoubtedly the most liberal-inclined" of the period's plantation movies (152).[2] Ostensibly, *Jezebel* is a film about the "taming of a shrew" (Bette Davis's Julie, another Southern belle with a mind of her own who refuses to conform to the Old South's restrictive codes). But it is also a film, Dyer writes, that contrasts the drama of the white characters with bare but extensive, and often significant, glimpses of black life "in which whiteness *is related to* blackness" (152, emphasis mine).[3] Dyer notes that such glimpses are often directed by the cinematography and composition, thereby troubling the margins of representation.

First, in several establishing shots Wyler's camera moves from a black character over or across to the white characters in such a way that their bodies leave traces on the "white drama" to come. For example, this happens when a young boy (Stymie Beard) operating a manual ceiling fan at a grand formal dinner suddenly cracks a great yawn, manifestly bored out of his mind. Second, black bodies frequently intrude into the frame while white characters speak, as if to interrupt or "intrude" (Dyer's word) on their discourse. In a noteworthy example of the latter, a slave serving at the table (of the same formal dinner) suddenly leans across our field of vision during a (somewhat heated) postprandial discussion about abolitionism, "literally embodying the fact of slave labour" (152), writes Dyer. Such moments have been viewed by critics like Dyer and Pines as highlighting the way Wyler visually frames the central "white" conflicts either by conspicuously marginalizing black bodies or by having those bodies "intrude" on the center from the margins.

I cannot fault a single word in Dyer's incisive and nimble analysis. However, the nature of the dining scene's subversiveness, as well as the depth and power of its progressiveness, is richer than his short piece can cover (another reason I want to open the example up is that this moment in *Jezebel* forcibly struck me long before I read Dyer's analysis of it). Consider that the two techniques Dyer highlights accomplish different, albeit complementary, effects: when Wyler's camera moves from a black body to "prick out" a white one, it forms part of the dramatic schema, even when that body is shortly eclipsed (either because the camera moves beyond or cuts away from them, or they leave the shot). In the second, however, the "intruding" black body reverses this process. It is as though Wyler understood that it was not enough to gesture toward the marginalization of black bodies by making them disappear into the "background." The process had to be reversed, the margins brought (however briefly) back into the center. Let us look at the dinner scene in more detail.

As with *Gone With the Wind*, *Jezebel* is set in the antebellum South (albeit Louisiana rather than Georgia). Twin dangers loom: an epidemic of yellow fever threatens to engulf the state, and a civil war with the North seems increasingly inevitable. The dinner scene is introduced via a high angled shot of a handsomely set table, brightly lit by ornate candelabra showing off blushing floral displays. A resplendent feast is in the process of being consumed with highly polished gleaming silverware. As the diners finish up their desserts, Wyler lingers just long enough on this establishing shot that our eyes are drawn to the margins of the frame where, standing around the edges of the room, the slaves wait to wait. Wyler cuts to a closeup of the (for now) convivial diners engaged in a postprandial discussion about the increasing momentum for abolitionism.

The "table talk" takes a serious turn when one of the diners breaks with the prevailing view. This is Pres (Henry Fonda), a progressive banker fresh from spending a year in the North who has clearly returned with strong abolitionist sentiments. Sitting across the table from Pres is Buck (George Brent), a genteel but hotheaded slave owner who literally has skin in the plantation game. Antagonizing both men is Julie (Bette Davis), who is using Buck (because he fancies her) to provoke Pres (whom she still loves). Julie is seething because Pres has returned to the Halcyon estate with a new wife from New York, Amy (Margaret Lindsay). As Julie goads Buck to challenge Pres on his abolitionist views, both men choose their words with care. Buck is proud of Southern customs, hidebound in his views on slavery, and quick to temper. But given his primary goal is to woo Julie, he must keep his cool and maintain decorum. Pres is likewise eager to avoid giving offense, especially as he is the guest of honor. But he must also be careful because (as Buck reminds him) abolitionist sentiments can get you hanged in these parts (the scene opens with those gathered around the table gleefully imagining the hanging of William Lloyd Garrison, should he ever venture this far South). Not for the first time in the film, old Southern etiquette seems to conspire against personal expression and freedom. After being warned to watch his tongue, Pres looks to oppose Buck's views on slavery without defaulting on his manners. "I think it was Voltaire who said," Pres carefully quotes, "'I disagree with everything you say and will defend to the death your right to say it.'" With his dander up, Buck presses Pres on his meaning. Sensing he is at the very limit of acceptable discourse at this table, Pres gives voice to a forthright but carefully worded thesis: "If you must have it," he says of the looming war, "it'll be a victory [for the North] of machines over unskilled slave labor," whereupon—at precisely the moment Pres says, "unskilled slave labor"—the hand of Uncle Cato (Lew Payton), one of the oldest (and most beloved) of the family's slaves, leans across to refill Pres's wine glass (see Figure 5.1).

When I first saw this film, the effect of Pres's words was stunning. To have the pluck to say such a thing in such company marked a moment of gritty defiance—classic Fonda, I thought. He appears to encapsulate that Southern quality of quarrelling without breaching decorum ("*passionately* calm" is how Louisa McCord described this quality of the 1850s Southern gentleman [qtd. in Fox-Genovese and Genovese 91]).

But to consider Pres's words alone weakens the effect considerably. A victory of machines over unskilled slave labor? Pres's emphasis on the "unskilled" labor of the slave is, one suspects, his way of protecting himself. This argument is already likely to get him into trouble; adding a moral insult to the economic injury will risk too much. It

Figure 5.1. Punctuating the point in *Jezebel*. William Wyler, Warner Brothers, 1938. Digital frame enlargement.

is rather better for him, and probably more effective in swaying the opinions of his companions (whom he loves, despite their politics), to stick to the "business case" (he is, after all, a banker). But if Pres's line of argument is less likely to risk his neck, it is perhaps not more likely to stick with a man like Buck (and it doesn't). One might even regard the phrasing as pusillanimous—as proof that Fonda, like Pres, was indeed caught in the iron maiden Baldwin imagined limiting his politic expression.

We know Pres doesn't believe Buck's slaves are either unskilled or mere labor. In the previous scene, Pres warmly compliments Uncle Cato for mixing his favorite drink, to which Cato replies that "the head might forget, but the hands remember." Pres smiles, urging his "old friend" to join him in a toast. Unnerved, Cato politely refuses ("Why, Mr. Pres, it ain't hardly proper"). Uncle Cato finally accepts, but with the concession that he will drink it alone out of sight in the pantry. The "impropriety" of Pres's offer is clear: he wishes

Uncle Cato to share a drink with him in a gesture, even a display, of bonhomie, mutual recognition, and solidarity. But at the dinner table, with all eyes upon him, Pres's sentiments are colder. It is an argument of the head, not the heart—uncharitably, one might call it a "banker's assessment."

But the scene simply doesn't read that way, and the reason is the timing of Cato's arm reaching (not to say "punching") into the frame to refill Pres's wineglass. Wyler orchestrates a consonance of rhetoric and action that is more than the sum of its parts. It is an "intrusion" that cannot be misconstrued as "improper," at least not in the diegesis. But all the same, it is the *cinematic* equivalent of Fanon's "'Fuck you,' madame." Cato's timing is, on the very surface, little more than a matter of pure, mechanical coincidence. As Pres has been speaking, we might have seen Cato passing from guest to guest, pouring and pouring. That he "appears" in this way at just this moment in Pres's speech can hardly be happenstance: the timing is too perfect, hence exceeds the purely cinematic arrangement of bodies onscreen. One might imagine Wyler blocking the shot with the actors as they rehearsed the scene over and over to get it just right: the timing of Payton pouring for each guest marking the beats in Fonda's delivery of the speech, beats which must culminate in this concluding statement.[4] Payton's movement is paced to the measure of Fonda's words; Pres's words appear, however, to be animated by Cato's movements. And this performative and profilmic harmony elevates Pres's speech; it "fills it out." Considered in isolation, Pres's speech is daring (in its own way), but essentially level-headed, cautious, and measured. With Cato's intrusion, however, it is resignified, repunctuated, even. Together in discourse and action, the two of them "speak" more than Pres alone can "say." It is the power of the cinematic gesture, writes Murray Pomerance in a different context, one that cannot be reduced or explained with reference to an actor's movement or a camera movement alone. Rather, it is the "little expressive move that has huge consequence, rendered on film because of the way it is performed, the way it is turned out to the lens, the way the scene itself lends it special light" ("Three Small Gestures" n.p.).

By punctuation, I mean something analogous to the point raised by Jacques Lacan of the therapeutic importance of waiting until the end of an analytic session for "the lasting word" of the patient's discourse to be "gathered" by a witness (the analyst), who is called forth to register the "man in his authenticity" (107). In the analytic situation, the analyst's interpretation doesn't just conclude the session; it gathers the patient's entire discourse, giving it meaning. It is like "punctuation," wrote Lacan, which "once inserted, fixes the meaning; changing the punctuation renews or upsets it; and a faulty punctuation amounts to a change for the worse" (108). In the silent era of Hollywood cinema, segregation led to black-owned and operated theaters showing predominantly "white" pictures. However, the live music added by black musicians offered the potential to overlay alternative (and often subversive) meanings to those intended (for example, rendering a serious political drama with the music of farce). Desirée J. Garcia notes that "movie theaters could be places for the assertion of 'consciousness' and 'social difference' in addition to the consumption of mainstream entertainment" (n. 23).[5] Such "progressive impolitics," as I want to call it, is subversive to its core. Uncle Cato's hand functions as subversive punctuation: it does not just intrude on but "interprets" Pres's speech. The head might forget, but the hands remember.

"Perhaps to be of colour is to have a brain," suggests William Brown, "since it involves not seeing the world as white or as cinema, with whites under capital becoming men of straw" (n.p.). And therein lies the glorious rub! On the one hand, Uncle Cato's intrusion into the "open region" (as Erving Goffman described the dinner table) cannot be construed as an incursion, intended to reinforce Pres's statement. But on the other hand, by breaking into the frame of the screen, this arm does seem to respond to Pres's remark. After all, as Margaret Visser noted, the dinner table is not just something to eat off but "something to lean on, to gesture over; it expresses what everyone has in common" (*Rituals*), or, in this case, what they don't. It is a gesture in the sense meant by Pomerance, one combining Wyler's camera placement, Payton's movement, and Fonda's delivery. It is subversive for simultaneously undercutting and supplementing what Pres says without lapsing into bad form. And that it is pulled off with such timing and panache marks the gesture as not only grasping the hidden meaning of Pres's speech but seizing its deepest intent.

Profaning the Table: Breaking Bakhtin's "Third Person"

The word "fane" referred to the temple (*fānum*) at which religious festivities (*fēriae*) would take place: that includes feasts. Hence, to be "profane" was to be outside of (pro-) such sacred spaces. The genius of Uncle Cato's intrusion in *Jezebel* is more clearly discerned by observing counterexamples in which the intrusions of servants and slaves at formal dinners leads not to the articulation of freedom but the disintegration of the festive situation. In these examples, the sudden gesture of the servant leads to the desecration of the sacred space of the table as "open region."

First, in Robert Altman's *Gosford Park* (2001), a servant girl, Elsie (Emily Watson), impulsively leaps to the defense of her boorish master (Michael Gabon) because he is being brow-beaten by his vituperative wife (Kristin Scott Thomas) during a formal dinner. Elsie's interruption consists of her saying no more than, "I have to say that is not fair. Bill . . ."—at which she stops herself, suddenly realizing her error. By leaping to her master's defense (especially against her mistress's accusations against him), and by using his familiar name, Elsie has revealed to all at the table that she and he have been having an affair. The dinner is ruined, and Elsie is dismissed.

Second, in Quentin Tarantino's *Django Unchained* (2012), a freed slave, Django (Jamie Foxx), and his abolitionist friend, Dr. Schultz (Christoph Waltz), bite their tongues throughout a formal dinner with a narcissistic slave owner, Mr. Candie (Leonardo DiCaprio), intending to charm him into selling a prizefighting slave. Django and Schultz are dining under false pretenses, however. They hope to seal the deal with the addition of a slave girl to justify the exorbitant price, a very specific slave girl—Django's beloved wife, Broomhilda (Kerry Washington), who is their prime objective. The cruel slaver will not part with Broomhilda, however, if he suspects her true relation to Django. While pouring wine for one of the guests, Broomhilda cannot resist casting a look in her husband's direction, unintentionally communicating to the rest of the room that she is in love with him, thereby blowing his and Dr. Schultz's cover—leading to a violent showdown.

And third, in Jordan Peele's *Get Out* (2017), Mr. Armitage (Bradley Whitford) tries to convince his daughter's new boyfriend, Chris (Daniel Kaluuya), not to read too much into the fact that, despite being a card-carrying white liberal, he embarrassingly employs a black maid and black groundskeeper. As they talk, the sweetly smiling maid (Betty Gabriel) reaches into the shot to fill Chris's glass. However, as the drink reaches the top of the glass, she just goes on pouring, iced tea sloshing over the table until the Armitages quickly invite her to take a rest. Alarmed, Chris begins to suspect all is not well with the Armitages.[6]

The difference between the example of Uncle Cato in *Jezebel* and these three is that the excessive gesture lacks all grace and coordination; it appears unrefined, closer to a breakdown, like the Freudian symptom disturbing and belying the appearance of "rude health" (as the British used to say). While Cato's gesture transcends its function as service (refilling a glass) to make a claim to freedom that neither he nor Pres is capable of authoring under these circumstances, all three of the above examples function oppositely: each servant is "exposed" in her situation of enslavement in such a way that she becomes an unwitting author of her own lack of freedom to speak freely at this table (to conduct a hidden affair with her master, to fool her master in order to obtain her freedom, or to undermine her master's claim to his liberal enlightenment). Perhaps it is always better that the truth will out, but all three of these films end with bloodshed.

Kierkegaard was right, declared Jean-Paul Sartre near the beginning of *Being and Nothingness* (1943), in distinguishing between fear "of beings in the world" and anguish "before myself." Sartre clarified the point by saying that while "a situation provokes fear if there is a possibility of my life being changed from without; my being provokes anguish to the extent that I distrust myself and my own reactions in that situation"—or, as he put it more provocatively, "vertigo is anguish to the extent that I am afraid not of falling over the precipice, but of throwing myself over" (53). When I feel anguished, I am "totally free," Sartre also claimed, and thus no longer "able to derive the meaning of the world except as coming from myself" (63)—with no justification or excuse. Moreover, I can neither hide from nor avoid anguish (67). All I can do is flee from it. This is what Sartre famously called "bad faith." In each of these cases the servant unintentionally appears to "throw herself," rather than simply fall over the precipice. Breaking character, she peeks out from behind the performative dimension of her role as a servant, thereby ruining the illusion that it is her pleasure to serve (or, in Broomhilda's case, that her pleasure is moot).

From the perspective of the servant, the need to go unnoticed at a dinner service is paramount. It is "most difficult to achieve that balance between attentiveness and the illusion of absence that is essential to good waiting," observes the butler, Mr. Stevens, in Kazuo

Ishiguro's *The Remains of the Day* (1989). "It is in this situation that one is rarely free of the suspicion that one's presence is inhibiting the conversation" (75). Of course, a butler cannot remain on the periphery, lest the diners soon discover their glasses empty; the successful butler has a presence *experienced* as absence by the diners. In Ishiguro's novel, a now elderly Stevens (played by Anthony Hopkins in James Ivory's 1993 film adaptation) reflects on his decades of service. Recalling an intimate dinner service for his lordship and a visiting dignitary, Stevens remembers the difficulty of attending to the needs of his masters while, at the same time, giving them sufficient privacy to talk. He solved the problem by withdrawing to a shadowy recess in the vast banqueting hall, giving them the illusion of privacy. Of course, Stevens's solution had a distinct disadvantage: when his services were required, the butler's footsteps echoed loudly in the empty hall, a noise he ruefully describes as "most ostentatious" (75–76).

What Stevens has in mind is that it is "highly impolite *to be observed* to eavesdrop," as Judith Martin wryly points out (758, emphasis mine). What Ishiguro describes here is the peculiar kind of eavesdropping power practically unique to the figure Mikhail Bakhtin described as the "third person." Encapsulated by Lear's Fool in Shakespeare, and by characters as diverse as jesters, courtesans, slaves, servants, butlers, handmaidens—and, more recently, personal assistants (in film, see Kristen Stewart's performances in Olivier Assayas's *The Clouds of Sils Maria* [2014] and *Personal Shopper* [2016])—Bakhtin's "third person" is one whose presence in rooms of prestige mark him or her out as occupying an almost unique position among their own social class: they are part of, but emphatically do not belong to, the spaces they occupy. And with eyes to see and ears to (over)hear—ears, especially, which cannot be closed—the "third person," who is not "seen" by his masters, can eavesdrop on those in high society, can discover their secrets—while never seeming rude. By contrast, he is being attentive in his role.[7] Any knowledge gleaned by a "third person" is intrinsically personal and private: "by its very nature there can be nothing *public* about it," wrote Bakhtin, because such conversations ". . . could not occur 'in the eyes of the world,' publicly, in the presence of a *chorus*" (122). However, in the presence of a "third person," the supposed privacy of the public figure is at once secured and compromised; or, as Bakhtin put it: "people are as little embarrassed in a servant's presence as they are in the presence of an ass, and at the same time the servant is called upon to participate in all intimate aspects of personal life . . . the figure of the servant retreats into the background but his significance remains the same" (125).

The Dignity of *The Butler*

> We both want our freedom. We just have our different methods.
> —Aimé Césaire, *A Tempest*

In Lee Daniels's *The Butler* (2013), the parvenu is far humbler in intention, and less self-deceiving than Ishiguro's butler. The film opens on an elderly Cecil Gaines (Forest Whitaker) awaiting the newly inaugurated president of the United States at the White House. The year is 2009. As he waits, Cecil begins to recount his life, starting with the day he witnessed the murder of his father on a Georgia cotton plantation. A stricken seven-year-old Cecil is quickly ushered indoors by a sympathetic caretaker, Maynard (Clarence Williams III), who instructs the young boy on the duties of the black house servant. "It's *his* world," Cecil is warned (referencing their white masters), "you're just living in it." When serving, silence is the rule: "I don't even wanna hear you *breathe*," Maynard stresses: "the room should feel empty when you're in it . . . You hear nothing, you see nothing, you *only* serve."[8]

Some years later, Cecil has worked his way up through increasingly prestigious positions before landing a butlering job at the White House during the Eisenhower administration in 1957. As he serves the president (Robin Williams) his tea, Cecil witnesses Eisenhower's reluctance to use federal troops to enforce school desegregation amid racial tensions. Meanwhile, rather than attend his classes at Fisk University in Nashville, Tennessee, Cecil's teenage son, Louis (David Oyelowo), joins a nonviolent student program protesting racial discrimination. In one scene, Louis and a group of activists passively refuse to leave a segregated diner, leading first to dismay and then to derision among the white diners. Editor Joe Klotz crosscuts (a technique often used in this film) between Cecil meticulously serving Eisenhower in the White House—polishing and inspecting silverware, serving, pressing clothes, and polishing shoes—and Louis and his friends being racially abused, spat at, physically assaulted, and finally arrested by the police. The rest of the film charts Cecil and Louis as they navigate their own political minefields. Cecil loyally serves under successive presidents and (apparently passively) observes their various attempts to tackle racism in America, including the Civil Rights Act proposed by President Kennedy (James Marsden) and enacted by President Johnson (Liev Schreiber) in 1964; the rise of the Black Panther Party in 1969 under President Nixon (John Cusack) and the 1986 Comprehensive Anti-Apartheid Act of 1986—vetoed by President Reagan (Alan Rickman). Cecil is "in the room" as each president wrings his hands over what to do and frets on which side of history his actions will place him. Through these same decades, Louis gets sucked into increasingly violent confrontations with racist America, including being attacked by the Ku Klux Klan on a Freedom Ride to Birmingham, Alabama, being assaulted by police with dogs and water cannons during the Birmingham Children's Crusade in 1963 (the very event that inspired Kennedy to propose the Civil Rights Act), co-founding the Black Panthers, and eventually campaigning against South African Apartheid. Louis's activism directly and indirectly inspires the presidents under whom Cecil serves—in 1965, he participates in the Selma voting rights movement, which moves Johnson (shown watching the violence on television) to enact the Voting Rights Act of 1965.

As the film progresses, both father and son become increasingly disillusioned at the sluggish speed of their country's progress toward equality, and each starts to question the other's methods. We see their relationship disintegrate as Cecil despairs at Louis throwing away an expensive college education for an increasingly aggressive militancy feeding the view of black Americans as not just uncivilized but "uncivilizable." Louis sees his father as an "Uncle Tom"—obsequious to a fault—and is hardly swayed by a young Martin Luther King, Jr. (Nelsan Ellis), who, upon learning that Louis's father is a butler (of which Louis is ashamed), claims that "the black domestic played an important role in our history." Louis interprets the comment as sarcasm. However, King insists he is being earnest: "Young brother. The black domestic defies racial stereotypes by being hard working and trustworthy. He slowly tears down racial hatred with his example of a strong work ethic and dignified character. Now, while we perceive the butler or the maid to be subservient, in many ways they are subversive . . ."—to which he adds, "without even knowing it." A key question is whether Cecil, as a Bakhtinian "third person" with access to the most powerful man in the world, can be subversive enough. To recall Ellison, is Cecil capable of only living with his "head in the lion's mouth," or can he also speak truth, as it were, in the lion's ear?

The relationship between father and son deteriorates precipitously in the years following Dr. King's assassination, during which time Louis's methods of resistance become increasingly violent. In a key scene, Louis unexpectedly turns up at his parents' house with his girlfriend, Carol (Yaya DaCosta). Cecil immediately bristles at their appalling table manners (Carol belches without excusing herself), both are skimpily dressed, and Louis refuses to remove his black beret while making irreverent and sneering remarks. They talk politics, and Louis and Carol enthuse about their new political party, the Black Panthers, which worsens Cecil's mood—especially when Louis's little brother, Charlie (Elijah Kelley), japes that they are aiming for the White House—with *their* manners (!). In a valiant effort to move the conversation onto neutral territory, Cecil's wife, Gloria (Oprah Winfrey), begins to wax lyrical about Sidney Poitier's recent performance in *In the Heat of the Night* (1967), but she has erred: Louis quickly interrupts, denouncing Poitier as "a white man's fantasy of what he wants us to be." Cecil counters that "his movies have him fight for equal rights." But Louis persists, "Only in a way that's acceptable to the white status quo," to which he adds, grinning, "and the brother can't act." Louis caps his riposte by denouncing Poitier as "nothing but a rich Uncle Tom," at which Cecil quietly but firmly demands that Louis and Carol leave. They assume he is jesting, but Cecil suddenly erupts, screaming at them to get out of his house. Gloria tries to smooth things over but when Louis mocks his father with a sarcastic apology—"Sorry 'Mr. Butler,'" he jeers, "didn't mean to make fun of one of your heroes"—she slaps him, hard, telling him he owes everything he is to "that butler," before reinforcing her husband's demand. (The scene ends with a smart joke by Charlie, who wonders about that "other Poitier film," before joshing that "*Carol* came to dinner.")[9]

The scene is strange, and we partly share Louis's shock at Cecil's volcanic eruption. He is not only clearly jesting about Sidney Poitier but is reiterating a claim about the star that was widely held by African Americans at the time. Cecil's reaction appears over the top, disproportionate to what is clearly a lighthearted remark. We might also share Louis's wide-eyed terror as his father suddenly seizes him, screaming, "I gave you this life and I can take it away!" (a line that echoes Cecil's earlier threat to his son, that he would "snatch the life" right out of him for skipping school in favor of joining protests). "To you your father should be as a god; / One that compos'd your beauties . . . / By him imprinted and within his power / To leave the figure, or disfigure it" (*A Midsummer Night's Dream*, 1.1.47–51). Here, the usually restrained and reserved butler explodes, one might conjecture, not just because Louis and Carol were rude, or because the Poitier comment was the proverbial "straw that broke the camel's back," but because Cecil is more invested in the subversive potential of Sidney Poitier than Louis (perhaps) recognizes. The image of Sidney Poitier goes, in this brief reference, to the heart of the Oedipal struggle raging between them, in the widening methods through which each tackles institutional racism.

The idea that Sidney Poitier became a political pawn in Hollywood "whitewashing" rested, write Robert Stam and Louise Spence, on the industry's insistence on providing "positive images" of black and minority ethnic characters to counteract their historical denigration onscreen. However, the result of such images, Stam and Spence write, "might at times be as pernicious as overtly degrading ones, providing a bourgeois façade for paternalism, a more pervasive racism" (878). Just as Renaissance humanism gave birth to the "vanishing point" in Western art, so too did this code of perspective give birth to the "rights of man" (879), they (rather witheringly) argue. Hence, in *Guess Who's Coming to Dinner*, the arrival of Poitier's Dr. John Prentice at the home of a pair of white liberals (Spencer Tracy and Katharine Hepburn) to ask for permission to marry their daughter (Katharine Houghton) represented more than their eventual acceptance of him out of recognition of the triumph of love over prejudice. Poitier was being invited "into the club of the truly human," as Stam and Spence put it, but "always on white terms" (883). Dressed in his neat, three-piece suit and with no discernible character flaws, Dr. Prentice was supposed to serve as a role model—the exception to demonstrate just how the well-adapted black man could be accepted into white society. Such views were expressed at the time.[10] In 1968, James Baldwin responded to the negative characterizations of Poitier—with whom he was good friends—as owing to the "sinister" fact that while "white Americans appear to be under the compulsion to dream . . . black

Americans are under the compulsion to awaken" ("Sidney Poitier" 225). As such, any positive image of blackness in popular culture, especially one as celebrated as Poitier's, was implicitly distrusted by black audiences who had "every reason in the world to feel themselves abandoned" ("Sidney Poitier" 224). For racist America, the problem was fatal: "*the black face, truthfully reflected, is not only no part of this dream, it is antithetical to it.*" Hence, the "Poitier syndrome," as African American playwright Clifford Mason coined it, became the prevailing view among black audiences of their first major film star.[11]

From this perspective, Louis's comments about Poitier were not only uncontroversial for the time but somewhat commonplace in black households. The problem for Cecil is his worry that he is suffering from the Poitier syndrome himself. In short, Cecil increasingly appears to doubt his own role in the civil rights movement, his own place in the history of this struggle as it is being written.

This dichotomy was described by W. E. B. Du Bois in *The Souls of Black Folk* in 1903 as the "double life" every black American must live: "Swept on by the current of the nineteenth while yet struggling in the eddies of the fifteenth century,—from this must arise a painful self-consciousness, an almost morbid sense of personality and a moral hesitancy which is fatal to self-confidence" (67). The world within and without what Du Bois called "the Veil of Color" were changing rapidly, but not at the same rate, and not in the same way. Such a double life, Du Bois lamented, must either "tempt the mind to pretence or revolt, to hypocrisy or radicalism" (68). With his slur against Poitier, Louis implicitly accuses his father of the former while Cecil, with his explosive reaction to his guests' bad table manners, rages against his son for the latter. But both men come to recognize the schism in their lives. For Louis this recognition arrives with his disillusionment at the shift to more extreme forms of violent resistance by the Panthers, especially when they begin to advocate murder (the taking of an "eye for an eye"). He subsequently embarks on an unsuccessful bid to become a politician. But for Cecil, the recognition of his "double life, with double thoughts, double duties, and double social classes" (as Du Bois put it) comes not as a sudden realization, as it does with Louis, but gradually, over time. At the beginning of the film, it can be detected only in the very smallest of Forest Whitaker's facial expressions as he serves his rich white guests. However, following the death of his youngest son, Charlie (killed in Vietnam), Cecil's entire posture and demeanor hardens. In one scene in the Oval Office, Nixon is plotting with his inner circle on the best way to tackle the Black Panthers. The president pauses mid-sentence to allow Cecil to place a cup of coffee down for him on the desk (the butler's white-gloved hands reaching into the frame, a la Wyler!), before he continues speaking, cynically suggesting they spin "Black Power" to mean "Black Businesses" to win votes while passing the buck on desegregation by letting the courts handle the legislation. When one of his aides asks about the Panthers, Nixon gasps, and jokes that he's already given the green light to Hoover to "*gut* them sons of bitches" (Cusack really emphasizes the word "gut"). Cecil looks disturbed. His face falls and his teary eyes search about the room while he continues to stand on ceremony (see Figure 5.2).

The president and his aides heartily chuckle until Cecil asks, politely—but with an edge in his voice: "Would there be anything else, Mr. President?" Their laughter falls dead. Nixon excuses Cecil but Daniels lingers on Nixon's face. The president seems troubled by the butler's remark. Cecil has succeeded in "appearing," not just as a "third person" dutifully attending the needs of his masters and privy to the private musings of the president, but as a black man, a black father, whose very presence—through the timing and intonation of his otherwise perfectly obeisant question—somehow violates that privacy.

Figure 5.2. Third person: Forest Whitaker in *The Butler*. Lee Daniels, The Weinstein Company, 2013. Digital frame enlargement.

Cecil is most obviously disturbed by his dichotomous existence, however, when, having advocated on behalf of the black staff at the White House for equal pay and career advancement, he finally discovers an ally in President Reagan (Alan Rickman). After winning his claim, he is celebrated at the White House, leading First Lady Nancy Reagan (Jane Fonda) to invite him and Gloria to be guests at a state dinner. However, while Gloria basks in the prestige, Cecil finds it stifling. At first, he is simply embarrassed to be served by his peers, who take good-natured delight in their old friend's apparent discomfiture by mocking him, either through exaggerated deference, or by making snarky comments under their breath. But Cecil's discomfort runs much deeper. "Cecil, we got two faces," his old mentor, Maynard, had informed him when he was training to be a butler: "ours, and the ones that we gotta show the white folks." As his friends and colleagues wait on their guests at the White House, Cecil witnesses, as if for the first time, the very two-facedness his old mentor had been describing. He is disturbed not by the realization that he wears the same two faces in his professional life, nor because he is seeing this two-facedness for the first time; what disturbs him is seeing it from the perspective of the masters themselves, the "principals," as Maynard had called them. It is a type of living Cecil now struggles to endure, and when he witnesses Reagan promising to veto any sanctions against South Africa for its use of apartheid, it is a two-facedness he can endure no longer.[12] To the shock of all, Cecil resigns his position at the White House.

This double-bind of the butler and the revolutionary is wonderfully expressed in Aimé Césaire's *A Tempest* (1969), which reimagines Shakespeare's final play from the perspectives of its colonized subjects: Caliban (who is here altered to be a black slave) and the spirit of the isle, Ariel (described here as a "mulatto slave"), who are both tormented by their master, Prospero. In perhaps the most memorable scene from Césaire's version, Ariel meets up with Caliban to warn him that Prospero intends to do him harm. Caliban responds by accusing Ariel of being an obedient Uncle Tom, kneeling and groveling like a coward for the promise of a freedom his master will never grant. Ariel replies that Caliban's aggressive resistance is as likely to get him killed as freed, since Prospero is much too powerful. And in any case, just because he is servile, Ariel reckons, does not mean he is necessarily submissive. "Listen to me," he urges, "Prospero is the one we've got to change. Destroy his serenity so that he's finally forced to acknowledge his own injustice and put an end to it." Induce Prospero to acquire a conscience (!), Caliban scoffs, "you might as well ask a stone to grow flowers" (27). The pair part amicably, as "brothers," but remain disunited. Their relationship echoes Du Bois, who wrote that "we have two great and hardly reconcilable streams of thought and ethical strivings; the danger of the one lies in anarchy, that of the other in hypocrisy" (68). And while we might initially think of Louis as the anarchic Caliban deriding his father as the traitorous Ariel, Daniels's film offers a subtler and more optimistic conclusion, one that chimes with the ambiguous ending of Césaire's play.

Having quit the White House, Cecil finds and apologizes to Louis at a rally before fully reconciling with his son in jail when they both get briefly locked up for protesting. Time passes. Gloria passes. An elderly Cecil is shown anxiously watching the televised coverage of the 2008 presidential election and, as the result is announced, calls to his son to celebrate the fact that Senator Barack Obama has become the first African American president-elect. They tearfully embrace.

On the dignity of butlering, Emily Post was unequivocal: "Would it have been so much better, so much more dignified," she asks of personal maids and butlers, "who live long useful years in closest association with every cultivating influence of life, to have lived on in their native villages and worked in a factory, or to have had a little store of their own? Does this false idea of dignity—since it *is* false—go so far as that?" (137). Just before Gloria passed away, Cecil returned to the plantation (long closed and left to ruin) on which he was raised. He has returned to remember his daddy. Gloria marvels at what he had made of himself, of the dignity her husband had attained. It is one of the few scenes in the film where Cecil is not dressed in his butler's uniform (the other significant example being the moment Cecil is informed of his youngest son's death—in which he is attired in a garish disco outfit). Here, Cecil and Gloria are dressed in matching tracksuits. He is not defined by his life of butlering anymore than he is restricted to wearing that butler's uniform, but he *is* identified with both the vocation and the attire.

This dignity in service is what I think the film means by eliding Cecil with Sidney Poitier. When news of Obama's election was announced, film critics Manohla Dargis and A. O. Scott celebrated his victory by pointing out that the trail to his success was blazed by icons like Poitier, whose powerful onscreen presence "helped expand the possibilities for fictional blacks, and real ones" (qtd. in Knight 161). At the end of *The Butler*, Cecil waits to meet President Obama in the Oval Office following his inauguration. He wears the tie pins given to him by some of the presidents he had served during his time as butler. He is greeted by Obama's chief usher (Stephen Rider), who says it is a great honor to meet him. However, when the usher indicates the way, Cecil gruffly responds, "I know the way!" before shuffling toward the office. It is an ending that suggests that neither Cecil nor Louis's methods constitute the way to end racism alone. Rather, to effect change, both were needed, along with some time. For while Audre Lorde was right to claim that *"the master's tools will never dismantle the master's house* . . . to bring about genuine change," she was no less right in prefacing this sentiment with the less well-known idea that "survival . . . is learning how to take our differences and make them strengths" (19). "Difference must be not merely tolerated, but seen as a fund of necessary polarities between which our creativity can spark like a dialectic. Only then does the necessity for interdependency become unthreatening. . . . Difference is that raw and powerful connection from which our personal power is forged" (18). Francis Ponge expressed this by adapting Descartes' *Cogito ergo sum*: "I speak and you hear me, therefore we are" (qtd. in Kristeva, "Word" 45).[13] The power to seek new ways of being in the world rests on such hearing. It provides the courage needed to act "where there are no charters" (Lorde 18), whether attained through the visibility of the revolutionary's suffering while attempting to smash the status quo or in the butler's quiet dignity as he upholds the values for and on which both must stand.

6

Racist Etiquette

Disservice

> Better to reign in Hell than serve in Heaven.
>
> —Milton, *Paradise Lost*

~

Volte-face: *In the Heat of the Night*

LET ME PLUNGE, AS IF through a hypertextual jump, into the film over which Cecil's wife, Gloria, was gushing in *The Butler*, for it seems to me that while Louis might be justified in condemning Sidney Poitier in *Guess Who's Coming to Dinner*, his arguments appertain less well when they are applied to Poitier's performance in *In the Heat of the Night* (a film that, unlike his parents, he clearly has not seen). In a (not uncritical) essay on Poitier, James Baldwin claimed that the black performer must find himself in a "rather grim bind. He knows, on the one hand he really has no right *not* to appear, not only because he must work, but also for all those people who need to see him. By the use of his own person, he must *smuggle in a reality* that he knows is not in the script" ("Sidney Poitier" 225, emphasis mine). But where does this "smuggled reality" appear? And what is the value of this "reality" if, to be smuggled effectively, it remains so effectively concealed that no one notices it?

Several years before he made *Guess Who's Coming to Dinner*, Poitier starred in the Broadway production of Lorraine Hansberry's *A Raisin in the Sun*.[1] Seeing that performance, Baldwin was struck by Poitier's ability to present a "life on that stage [that] said something to them [black audiences] concerning their own lives ... they nourished and re-created each other" ("Sidney Poitier" 224). Against such vital performances, the "tepid liberalism" (as Frances Gateward calls it [174]) into which his characters were forced during the 1960s culminated, perhaps most problematically, in *Guess Who*. By contrast, this film was intended to say something to white liberal audiences. As Baldwin laments, "There was really nothing it *could* say to black people—except for the authority of Sidney's performance" ("Sidney Poitier" 226). But this authority was more than nothing. Of Poitier's performance in *The Defiant Ones* (1958), Baldwin noted a "quality of pain and danger and some fundamental impulse to decency that both titillates and reassures the white audience." But when in closeup his character speaks about his wife—who wants him to "be nice"—Baldwin was struck by the expression on Poitier's face as he delivers the line, "She say, 'Be nice. Be nice,'" which, noticed he, "conveys a sorrow and humiliation rarely to be seen on our screen" ("Sidney Poitier" 226). A smuggled reality.

Furthermore, Gateward argues that such realities were more liberally smuggled into the film over which Cecil's wife is gushing in *The Butler*; smuggled, that is, with such brazenness as to hardly befit the word. *In the Heat of the Night* opens with a train pulling into the station at a small town, Sparta, Mississippi. From the carriage steps a well-dressed black man in a tailored suit, his hands clasped around an expensive travel bag. He walks to a room to await a connection. We do not see his face, though we are left in no doubt that this is Poitier. Director Norman Jewison cuts from this figure to a patrolman, Officer Wood (Warren Oates), who stumbles across a murder victim lying in the street. He quickly raises the alarm with Chief Gillespie (Rod Steiger), who confirms the identity of the victim as a Phillip Colbert, a wealthy Northern industrialist planning to build a factory in this small town, bringing jobs and prosperity into the community.

Mindful of the political sensitivity surrounding this crime, Gillespie urges his officers to apprehend a suspect quickly, lest Colbert's widow (Lee Grant) renege on her husband's planned investment in the town. Thus, when he stumbles across Virgil Tibbs (Poitier) awaiting his connecting train to Memphis, Officer Wood's racist prejudices, coupled with the urgency to collar the perpetrator, establishes Tibbs as a main suspect. "On your feet, boy!" Wood demands. Tibbs reaches into his pocket for his identification but Wood, almost breathless with exhilaration, draws his gun before forcing his suspect to "assume the position." Pinned against the wall, Tibbs (who knows "the position" only too well) is roughly frisked. Gateward points out that having withheld from the audience the revelation of his star's face, Jewison builds the anticipation and excitement appropriate for the entrance of a big star (recall Welles in *The Third Man*). But when it comes, this reveal proves fraught, not to say troubling (173). Our star is insulted and demeaned, even abused, and "when he is forced to raise his hands," writes Gateward, "in that compulsory pose that too many innocent black men have been coerced to strike—now, as then—it is an affront to the dignity and humanity deserving of every person" (175). Gateward emphasizes the low-angle closeup of Tibbs with his hands against the wall: "Yes, it reveals the silent anger Poitier expresses so well, but also profound humiliation and wariness, as there is no guarantee he will survive the encounter" (173). Following Wood's frisk, Tibbs is triumphantly manhandled—paraded, even—through the station. He is presented to Chief Gillespie, a man, Gateward points out, who is in every way the opposite of Tibbs: "When Gillespie is gruff, Tibbs is mannered. When Gillespie is boorish, Tibbs is civil. When Gillespie is presumptuous, Tibbs is thoughtful" (172). Gillespie quickly discovers his chief suspect is a highly skilled forensic murder investigator from Philadelphia (although not before he perpetuates many of the racist assumptions that led to Tibbs being wrongly collared by Wood in the first place). However, with orders from an anxious mayor (William Schallert) to solve the crime, and with Tibbs ordered by his superiors to help, the unlikely pair team up to discover the real perpetrator.

Poitier's performance is suffused with characteristic restraint, authority, poise, posture, reasoned thinking, and above all decorum. However, it is also a performance punctuated by moments in which the effort of his restraint is telegraphed. Before replying to each insult and effrontery, he must almost literally bite his tongue. He pauses to collect himself. He bristles without ever rising to the bait. But in these early, fiery exchanges with Gillespie, Poitier smuggles in moments of subversive etiquette. "What d'ya hit him with?" Gillespie demands prior to discovering that Tibbs is not his man. "Hit *whom*?" Tibbs curtly responds. Still believing he will have the last laugh, and possibly even delighting that Tibbs's fall will be all the greater on account of his high social class, Gillespie mocks Tibbs's education ("*Whom*?!"). The smile is wiped from his face, however, at the revelation that Tibbs is a lawman, and Gillespie's inferiority is further reinforced when he realizes that Tibbs's salary is significantly higher than his. Hence, when Tibbs invites Gillespie to confirm his identity with his superiors in Philadelphia and offers to pay for the call, Gillespie's only means of defense is to insist that *he* pay. It is the first moment Gillespie attempts to claw back some of the dignity for which Southerners wish to be known, especially having so egregiously jettisoned it both in his manners and his deportment (in these early scenes, Steiger plays Gillespie as a slack-jawed, gum-chewing, and chair-slouching yokel).

Poitier's performance here is perhaps the epitome of torturous etiquette. Much of it is gestural. Mark Harris notes that Jewison and his screenwriter, Stirling Silliphant, pared a lot of Poitier's dialogue from the script to render Tibbs "someone who uses silence, withholding, and watchfulness as a weapon" (qtd. in Gateward 172). However, Tibbs's most memorable reaction occurs when he and Gillespie follow up on a clue—traces of fern root, discovered in the victim's car—leading them to Endicott's Cotton Plantation. On their approach, Gillespie gestures to the black farm workers picking cotton in the morning heat, sniping, "None of that for you, huh Virgil?" Jewison lingers on Poitier's face as he burns with anger, but his expression soon changes. "Is it a sense of shame," asks Gateward, "for letting the comment rile him, or is it class-guilt?" (173). When they arrive at the plantation house (grand, white-pillared, in the style favored by the South), they are greeted by a black butler (Jester Hairston), who ushers them into the house to speak to the owner of the farm, Eric Endicott (Larry Gates).

Endicott is courteous and offers both men a drink. Unwilling to impose, Gillespie refuses, but Tibbs pointedly accepts (he specifically requests "something cool, something soft"). No matter how graciously he does it, Tibbs's acceptance of the drink undermines

Gillespie's authority to establish himself as the lead in the questioning to come. On the one hand, Tibbs is already convinced (incorrectly, it will transpire) that Endicott is responsible for Colbert's murder—his motive: to drive (indeed kill!) off a powerful new competitor. On the other hand, however, Tibbs is clearly riled by the racist iconography on and of the farm (as Tibbs and Gillespie approach the house, Jewison frames their arrival against a black lawn jockey ornamenting the front garden). As Endicott invites Tibbs into his orchidarium, a conversation between them ensues that is unfalteringly gracious and polite: Tibbs begins by professing his admiration for orchids and demonstrating some floricultural understanding; Endicott responds by inviting him to look around. Tibbs compliments him: "It's beautiful, it's breathtaking." Then Endicott asks Tibbs what his favorite species is, and when Tibbs claims he is partial to the epiphytic, Endicott smiles to himself. How apt, he drawls: "Because, like the nigra, they need care, and feedin', and cultivatin'. And that takes time." Clearly, such a comment is designed to rankle Tibbs, not to say put him back in his place (given that Tibbs is manifestly thriving on his own). Endicott insinuates Tibbs is the exception proving the rule. "That's something you can't make some people understand," continues Endicott. "That's something Mr. Colbert didn't realize." Tibbs now picks out some of the fern roots from one of Endicott's flowerpots and holds it aloft. Playing dumb, he asks what it is called. "Osmunda—fern root," Endicott answers, at which Gillespie jolts in his seat. Recollecting that Tibbs found the same root in the victim's car, Gillespie suddenly registers that his partner is working up to accusing Endicott of murder. He politely excuses them both and makes to leave, but Endicott's suspicions have been raised. He demands to know why the officers have come, his expression turning quickly to disgust when Tibbs delicately asks questions about Endicott's whereabouts the night of the murder. Endicott steels his gaze and walks over to Tibbs, slapping him across the face. Without missing a beat, Tibbs slaps Endicott back, harder. It was the "slap heard around the world" (qtd. in Gateward 169).

"The use of all this racist iconography," Gateward argues, "coupled with the slave imagery of the cotton fields and insidious comments by Endicott . . . creates a sense of tension and foreboding that demands release" (173–74). She is right, and that tension is ratcheted as much by the faux decorum of both men: for Endicott, in the insincerity of his hospitality and the sincerity of his patronizing manner; and for

Tibbs, in his cynical dissemblance and feigned ignorance. It was the first time a black man had struck a white man in a modern context without consequence, writes Gateward, and it signified to contemporary audiences that the times were changing. After reeling from the shock of the unexpected blow, Endicott appears visibly shaken. But the hand raised to his mouth is less protective of a secondary assault than an (instinctive) attempted reclamation of something he seems to have lost (see Figure 6.1).

"You saw it," Endicott confirms with Gillespie, but the chief of police makes clear his intention not to act. Gillespie's prevarication adds insult to the injury, and Endicott's rancorous expression turns almost mournful as he tearfully notes that "there was a time when I could have had you shot." Tibbs says nothing but powerfully stares back. After all, he not only expected Endicott's slap; he provoked it. Poitier's eyes are ablaze with hate, his clenched jaw parts ever so slightly (not quite enough to bare his teeth), but he remains composed. He leaves, partly clattering the butler—who had pointedly returned with Tibbs's lemonade just before the slap (the butler ruefully shakes his head in sympathy with his employer before chasing after Tibbs to scold him for his impertinence).[2] But that line, "There was a time. . . ."—what Endicott's expression betrays is the knowledge, if not acceptance, that "that time" really has passed. It is

Figure 6.1. The slap heard around the world: *In the Heat of the Night*. Norman Jewison, The Mirisch Corporation, 1967. Digital frame enlargement.

not despite the renunciation of slavery that Endicott perceives the decline of Southern values but because of it. In this, he is not unlike John Taylor, who in 1818 argued that "personal slavery has constantly reflected the strongest rays of civil liberty and patriotism" (qtd. in Fox-Genovese and Genovese 94). In the modern era, men like Endicott have not only lost slave labor (and the right to slap and kill their "property" with impunity); they have lost dignity in the world. And worse, lost it to men like Tibbs.[3]

If, to return to the "Poitier Syndrome," such a vision of the modern world rings hollow given so many police killings of young black men, then perhaps it is in the smaller gestures than the bigger ones that Baldwin's "smuggled reality" is to be perceived. Earlier in the film, Tibbs had returned to the police station, desperate to leave the bigotry and catch the next train out of Sparta. He is warned not to enter Gillespie's office—the chief is away, and waiting for him is Colbert's widow, still ignorant of her husband's death (the white police officers all lacking the courage to tell her). Tibbs moves to walk out but an impulse stops him. Instead, he directly strides into Gillespie's office, ignoring the desk sergeant's pathetic protests, and curtly informs Mrs. Colbert that her husband is dead. He offers his hand in consolation and she eventually grasps it. For Gateward, the image of Poitier's black hand joining in compassion and empathy with Grant's white hand was no less a key image in the history of African American images onscreen than the slap heard around the world. Both seem to transcend, she argues, and at the same time to emphasize, race: with his intelligence, dignity, and impeccable sense of good form, Poitier makes his blackness a "fact of life." "By reaching out his hand to comfort a grieving woman but also in a lightning-quick backhand across the face of a rabid racist," we get "an image of a black man so rarely seen and even less well understood" (Gateward 176). While for Baldwin it was Poitier's face, for Gateward it was his hands. In both cases, his performance in *In the Heat of the Night* appears to substantiate Baldwin's hope that such "smuggled realities" might be capable of inducing white (liberal) audiences "to *think*, in any real way, of the *reality*, the presence, the simple human *fact* of black people" ("Sidney Poitier" 227). What is most important, Baldwin noted, was the "presence" of Poitier. The precedent he set "is of tremendous importance for people coming afterward. And perhaps that's what it's really all about—just that" ("Sidney Poitier" 228). It is a conclusion echoed by Gateward, who writes that while Poitier never lost the "syndrome that had so long plagued him," at least "some of what lies beneath could come to the light of day" (176). It is on this basis that Baldwin ultimately resisted the idea of "Poitier syndrome," observing that the black actor is not born an actor: all his experiences of racism will have made "his blood thick with humiliations," such that "whatever his training, he is not there to get a role he really wants to play: he is there to get a role which will allow him to be seen" ("Theater" 23).

I think what Baldwin referred to as "smuggled realities" is another way of describing the appearance of that historic humiliation. Such impolitic gestures are impolitic because they cut, however briefly, against the phantasmic "grain." For their capacity to arrest us, to captivate and capture us in often indelible film moments, Poitier's facial expressions and hand gestures seem to recapitulate, however briefly, something of that commanding stage presence both celebrated and mourned by Baldwin. When Stanley Kramer—who directed Poitier in *The Defiant Ones* (1958) and, of course, in *Guess Who*—reflected on Baldwin's critique of his films, he tried to account for the reaction by reflecting on his own identity. "The fact is that I am a white man who made films about human beings who happened to be black. I understood the problems of black men and women morally, socially and intellectually, but"—and here he references Du Bois's famous phrase, "the souls of black folk" (1903)—"the damn soul kept slipping between my fingers" (563). Kramer felt so vulnerable making these films, he likened it to getting undressed and, standing naked, declaring, "Well, look, this is where I'm vulnerable. Stab me there" (563). But in that same interview, Kramer also claimed that Poitier's power was the truth of his face, which he often treated like a landscape. "When you deal with people with this kind of power," Kramer concluded, "who have that kind of personality, just showing their face has a certain validity" (572).

I like Gateward's analysis of the way Tibbs's hand reaches forth and takes Mrs. Colbert's in sympathy. I like it very much. But if it works as an enduring image—the recognition of our common humanity, an image of the future—then it works as an image haunted by the look in Endicott's face of bitter hatred as he laments rather than celebrates the very same future. While we might have little sympathy for Endicott and his pain—might even celebrate the flicker of glee that flashes across Tibbs's eyes as he inflicts it—we can ill afford to simply ignore the suffering of men like Endicott, who (his innocence in the murder proved) will go on calling the shots in towns like Sparta. At the end of their investigation, Tibbs and Gillespie have worked through their differences and come to respect one another. Tibbs finally boards his train out of Sparta, and Gillespie, struggling to find the right words to say goodbye, simply calls to him, "You take care, you hear?" Tibbs smiles. It is a moment Baldwin read as an equivalent of the "fade-out kiss," but one that gave him the impression of "something strangling, alive, struggling to get out" (qtd. in Knight 175). Both men remain trapped in their history, because for every embracing reassurance of the future is an image of that same future being smothered. Today, we live in a world that is markedly different, but a new vocabulary with which to talk about racial difference has struggled to materialize. That image of strangulated love has lingered. But the "validity" of Poitier's face, the "rightness" of his performance, must go some way toward changing those historical parameters if for no other reason than that those images of dignity and defiance—and power—have now become part of our history.

White Looks: *Ma Rainey's Black Bottom*

There is power in looking.

—bell hooks, *Reel to Real*

Building on his screenplay for Robert Altman's murder-mystery drama *Gosford Park* (2001), series showrunner Julian Fellowes penned *Downton Abbey* (2010–15) as an update to the British drama series *Upstairs, Downstairs* (1971–75), which charted the early twentieth-century decline of the British aristocracy through the lives of both the masters "upstairs" and their servants "downstairs." Katherine Byrne notes that the "mutually respectful, contented, and even affectionate, existence" between the servants and their employers has led to criticisms that the show is idealized and "ideologically indefensible" in its portrayal of historical "truth" (177). She wonders whether the darker turn of the later series, especially following the brutal rape of Anna (Joanne Froggatt) in season four, marked a shift in the drama toward a more ominous, more volatile, vision of society. Byrne considers the lingering ambiguity over whether this marked a response by Fellowes to the charge of social conservatism or whether it redoubles that attitude. In keeping with the show's conservative theme, the darker turn might be viewed as nostalgic for the old hierarchies (a statement of the kind that "society begins to crumble when the old order is challenged or subverted"). On the other hand, perhaps it is meant to reflect the dark reality of that very "order" (acknowledging that such brutal violations subsist in that order—which is no order, for some) (185). Byrne settles on a more nuanced interpretation. What if social disorder is the price to be paid for new freedoms, she asks? "The cost of a movement away from the conventional, nostalgic heritage drama is that the world offered instead is less comforting and more disturbing." With fans around the world denouncing the darker storylines as unpalatable, as too difficult to bear, Byrne concludes that this more disturbing world must be one that "many viewers do not wish to inhabit for it resembles too closely their own" (188).

It is a perspicacious analysis, but I want to flip the idea on its head by looking not at the crumbling of social conservativism but its opposition.

Based on August Wilson's play (1982) of the same name, *Ma Rainey's Black Bottom* (2020) introduces us to the "Mother of Blues," Gertrude "Ma" Rainey (Viola Davis), whose (white) manager, Irvin (Jeremy Shamos), has secured a recording contract with (also white) producer Mel (Jonny Coyne) to cut a record they all know will sell to a (mostly white) public hungry for the "authentic" sound of the (quintessentially black) blues. This takes place in Chicago during the summer of 1927, and jazz records are the latest must-have in popular music. There is, however, a snag: Ma is ever so late, and their expensive studio time is ticking away. As Irvin anxiously paces and Mel quietly seethes "upstairs," Ma's band members are ordered to wait "downstairs" in a stuffy, sweltering little practice room. The July heat has frayed everyone's nerves, and the lightly bantering musicians soon begin to press more heavily on one another's flanks. When Ma finally turns up over an hour late, she is unrepentant and uncooperative, fiercely demanding the ice-cold Coca-Cola she had been promised. Not one note will she sing without it. Her diva-like behavior worsens when, having slaked her thirst with the freshly bought cola, Ma insists on her nephew Sylvester (Dusan Brown)—a boy with a pronounced stutter—speaking the spoken-word opening to the album. Mel silently fumes. Irvin wrings his hands. The band members stand idly. In take after take, the boy stumbles over his lines. The song is "Ma Rainey's Black Bottom," and with each failed attempt Ma patiently insists he will get it right soon enough. Finally, Sylvester nails the intro and the band nails the song—to the relief of the near exasperated manager and producer. As they take a break, Ma sits with her trombonist, Cutler (Colman Domingo). Gesturing up at Mel and Irvin in the mixing booth, she offers an insight into her recalcitrant behavior: while they treat her like a big star, she confides, and give into every demand no matter how whimsical, their obsequiousness is nothing more than an act. It is a false etiquette, and Ma knows that those white men are up there right now (she gestures up to the booth) cursing her name. If they didn't have my voice, Ma reasons, they would treat her no different than "a dog in the alley." Cutler sympathizes.

As the false etiquette "upstairs" becomes strained, so too do tensions fray "downstairs," as the band's ambitious young trumpeter, Levee (Chadwick Boseman), voices his plans to leave Ma's band and become a star on his own terms. The others find him arrogant and lacking in respect. In turn, he mocks one of the other musicians, Toledo (Glynn Turman), for having faith in God but no personal aspiration. Toledo fires back, ridiculing Levee's flashy new shoes and heaping scorn on his belief that a producer like Mel—from whom Levee is hoping to secure a record deal—would ever make a black man like him a star. Agitated by Toledo's stinging remarks (and fearful they might be true), Levee finds Mel and presses him for a response to his demos, but the producer dismisses his songs, claiming they're worth just five bucks apiece because there's no market for them. Brokenhearted, Levee sells his songs and slumps dejectedly back into the practice room. Baldwin wrote that no matter how servile an individual appears, "there is always a murderous rage, or a murderous fear, or both, not quite sleeping at the very bottom of their hearts and minds" (Baldwin, "Theater" 21). It proves as much when Toledo inadvertently steps on one of Levee's shiny yellow shoes. He apologizes, but Levee refuses to accept his apology. Blinded with rage, Levee stabs Toledo in the back. He realizes with horror what he has done and breaks down, cradling his dead friend as the rest of the band looks dolefully on.

The film ends with three powerfully deflating performative reactions. The first is Boseman's crestfallen expression as Levee registers that his friend is dead by his own hand, and that his career aspirations are over (it is a moment with added pathos: Chadwick Boseman died in postproduction, making this performance his last). The second reaction takes place outside the studio where, having finally finished recording, Ma has left without signing the release papers. Irvin hurriedly follows her out, begging and squirming as he desperately tries to convince her to sign the paperwork here and now—without which he and Mel cannot sell the record. At the very last moment, Ma relents and signs. But with her signature secured, Irvin's entire demeanor changes: the balance of power now shifted, he brusquely snatches the papers up and waltzes away without so much as a kindly glance, let alone a word of gratitude. By contrast, Ma deflates, both in body and spirit. Her face weighs with the confirmation of what she already knew, perhaps has always known: to these white men she is like the bird in the story told by Plutarch of a man who plucked a nightingale and, finding but little to eat, exclaimed, "You are a voice and nothing more." As she is driven away, Ma exhaustedly slumps in the backseat wearing a lost, glazed expression that sags her features.[4]

But there is a third reaction at the end of the film—namely my reaction. Before I can explain it, I need to explore a little of the context underpinning the film's approach to cultural appropriation.

White supremacists "worship at the throne of black mediocrity," bell hooks noted, for it confirms their sense of innate superiority. And when that belief is challenged, as it abundantly is in music—for "music is a terrain where black people in fact do push to the limit, do always go everywhere there is to go and beyond that" (*Reel* 190)— it is there that we especially discover the egregiousness of cultural appropriation. Already reeling at the end of *Ma Rainey* from these two deflated reaction shots of Boseman and Davis, both drained of their vivacity and vitality—drained of life, a sucker-punch landed for this viewer when, in a chilling coda, we return once more to the same recording studio in which the entire film has taken place. Except now, all the warm colors appear desaturated (the film was photographed by Tobias A. Schliessler). We hear Levee's song being sung by a white singer accompanied by (we soon discover as the camera pulls out) an all-white band. Mel is recording it. It doesn't matter that this version of the song is as sapped of Levee's energy as the room is of color. It doesn't matter that the song, while slickly played and silkily sung, seems vapid, soulless, and *blues-less* after what we have witnessed Ma do with her band (Ma's singing voice was performed by "the goddess of wind," Maxayn Lewis). What matters is the erasure of Levee and Ma, and the construction of this white fantasy band to effectively "cover" it. The coda raised in me a strange feeling of . . . shame.

In *Being and Nothingness*, Jean-Paul Sartre described shame as a useful means to explore the problem of the existence of others. It is a curious mode of consciousness, he wrote, a "shameful apprehension *of* something and this something is *me*. I am ashamed of what I *am*. Shame therefore realizes an intimate relation of myself to myself. Through shame I have discovered an aspect of my being" (245). What makes it curious, Sartre thought, is that I do not feel shame in isolation: I feel shame *before somebody else*. When I make a vulgar gesture that gesture "clings to me," but I don't judge it; "I simply live it." "But now suddenly I raise my head. Somebody was there and has seen me. Suddenly I realize the vulgarity of my gesture, and I am ashamed . . . I am ashamed of myself *as I appear* to the Other." "Shame is by nature *recognition*. I recognize that I *am* as the Other sees me . . . Nobody can be vulgar all alone!" (246).[5] Nothing new is added, except the gaze of another person. The Other is an "as if" in my experience. Since I cannot know what they think of me, I experience their gaze "as if" they thought of my vulgarity the way I am moved by their presence to think of it now. But the contradiction is that I only think my behavior vulgar, am only ashamed of it, because I treat the Other "as if" she sees, and judges, me doing it (Sartre 251).

One way of reading the final scene in *Ma Rainey*, then, is to think of it in terms set out by Ron Scapp, who writes that "liberals may pride themselves in their ability to tolerate others but it is only after the other has been redescribed as oneself that the liberal is able to be 'sensitive' to the question of cruelty and humiliation" (qtd. in hooks, *Black Looks*). The white performers clearly undermine this sensitivity because of the way this space is cleansed of color. We remember Levee's voice, its timbre and passion, just we recall the urgency of his ambition, and how unjustly he was cheated of his songbook, through their very absence. But why did I feel personally ashamed at seeing this act of cultural appropriation? Why not a (very liberal) rage at the cruelty of Mel's theft from and humiliation of Levee when he knew the true value of his music?

The moment elicits shame, I think, because director George C. Wolfe has constructed the entire film around different modalities of power. This power is clearly connected to space and to looking. First, space. The "upstairs, downstairs" division ultimately boils down to Levee's desire to become Ma Rainey—to have her clout over men like Mel and Irvin and sell as many records as she does. Unlike the rest of the band, Levee wants to be "upstairs." But things aren't much better up there. As Ma resignedly points out to Cutler, there is another hierarchy of power "above" her, too. The recording booth is where the real power begins. Her voice might be its chief resource—the fuel of their success—but despite the money and flattery hers is a resource to be cynically used up and discarded (while being privately disrespected into the bargain). Second, and perhaps more important, we get looking. hooks wrote that parents punish children for staring because, unlike looks, gazes are "seen as confrontational, as gestures of resistance, challenges to authority" (*Reel* 197). The gaze is political, but the parental injunction to the child also creates a kind of terror: staring can, parents warn, be dangerous. The child learns to look the other way, hooks wrote, and so is afraid to look when the punishing parent enjoins them, "Look at me when I talk to you."[6] "Afraid to look, but fascinated by the gaze" (*Reel* 197). hooks recalled learning that slaves were denied the right to look, too, and were punished—just like children. Later, she reflected that the domination of parents and slaveowners alike was not so absolute that the child or slave never sneaked a peep, dared to "stare dangerously." For such people, the gaze becomes an act of rebellion, an "oppositional gaze" (*Reel* 198). For hooks, this feeds Stuart Hall's conception of the black spectator, who must shed the construction of blackness onscreen by whites as a snake sheds its skin. Such freedom depends on the agency, writes Manthia Diawara, of the spectator who resists "complete identification with the film's discourse" (qtd. in hooks 199). These are moments of progressive rupture.

But what was so subversive, at least for me, about the final moment in *Ma Rainey* was the way Wolfe already positions his viewers in a black perspective. We never see the film through the eyes of Mel or Irvin. And given Ma is not much more empowered than Levee, we never get the perspective of a true "upstairs" (unlike *Downton Abbey*)—*until that final shot*. The rupture, as it were, goes the wrong way. Instead of cinematic pleasure being defined in relation to stereotypical images of blackness—as degraded and dehumanized, as hooks warns—this film presents the warmth and color of black lives that matter. When those lives are exhausted (or in the case of Levee and Toledo, destroyed), we mourn those losses as though they were ours. But the final shot reminds white viewers that these lives do not belong to, nor are they assimilable to, a white perspective. One lacks the proper "lived experience," as James Baldwin and others have put it ("Theater" 22).[7] Instead of moving from an act of consumption to one of acknowledgment, we go in the opposite direction, echoing Ma's comment from earlier in the movie, that "white folk don't understand the blues. They hear it come out, but they don't know how it got there," and that "this be an empty world without the blues."

From this perspective, the territorial violation at the end of *Ma Rainey* reminds us of that emptiness. It is as though this space has been "invaded" by the white musicians, as if—like Levee's song—it does not belong to them. I attribute my feelings of shame in this final volte-face to the unexpected experience of finding myself reflected in their transgressing faces—the white faces of white performers covering black music while erasing the black artists who invented it. The wounding "rupture" had been covered over, plastered over, as if it had never happened. If there is an oppositional gaze in *Ma Rainey*, then it is a kind of "white look" that reverses hooks's "black look"—a look numb to the pain of black history and deaf to the sound of the blues. It was a reassuringly uncomfortable experience.

Author's Note

This chapter is dedicated to the memory of Sidney Poitier, who passed away as I finished writing it.

(January 7, 2022)

Part III

Dissolution

7

Garments of the Mind

Clothes

> Behaviour is the garment of the mind and ought to have the conditions of a garment.
>
> —Francis Bacon, *The Advancement of Learning*

~

WHILE EARLY GUIDES ON civility like Erasmus's *De civilitate morum puerilium* (published in 1530) sought to instruct young men on the disgusting habits and behaviors (farting, scratching, spitting, vomiting, belching, and nose picking) ill-befitting the royal court (whence, "courtesy"), later guides focused more on habits one should adopt—"positive features," such as good deportment and grace, as well as the means to redress social slights and wrongs. Those later manuals aimed to define the "man of quality," as the seventeenth-century French diplomat Antoine de Courtin put it. Thus, in moving from general instruction on mannered behavior to a description of the mannered type, later etiquette guides gave birth to the concept of "the gentleman," a concept invented, quipped Bertrand

Russell, to keep the expanding middle classes in order. The gentleman, then, was invented as a class fantasy, with national deviations. Theodor Fontane, for instance, distinguished the German character from the English by the latter's emphasis on "outward packing," on which he remarked that in England "you need not be a gentleman, you must only have the means to appear one, and you are one. You need not be right, you must find yourself within the forms of rightness, and you are right" (quoted in Elias, *Civilizing Process* 30). Emily Post disagreed, noting of the American male that if he was "well-bred," he can never deteriorate in manner: "A gentleman may be in his shirt sleeves actually, but he never gets into his shirt sleeves mentally" (446). In other words, a gentleman "dresses down" in appearance only, never in his decorum. If his manners "slip," he does not just cease to be a gentleman—he never was one.[1]

Nonetheless, a gentleman can be discerned from what he wears. In Edith Wharton's novels, writes Hildegard Hoeller, "you wear your manners on your sleeves, so to speak; or even better, your choice of sleeve reveals the manners but so does the shape of the arm it covers. Indeed, manners are expressed most perfectly by the way in which the sleeve is chosen to tastefully reveal and cover the arm. . . . Manners are about exhibition" (139). This chapter considers the exhibition of gentlemanliness as a version of the basic problem of etiquette: is anyone capable of being a gentleman, determined as such by how they "fit the cut" of their cloth? Are some "born gentlemen," while others condemned by birth never to "measure up"? Following this discussion, the chapter considers an analogous argument apropos of the lady. I return to William Wyler's *Jezebel* (1938) to consider a female fashion faux pas resulting in social (and literal) death. Here, it is less a question of whether the lady can be "made" but "unmade" by a sartorial choice.

Playing a Gentleman: *Our Man in Havana*

All men are equal—all men, that is to say, who possess umbrellas.

—E. M. Forster, *Howards End*

The exhibition of manners is crucial to Carol Reed's *Our Man in Havana* (1959), in which a vacuum cleaner salesman, Jim Wormold

(Alec Guinness), struggles to make ends meet in pre-revolutionary Cuba. Wormold is a single parent who cannot resist giving in to his spendthrift teenage daughter (Jo Morrow) while dreaming of a better life for her (a finishing school in Switzerland). One day, Wormold catches sight of a well-dressed man who, despite the Cuban climate, dresses in a suit and bowler hat, and walks everywhere clutching his umbrella—as though it were an extension of his arm ("An Englishman walks in a pouring rain," wrote Emerson, "swinging his closed umbrella like a walking stick. . . . And he has been doing this for several generations, it is now in the blood" ["English Traits" 519]). The well-dressed man introduces himself to Wormold as Hawthorne (Noël Coward), and the salesman's instinct is to try and close a sale. But Hawthorne slips distractedly away, apparently having come with other ideas. They meet again in a bar, and this time Hawthorne ushers Wormold into the men's room to reveal that he is part of the British Secret Service and Her Majesty's Government would like Wormold to enlist. Utterly bemused, Wormold politely declines, wondering aloud what MI6 could possibly want with a man like him. He is tempted, however, when Hawthorne mentions the generous tax-free salary. Wormold's mission, Hawthorne explains, would be to use his vacuum cleaner business as a front to recruit new agents and report on any fluctuations in the economy. Think it over, he says as he departs, forgetting (intentionally?) his umbrella.

Could he, Wormold, become a secret agent? Taking up Hawthorne's umbrella, Wormold begins to dream. That night, his daughter asks where the umbrella came from. Wormold opens it up (indoors—bad luck) and places a lampshade on his head to perform a little circus routine, a reference to a time when they saw a clown perform (see Figure 7.1).

But Wormold wants to play the gentleman. He resolves to accept Hawthorne's offer. He buys a suit and joins an expensive country club to search for agents to recruit. However, Wormold has exactly zero success and soon fears that Hawthorne and his superiors back in MI6 will grow impatient and cut the salary to which he and his daughter have quickly become accustomed. On the advice of his German pal, Dr. Hasselbacher (Burl Ives), Wormold begins to invent the agents, and, to his delight, he is believed. Now Wormold begins to turn his talent for inventing fictional spies to writing fictional spy novels. But when MI6 see Wormold's drawings for a fictional superweapon (based on vacuum cleaner designs), they believe them to be real.

Figure 7.1. Gentleman or clown? Alec Guinness in *Our Man in Havana*. Carol Reed, Columbia Pictures, 1959. Digital frame enlargement.

They dispatch a well-trained secretary, Beatrice (Maureen O'Hara), to support Wormold and his "agent" in the field. Beatrice is sharp as a tack, and Wormold must now cover his tracks by "killing off" this imaginary agent. But when a real man with the same name turns up murdered and Hasselbacher's lab is trashed, Wormold begins to fret that his fictions are somehow bleeding into reality.

The tension in the film is held in Wormold's attempts to keep his lies from unraveling while also being thrust into the middle of a very real spy drama for which he feels hopelessly inadequate. The stakes are raised further when he and Beatrice are arrested by a corrupt police captain, Segura (Ernie Kovacs), who suspects he is involved with the murdered "agent." Despite believing himself to be a man of considerable social grace, Segura is a vulgarian and notorious sadist. Concerned Wormold will be tortured into revealing his knowledge of the superweapon, Beatrice plays for time by asking how Segura got one of the engineers to talk. "Thumbscrews?" she sardonically suggests. Segura chuckles, missing the inference (that he is not the suave gentleman he presents himself to be, but a brutish thug). "The engineer does not belong to the torturable class," Segura observes (as though sharing a brilliant insight). Surprised, Beatrice asks if there are really "class distinctions in torture." Missing (or else indifferent to) her sarcasm, Segura earnestly confirms her suspicion, "Yes, some people expect to be tortured. Others are outraged by it. One never tortures except by mutual agreement." Astonished, Beatrice wonders who would ever *agree*, to which Segura casually responds, "Usually the poor," adding that "in your [British] welfare state, you have social securities, therefore you have no poor. Consequently, you are untorturable."[2]

Torture by mutual consent? The idea seems preposterous, but cinema history seems to confirm it. When Sam Spade (Humphrey Bogart) is threatened with torture in *The Maltese Falcon* (1941), he makes clear he is having none of it, and patiently explains why torture won't work on him. Impressed, his would-be torturer (Sidney Greenstreet) joyfully exclaims, "By gad, sir, you *are* a character!" Likewise, James Bond appears to be untorturable, even when he is being tortured. Consider Daniel Craig's "scratching my balls" line in *Casino Royale* (2006). And to take one further example, Dr. Lecter (Anthony Hopkins) is entirely unmoved at the thought of being fed "feet first" to pigs specially reared by mercenaries to devour human flesh in *Hannibal* (2001). He jeers at and taunts his captors and, when Agent Starling (Julianne Moore) arrives to rescue him, shows no surprise but purringly greets her with impeccable courtesy ("Good evening, Clarice,") before complimenting her ("You look well").[3] Contrastingly, some scenes depict men who *believed* themselves untorturable but had this belief proven wrong. In *Scarface* (1983), when a mid-level drug dealer, Tony Montana (Al Pacino), avenges a botched assassination attempt ordered by his boss, Lopez (Robert Loggia), he finds his target in the middle of a meeting with a corrupt cop, Bernstein (Harris Yulin), who has been extorting money from Tony. Bernstein barely flinches when Tony executes Lopez and sits, aloofly watching the drama. But when Tony rounds on him, a flicker of uncertainty crosses Bernstein's brow as he issues a warning, "Don't go too far, Tony." Tony shoots him in the gut. "You can't shoot a *cop*," Bernstein gasps in disbelief.

These examples feature individuals who either uphold their social role, change it (upwards), or have that (higher) social role undermined. But in *Our Man*, Wormold is only "playing" at being a classy spy. The ingenuous Segura never suspects him of being a fake, and the more Wormold denies being an agent (to avoid being tortured), the more Segura believes the lie. Even Beatrice, who is initially skeptical of Wormold's reported successes in Havana, is won over by the sheer audacity of his fabulations. The film explores the idea that Wormold can fantasize himself into a higher social class by, first, saying the right things and wearing the right clothes (and possessing an umbrella); and second, by denying that he is in fact what he claims to be. In constructing this image of himself "as an agent," Wormold fails when he acts truthfully (that is, genuinely attempts to recruit agents) and succeeds when he falsifies (invents) them. Then, when the fantasy becomes reality, the more he attempts to distance himself from the lies and affirm his true humbleness, the more his constructed self is bought into. Spy craft, after all, depends on dishonesty and dissimulation.

To paraphrase a famous construction by Jean-Paul Sartre, Wormold is playing *at being* a secret agent (*Being and Nothingness* 82). "Nothingness," or the performance resting on it, produces "being." This is proved in the final third of the film when, as was inevitable, Beatrice discovers Wormold's deception. She forgives him (they have fallen in love), and together they resolve to complete their mission before returning to London to face the music. But as he stares down threats from Segura and enemy agents who have targeted him for assassination, Wormold discovers that he now possesses the attributes of a real secret agent. He shows wiliness and resourcefulness in besting Segura. He is dignified in the face of death and turns the tables on the enemy agents (not to mention that Alec Guinness looks dapper in a suit!). He is just like the child who, as Sartre put it, "plays with his body in order to explore it, to take inventory of it . . . [who] plays with his condition in order to *realize* it" (82). The cloth of the film hangs on the gap between "playing at" and "being." At least this is where the film's comedy derives from. If Wormold is merely a secret agent, the story ceases to be funny (it becomes another James Bond film). *Our Man* is far richer. It is a film about performance and performativity, about the power of performative dreaming. Wormold cannot simply take Hawthorne's umbrella; he must seize it. "I'm not the stuff of secret agents," he rues. But the point of the film is that no one has the stuff of secret agents. It is always a performance. One either performs well or badly in the role. Just like a gentleman.

Born Gentlemen: DiCaprio's Conmen

> One way of looking at speech is to say that it is a constant stratagem to cover nakedness.
>
> —Harold Pinter, *Plays One*

Steven Spielberg's *Catch Me If You Can* (2002) begins with the disillusionment of a teenager, Frank Abagnale (Leonardo DiCaprio), whose world falls apart when the family is forced to downsize to pay his father's tax debts and his mother admits to having an affair. To cope with his parents' subsequent divorce, Frank escapes into a fantasy world pretending to be various figures of authority. Initially, his scams are spontaneous (on his first day at a new school, he poses as a substitute teacher), but with each successful con he orchestrates larger and more complex cheats (including banking fraud). In one scene, having plagiarized a medical certificate and obtained a job as a night supervisor on a quiet ward, Frank is interrupted (in a tryst with a hospital worker!) by an emergency call. Reluctantly, he attends and is immediately confronted by blood and gore that turns his stomach. A young boy has a fractured tibia from a bicycle fall and two junior doctors (Jonathan Brent and Shane Edelman) want his advice. Not only does Frank have zero clue about what to do, he is nauseous at the sight of the broken bone poking out of the wound. One of the junior doctors explains what happened, but Frank can do little more than ask the other, "Do you concur?" It is a line he has gleaned from watching medical dramas on television. Confused, the junior queries the question ("Concur? With what?!"). Caught in a bind, Frank doubles down. "Do you *concur*?" he asks again, more firmly. The first junior doctor then proposes a course of treatment with which Frank quickly agrees. With one last glance at the protruding bone (which Spielberg and editor Michael Kahn cut to in closeup), Frank queasily compliments the junior doctors on their excellent work before scurrying from the emergency room to puke in a nearby janitorial cupboard. However, any thought that Frank has blown his cover with these junior doctors is shortly belied when the one who had hesitated to concur reflects to the other, "I blew it, didn't I?" he self-chastises. "Why didn't I concur!?"

With every "Mm" and "Yes" as he plays for time, Frank conceals his utter lack of training behind a performance of suppressed knowledge. He doesn't tell these junior doctors he is testing them; they just assume it. One is reminded of the scene in *Titanic* (1997) in which a young man from steerage class, Jack Dawson (DiCaprio, again), is (grudgingly) invited to dinner in the first-class dining saloon on the upper decks by the snobbish Cal Hockley (Billy Zane) to reward him for rescuing his fiancée, Rose DeWitt Bukater (Kate Winslet), from nearly falling overboard. Jack is lent a dinner jacket by a sympathetic passenger, Molly (Kathy Bates), and warned to expect some rough treatment. Considered *nouveau riche* ("new money," hence vulgar), Molly is also something of an outsider in this company of "aristocratic" (i.e., "old money") Hockleys and Bukaters. She warns Jack that dinner will be like entering the "snake pit." However, when Jack appears he exudes charm and sophistication. Against the stuffily miserable and boorishly narcissistic Hockley, Jack shines. But it is all an act. While waiting for Rose at the foot of the stairs, Jack checks his tie and waistcoat before glancing around the room to see how the other gentlemen carry themselves, imitating their gestures and general deportment.

When Rose appears and descends the staircase in a radiant gown, he beams up at her. When she reaches him, she cannot help gushing as he bows, offers his arm, and delicately kisses the back of her hand (see Figure 7.2). Astonished not just at how well Jack has "scrubbed up" but at how well he is imitating a gentleman, Rose raises an eyebrow in response to which he confesses that he learned such mannerisms from watching the Nickelodeon.

Just as it is Frank's white coat and stock phrases (more than his forged credentials) that enable him to "pass" as a doctor, Jack's loaned dinner jacket and plagiarized affectations enable him to "pass" for a gentleman. And we know Jack passes because the viperous Cal feels it

Figure 7.2. Class act: Leonardo DiCaprio in *Titanic*. James Cameron, Paramount Pictures, 1997. Digital frame enlargement.

necessary to scoff at the sight of him: "Well, it's amazing! You could almost pass for a gentleman," to which Jack smartly retorts, "*Almost.*" Jack picks up what he can and improvises the rest. When he quietly balks at the number of knives and forks surrounding his plate, Molly surreptitiously advises him to begin at the outside and work his way in. On the surface, Jack is a "veneered gentleman, not a real one," as Emily Post would have put it—a man "whose social position is self-made." Of such men, Post had this simple advice for those in "best society": "*Shun him!*" He is not the "born gentleman," a "man of breeding," or a "thoroughbred" (508)—clearly belying her claim that good etiquette concerns behavior rather than breeding. But Jack proves himself better bred than the repulsive Cal, who, when informed that the iceberg collision will mean that half the passengers on board the Titanic will drown, simply smirks and replies, "Not the better half."

The problem with Post's contradictory view of the gentleman is even more clearly elaborated in *The Talented Mr. Ripley* (1999), in which a low-class piano tuner, Tom Ripley (Matt Damon), is mistaken for a Princeton graduate by a wealthy businessman (James Rebhorn), who then tasks him with traveling to Italy to convince his listless son, Dickie (Jude Law), to return home from a life of frivolous luxury. Tom falls in love with Dickie's fine clothes and Italian lifestyle—indeed, with Dickie himself—and his lies spin out of control as he struggles to stay afloat in a world of snobs and sneers. Murray Pomerance describes the dynamic as a "double desire and a double infraction: Tom wants Dickie (the film is set in 1955 in Italy and homosexuality is vigorously denied by the state); and Tom wants Dickie's class." He penetrates (or at least threatens to penetrate) the boundaries of masculinity, heterosexuality, and privilege all at once ("Tom Ripley's Talent" 316). Tom is especially despised by one of Dickie's repulsively louche friends, Freddie (Philip Seymour Hoffman), who hates Tom because he whiffs of social inferiority. Freddie believes, writes Pomerance, that privilege "should continue indefinitely because it is not only beautiful—and therefore desirable to those who lack it—but also natural, the birthright of those who claim it," and what irks Freddie the most "is not that Tom has acquired a taste for the good life . . . but that Tom has begun to make a claim upon that taste" ("Tom Ripley's Talent" 328).

Likewise, DiCaprio's conmen threaten high society because they possess talents enabling them to "pass" as gentlemen, thereby undermining the gentleman's claim to be distinct by dint of his noble birth. It is not merely that DiCaprio's conmen "work" high society like grifters; it is that their work in high society cannot be separated by observable measures, their comportment or deportment. No one could be more dangerous to a man like Cal Hockley, whose sense of belonging to the "better half" of the ship hinges on his ability to distinguish himself from his social inferiors. Perhaps Jack's talents are signified by his extraordinary facility for life-drawing. It is through Jack's sketch of Rose in the nude that Cal discovers his fiancée is having a passionate love affair with him. When the ship begins to sink after striking the iceberg, Cal accuses Jack of theft and has his valet (David Warner) chain him up below deck—condemning him to drown along with the "lesser half" of the ship. But Jack, like Frank in *Catch Me If You Can*, proves that despite his low birth he is the true gentleman (sacrificing himself so that Rose can live her life freed from Cal and his repugnant class). In these roles, DiCaprio plays a figure like Baudelaire, of whom Walter Benjamin wrote that "he catches things in flight; this enables him to dream that he is like an artist. Everyone praises the swift crayon of the graphic artist. Balzac claims that artistry as such is tied to a quick grasp" (41).[4] DiCaprio's characters make themselves gentlemen, because beneath the surface of their finery beats a heart that is good and moral. They are (like DiCaprio himself) artists—and as Danish author Isak Dinesen (Karen Blixen) wrote in her short story "Babette's Feast" (1958), "An artist is never poor." Rather, they correspond to the individual described by Emerson,

> whose manners, though wholly within the conventions of elegant society, were never learned from there, but were original and commanding, and held out protection and prosperity; one who did not need the aid of a court-suit, but carried the holiday in his eye; who exhilarated the fancy by flinging wide the doors of new modes of existence; who shook off the captivity of etiquette, with happy, spirited bearing, good-natured and free as Robin Hood; yet with the port of an emperor,—if need be, calm, serious, and fit to stand the gaze of millions. (qtd. in Cavell, *Pursuits of Happiness*)

A Burst of Color: Will Smith in *Six Degrees of Separation*

> Stars, hide your fires;
> Let not light see my black and deep desires.
>
> —*Macbeth*

If Tom Ripley has two strikes against his character (his social class and his sexuality), Paul Poitier—a black man—has three. Fred Schepisi's *Six Degrees of Separation* (1993) begins with an art dealer, Flan Kittredge (Donald Sutherland), and his wife, Ouisa (Stockard Channing), agitatedly flapping around their Fifth Avenue apartment on the Upper East Side of New York. They appear to have been burgled and scramble to locate various prized possessions while grimly reflecting on how much worse it could have been (What if our throats had been slashed in our sleep, Ouisa gasps? Would we have awoken?). Schepisi and editor Peter Honess cut to the Kittredges at a wedding sometime later, somewhat self-indulgently regaling their upper-class pals with the story of what happened. As they speak, we cut back to the Kittredges in their apartment the evening before the robbery took place.[5] They are preparing to go to dinner with a wealthy white South African friend, Geoffrey (Ian McKellen), from whom they hope to secure a loan of two million dollars to purchase a Cézanne. A generous commission from the onward sale of this painting will save the Kittredges from insolvency (although Flan has kept from his wife just how dire their finances are). With so much at stake, the couple nervously entertain their guest: Ouisa makes dinner reservations while Flan waxes lyrical about a Kandinsky painting ("Mid-period, Landscape of a dark green forest," he comments ostentatiously, "in the far distance you see the sunlight . . . a burst of color asked to carry so much"). Mid-flow, Flan is interrupted by the sudden arrival of the doorman carrying a young, handsome black man dressed in a two-piece suit. He has been stabbed in an apparent mugging in Central Park. The stranger is Paul (Will Smith), who tells the Kittredges that he is a friend of their children at Harvard and asks if he might impose on their hospitality just long enough to patch up his wounded torso and recover from his horrible experience.

The Kittredges are thrown. Keen to help (and be seen by Geoffrey to help), but equally anxious not to let this intrusion derail their crucially important evening, they rush around, cleaning and dressing Paul's wound and loaning him a pink shirt while continuing to woo Geoffrey. On the one hand, Flan worries he is losing his investment as their South African guest's attention begins to wander. On the other, he appears no less fearful that Paul will bleed on their expensive rug. As Ouisa tends to Paul's stab wound, he calls to her, "Where is the medical book?"—but mimes to ask her to fetch medical gloves. His mime betrays a fear concerning blood contamination at a heightened time in the AIDS epidemic. He is also chary of giving offense.[6] All appears lost as Geoffrey motions to leave, but the tide turns as a newly patched up Paul thanks them for their hospitality, warmly compliments the Kittredges on their apartment, mentions his fondness for their children, and comments knowledgably about the double-sided Kandinsky hanging in the apartment. The young man has unimpeachable manners. Somewhat impressed, Ouisa, Flan, and Geoffrey become intrigued by him. Paul tells them his father is a well-known film director arriving in New York to begin work on an adaptation of the musical *Cats*. Can one do a film adaptation of *Cats*? they jest. And who is your father, asks Flan. "He named the greatest black movie star of the fifties and sixties," Ouisa gushes to their (now growing) wedding crowd of listeners. He named Sidney Poitier.

Any lingering thoughts of getting rid of this interloper suddenly vanish. "Your father means a great deal in South Africa," Geoffrey enthuses. Sensing that Paul's intrusion on their evening might prove serendipitous for their deal, the Kittredges work to resolve the problem of dinner. Having lost their reservation, Paul insists on cooking for them. And what a gourmand he proves! He watches them devour his cooking as he sits and watches ("the cook never eats"). They gulp back red wine and listen to him talk about his father. Paul seems satisfied by their satisfaction (see Figure 7.3). The evening is rescued and more.

After dinner, as they drink coffee and liqueurs in a plush sitting room, Geoffrey begs Paul to tell them about his thesis—the only copy of which was stolen in the mugging. Paul soon captivates them with a moving speech about his research into J. D. Salinger's *The Catcher in the Rye* (1951), explaining that this novel about fear of phoniness ("What scares me most is the other guy's face") reflects a modern paralysis (he references Chekhov and Beckett) experienced

Figure 7.3. Will Smith in *Six Degrees of Separation*. Fred Schepisi, MGM, 1993. Digital frame enlargement.

as the "death of the imagination." We no longer share a link to the inner world, laments he, concluding, "I believe the imagination is the passport that *we* create to help take us into the *real* world. I believe the imagination is merely another phrase for what is most uniquely *us* . . . To face ourselves. That's the hard thing. The imagination: that's God's gift to make the act of self-examination bearable." Ouisa gasps, while Flan (a tear in his eye) chokes, "I hope your muggers read every word." Geoffrey delightedly declares the evening a triumph, and before leaving he pledges the money to buy Flan's Cézanne. Ecstatic, the Kittredges insist Paul stay the night rather than check into some fleabag hotel. They loan him fifty dollars ("a commission," they joke). Confused about the celebratory atmosphere, Paul checks he hasn't encroached on their evening ("Did I intrude?"). They explain how important Geoffrey's investment was while Paul insists on washing the dirty dishes as Ouisa watches ("It gives me a thrill to be looked at," he smooths). They bid one another "good night" before retiring.

In the morning, however, things take a sinister turn for the Kittredges when Ouisa wakes early, only to be confronted by a naked blond hustler (Lou Milione), apparently solicited by Paul after they had retired to bed. The hustler reacts aggressively while Paul apologizes and attempts to explain. But the Kittredges will not be calmed. "You brought this . . . this *thing* into our house! Thing! Thing!" Flan yells as he shoos the hustler from the apartment.[7] As Paul is also thrown out, he begs them not to tell his father, offering the excuse that he had been afraid and lonely. Later, the Kittredges receive an elaborate bouquet of flowers and a pot of jam with a card that reads, "To thank you for a wonderful time, Paul Poitier."

We return to Flan regaling the wedding party with the story (by now even the bride is listening), and as Donald Sutherland's blue eyes twinkle, he teases a delicious twist in the tale.

After reassuring themselves they had not been robbed, the Kittredges' panic turns to puzzlement regarding Paul's intentions. They go to lunch with their neighbors, Kitty (Mary Beth Hurt) and Larkin (Bruce Davison), only to discover that they too had taken in a mugged stranger named Paul, whose father was a movie icon adapting *Cats* . . . The foursome phone their kids who claim never to have heard of Paul Poitier. Following some amateur sleuthing by the Kittredges' bratty and resentful teenager, Tess (Catherine Kellner), an old high school friend, Trent (Anthony Michael Hall), becomes a prime suspect in this unfolding mystery. Trent admits to meeting Paul several months before, at which Honess cuts to Trent's apartment at that time.

Paul now cuts a very different figure. He wears jogging bottoms and sneakers and no longer speaks with a preppy accent. Utterly infatuated, Trent begins schooling Paul on upper class manners ("Rich people do something nice for you, you give them a pot of jam"). He teaches Paul how to speak ("This is the way you must speak," he says. "Hear my accent. Hear my voice. Never say you're going 'horse-back riding.' You say you're 'going riding.' And don't say 'couch.' Say 'sofa'"). He schools Paul on his pronunciation (not "bodd-ill a bee-ya," but "bottle of beer"). Practicing in the mirror, Paul proves a quick study. He quizzes Trent about an address book filled with the names and addresses of his rich friends and their parents, offering to give Trent an item of clothing for every name he spills the beans on. Ecstatic, Trent collapses onto the bed, claiming he feels like Scheherazade. He tells Paul about the Kittredges' Kandinsky. Paul balks ("a Kan-what-ski?") but is intrigued by the lives of these "rich folks." Trent's striptease revelations about New York's upper classes continued for three months or so, until one day, he ruefully admits, Paul simply left—taking Trent's stereo, sports jacket, word processor, printer . . . and the address book.

Like Sidney Poitier, writes Willie Toliver Jr., Will Smith "does not fit the prevailing stereotype so often purveyed by popular culture of black men: a figure associated with violence, social aberrance, and hypermasculinity" (254). Quoting Donald Bogle, Tolliver recalls that in the fifties and sixties (and especially in Stanley Kramer's *Guess Who's Coming to Dinner*), Poitier was seen as the "model integrationist hero.... He spoke proper English, dressed conservatively, and had the best table manners." He played characters who were the "perfect dream for white liberals anxious to have a colored man in for lunch or dinner" (qtd. in Tolliver 255). Both Paul in *Six Degrees* and Poitier in *Guess Who* "offer performances of blackness that dexterously engage race at the same time that they mask it, making it possible for them to get through the door and into the dining room of White America" (258). Paul affirms a positive vision of black education. He charms and beguiles the Kittredges, and even turns them on (when Paul is being patched up by Ouisa, Schepisi shoots Smith's naked torso in such a way that suggests a frisson of sexual excitement in the room—for the men as much as for her). Paul's "betrayal" of their hospitality is the more egregious for having disarmed their (unconscious) prejudices.

Paul is both a fantasy and a fantasist, and Trent is a contemporary Henry Higgins.[8] In Poitier, writes Tolliver, "Paul could not have a better model for fashioning an identity that would give him access, not only to the right clubs, but to Fifth Avenue as well" (255).[9] In his college-style suit, Paul is neutralized as a threat.[10] The possibility of Smith's stardom, Tolliver argues, rests on his "ability to negotiate these images and to defuse them" (266), on his ability to be "post-racial" (260). But in Trent's apartment, Paul is neither deracinated nor desexualized. Toward the end of the scene, Trent tells Paul he should never leave, tells him he will go through every name and every family and teach him how to woo them. "You'll never not fit in again," he says dreamily, gazing off into space. "I'll make you the most eagerly sought-after young man in the East. And then I'll come into one of these homes one day—and you'll be there and I'll be presented to you. And I'll pretend to meet you for the first time and our friendship will be witnessed by my friends, our parents' friends. If it all happens under their noses, they can't judge me. They can't disparage you. I'll make you a guest in their houses." It is a powerful but also melancholic moment, for Trent secretly knows that his fantasy is just that. For Paul to pass would take a miracle, and yet pass he does.

Let us compare the examples. With DiCaprio's characters, we have individuals who pass muster but only on the surface. Were Jack on the *Titanic* to be tasked with performing any delicate skills with his knife (filleting a fish, for example), or to show any awareness of the intricacies of a dinner service (ordering white wine with said fish), he would, like Frank in the emergency room, be immediately exposed. But with Tom Ripley and Paul Poitier the situation is different. They both exhibit refinement and "talent" that demonstrates an ability to perform the intricacies of upper-class life, notwithstanding minor slips. Roland Barthes asked us to imagine someone "who abolishes within himself all barriers, all classes, all exclusions, not by syncretism but by simple discard of that old specter: *logical contradiction*. . . . Such a man would be the mockery of our society: court, school, asylum, polite conversation would cast him out: who endures contradiction without shame?" (*Pleasure* 3). Echoing this, Erving Goffman remarked that the conman's true crime is "not that he takes money from his victims but that he robs all of us of the belief that middle-class manners and appearance can be sustained only by middle-class people" (*Presentation* 29). This is Paul's true crime in the eyes of his upper class marks. While he steals information and cons them out of money, his worst offense is to rob them of the belief that people like them, the Kittredges (who are also confidence tricksters, but "on a higher plateau"), are discerning—people of refinement. He robs them of their belief in themselves. It is little wonder the film ends with Paul inspiring Ouisa to leave Flan, eager to live a more honest life.

Offending the Definitions: On Wearing Red

Visibility is a trap.

—Michel Foucault, *Discipline and Punish*

Early on in Howard Hawks's *Rio Bravo* (1959), the hypermasculine image of John Wayne is playfully teased by a comic misunderstanding concerning a little red dress. Sheriff Chance (Wayne) is on edge as the gang of a local murderer looks to spring their man free, most likely using violent means. His shotgun by his side, Chance strides from the jailhouse to the saloon searching for any weaknesses in their security. He interrogates a cocky shootist (Ricky Nelson) newly arrived on a stagecoach, concerned the young man's skills might be pressed into service by the gang. In the middle of this tension, a package arrives from a courier. After allaying his suspicions about this package (and the rider who delivers it), Chance takes the package to its addressee—his pal, Carlos (Pedro Gonzalez Gonzalez), who gently teases Chance on his naivete around women while bragging about his own knowledge and experience. "Wait 'till I show you what is in this package," Carlos excitedly tells Chance (as Wayne comically looms over the diminutive Gonzalez). He adds that it is not the kind of item a man would want others to see him buying (hence the discreet delivery). Carlos opens the package and delightedly pulls a pair of bright red lacy pants from the box—a gift for his wife. "Are they not beautiful, senor?" he gushes, as Chance cracks a much-needed smile. Carlos then holds the pants up to Chance's waist to "make the picture of how she will look," and his model's smile quickly turns to discomfort. Suddenly, that discomfort turns to embarrassment when a woman's voice offscreen cuts in with, "I beg your pardon, gentleman but I'm looking for a . . ." She stops mid-sentence as Hawks (with editor Folmar Blangsted) cuts to the stranger (Angie Dickinson) standing in the doorway, utterly bemused at the sight of Chance modeling the lacy underwear. A smile spreads across her face as she teases the sheriff by telling him that such garments "have great possibilities, but not for you." Hawks cuts back to the men looking rather sheepish, the red pants snatched away by Carlos. Wayne blushes, his face turning the color of his trademark red shirt. He gruffly recomposes himself to storm from the room, briefly pausing when the woman jestingly calls, "Don't forget your pants."

It is a comic moment to cut through the macho tension, elevated by Wayne's self-reflexive teasing of his own macho star persona. But Chance's embarrassment also raises its own tension. It is not just that he has been "caught out" modeling racy womenswear—exposed in a private moment that was supposed to be just the fellas; he has been caught out by a woman to whom he is evidently attracted. And what is worse, the lace pants aren't just womenswear; they are bright red, and red is a color with some infamous symbolic connotations, especially regarding women and desire.

In the opening scene of Martin Scorsese's *The Age of Innocence* (1993), Countess Olenska (Michelle Pfeiffer) arrives late to a performance of *Faust* and all eyes are quickly upon her as the men turn their opera glasses to hold her in their sights: and by "sights," I mean both in the sense of seeing and in the sense of taking aim. The countess' marriage has ended, so she is regarded as a "fallen" woman. "What can you expect," one of the onlookers vituperatively snipes, "of a girl who was allowed to wear black satin at her coming-out ball?" The countess gets tongues wagging once more when she arrives at an elaborate dinner party with a somber dress code thrown by the esteemed Van der Luydens. Late again, and without apparent haste or embarrassment, the countess enters the party in a dazzling red dress. As Pamela Knights memorably put it, "Ellen has only to walk alone across a drawing room to offend its definitions" (32), yet onscreen her red dress is a fashion feast for our eyes (see Figure 7.4).

It recalls Vivien Leigh's red dress from *Gone With the Wind* (1939), the red dress worn by Natalie Wood when she and Richard Beymer first catch sight of each other in *West Side Story* (1961), and the moment Olivia Hussey burst through a crowd of drably dressed dancers to catch Leonard Whiting's eye in blazing red in *Romeo and Juliet* (1968)—Romeo gasps at the sight of her, unable to speak the line from the play: "O, she doth teach the torches to burn bright!" (1.4.42). Perhaps even more dazzlingly, the sudden appearance of a red dress gives us a jolt for a different reason when a middle-aged divorcé, Arthur (E. G. Marshall), introduces his new girlfriend, Pearl (Maureen Stapleton), to his adult children for the first time in Woody Allen's *Interiors* (1978). The shock of Pearl's bright red dress marks a sharp contrast with the desaturated color palette favored by Arthur's ex-wife, Eve (Geraldine Page)—an interior designer whose passion for

Figure 7.4. Offending the definitions: Michelle Pfeiffer in *The Age of Innocence*. Martin Scorsese, Columbia Pictures, 1993. Digital frame enlargement.

beiges and off-whites, soft pastels and a clean minimalism resulted in the strict décor that has hitherto dominated the film (for which Allen worked with production designer Mel Bourne). As well as marking a visual break from the color schema of the film, this burst of red signifies the finality of Arthur's break from Eve, with whom his children had been hoping he would reconcile.

Michel Pastoureau writes that red has a complex history as a color. It fell out of fashion around the time of the Reformation because it was "too garish and costly a color, indecent, immoral, depraved," and by the time the pope began to favor white, red "hardly held the place of honor for a good Christian anymore" (Pastoureau 94). The color was further tarnished by its association with the "flames of hell, original sin, and a whole parade of major vices, among them pride, falsehood, and lust" (94). In clothing, red held special significance as the color of decadence, luxury, or immorality. In many Western cities, a piece of red clothing (dress, hood, scarf, aglet) was mandated to distinguish prostitutes from "honest women." Other examples of individuals "branded" thus included butchers, executioners, lepers, convicts, and outcasts—including non-Christians, i.e., Jews and Muslims (Pastoureau 108). The color evoked the image of the Whore of Babylon (the "Scarlet Woman") from the book of Revelation and in the eighteenth and nineteenth centuries was considered "dangerous."

Hence, in addition to being scandalous, red is also the color of punishment. As such, it is a color that offends against order and etiquette (which, if it has a color, would be clean, virginal, innocent white). This is expressed most painfully and devastatingly in a major fashion faux pas in William Wyler's *Jezebel* (1938), a film already discussed in chapter 5 for its treatment of race. Here, the discussion turns to a sartorial blunder from which the film's heroine will not recover.

Seeing Red in *Jezebel*

One might suppose that a ballroom is always a chamber of torture.

—Emily Post, *Etiquette*

"Merely to think of the way Bette Davis makes her entrance in *Jezebel*," wrote Stanley Cavell in *The World Viewed*, is to "provide us with a fair semblance of ecstasy" (*World Viewed* 5–6), an ecstasy Martin Shingler notes will force her character "to learn some painful lessons in how to deport herself and how to exercise self-control" (36). Prior to her arrival, Miss Julie (Davis) is conspicuous in her absence at her own party, for which she is terribly late. Southern manners are the focus of much of the discussion, as we learn from one guest whose rather formal curtsy causes her teenage daughter to scoff, "Girls don't curtsy anymore!" Her mother quickly shoots back that "they do in New Orleans!" before warning her daughter not to get involved in what she calls "Yankee manners." The film is set in 1850s Louisiana, and war with the North is looming. As the guests go on waiting for their host, Wyler cuts to an exterior shot as Julie bounds in on her braying and rearing horse, over which she maintains complete control. She confidently leaps (as opposed to demurely dismounting) from the horse and thrusts the reins into the hands of a terrified looking slave child (Stymie Beard). Regarding him with a smile, Julie asks him what's wrong. He fearfully replies that her horse bites, at which Julie grinningly retorts that if he does, "just plain bite him back!"

Julie strides into the house where her handmaiden, Zette (Theresa Harris), offers to help her dress, but Julie dismisses her, saying she'll go in as she is. "In your *riding* clothes?" Zette incredulously asks. Julie enters her party with a fanfare, and the gossiping intensifies at the sight of her in riding outfit. She smiles with satisfaction.

The limit to Julie's power appears to stop with her fiancé, however. Pres Dillard (Henry Fonda) is an equally headstrong banker making a strong impression with civic leaders and has little time for Julie's childish shenanigans, which include ordering him out of a business meeting with the partners at his firm, and then, after he refuses to come, barging into the bank (where women were not allowed to be in 1852). Irritated that Pres won't see her, Julie storms off to a dress fitting for the upcoming Olympus Ball with her Aunt Belle (Fay Bainter). While her gorgeous white dress is being adjusted, Julie spies a stunning red dress and joyously declares it "saucy!" to which Aunt Belle adds ". . . and vulgar!" But Aunt Belle's reaction only interests Julie more. "Yes, isn't it," she demurs, before adding that "this is 1852, not the Dark Ages. A girl doesn't have to simper around in white just because they aren't married." As it dawns on her that Julie is serious about wearing the red dress to the debutante ball, Aunt Belle chides that "in New Orleans they do—you'll insult every woman on the floor." Thinking the matter closed, they buy the white dress, but Julie also buys the red one, just in case.

Later that evening, Pres calls on Julie and finds her aunt and uncle still simmering at Julie's behavior. He too remains sore at her embarrassing intrusion into the bank, and with the words of one of his superiors still ringing in his ears ("These days women need discipline!" the older man had declared, "your father . . . would've cut him a hickey, and he'd have flailed the living daylights out of her!"—to which Pres had smiled), he heeds his uncle's advice not to "spare the rod," and takes a cane with him up to Julie's room. Of course, Pres has no intention of beating Julie and merely uses it to rap lightly on her door. Wyler cuts to Julie in her room, clearly able to hear her fiancé but happy to ignore him. He calls out for her, but she goes on ignoring him. Getting impatient, Pres knocks and knocks and calls and calls, but still she ignores him (a smirk alights on her face). With Pres on the verge of kicking the door down, Julie sweetly inquires, "Who is it?" before letting him in. Fuming, Pres tells her to grow up. Then he sees the dress. "You . . . can't wear *red* to the Olympus Ball! You never saw an unmarried girl in anything but white!" he despairs. He warns Julie that there will be no ball for her if she wears that dress. As he leaves, she points out that he didn't use his cane (clearly a sexual innuendo).

Sure enough, like a red rag to a bull, Pres's pep talk has had the opposite effect, as Julie greets him wearing the red dress. His first instinct is to refuse to take her. But then an idea flashes across his eyes, which is quickly registered by Julie's aunt and uncle. While Aunt Belle begins to warn against doing what he plans, her uncle nods in silent consent. Pres *will* take Julie to the ball but as punishment for her behavior, knowing she will be humiliated. Indeed, Julie's confidence saps from the moment she walks through the door as a scandalized murmur sweeps through the room. Every couple they approach finds a swift excuse to be elsewhere; Julie's friends turn their backs. Pres challenges the men to say something out of turn, brimming with embarrassment and quivering with muted rage. Hoping to salvage some dignity, Julie urges Pres to take her home, but in a final humiliation he forces her to dance with him—her red dress figuratively staining the dance floor as the girls in white quickly move to the edge of the ballroom. Even the band stop playing, but Pres urges them on. They waltz alone in shame and misery (see Figure 7.5).

Figure 7.5. Shameful red: Bette Davis and Henry Fonda in *Jezebel*. William Wyler, Warner Bros., 1938. Digital frame enlargement.

Julie's fashion faux pas strikes a crushing blow to her social standing and proves fatal to her engagement with Pres, who breaks off their planned nuptials and moves away to New York for business. Her "ordeal by ballroom," as Emily Post put it (263), does not end with the party. Julie develops a social phobia and falls into long and deep depression. But why is it the case that "a woman can never be too fine while she is all in white," as remarked one of Jane Austen's characters in *Mansfield Park* (or, as the same sentiment is expressed in *Singin' in the Rain*, "White is right when you're a bride and you want to impress . . ."). The etiquette manuals emphasize the importance of wearing white (Miss Manners, for example [639–40]) but stop short of giving a reason. Kassia St. Clair points out that the whiteness of a dress is symbolic of sexual purity (41); red, prostitution (136). Starched whites are the kind of white, as David Batchelor puts it, "that repels everything that is inferior to it, and that is almost everything" (10).[11]

In *The Second Sex*, Simone De Beauvoir quoted C. A. Porter's observation that when they were due to attend a ball, girls in the

American South used to make themselves sick eating mixtures of salt and lemon to halt their menstruation period, fearful that otherwise the young men "might discover their condition from the appearance of their eyes, contact with their hands, or possibly an odour, and this idea horrified them" (380). The problem, De Beauvoir wrote, was that the debutante could not very well "play the idol, the fairy, the faraway princess, when one feels a bloody cloth between one's legs; and, more generally, when one is conscious of the primitive misery of being a body" (380). Hence, red did not just signify prostitution, it also signified sexual maturity, and worse: sexual history. Again, there was a double standard here. While on her wedding night a bride was expected to come from a state of ignorance and innocence having had no "past," it was well accepted that her husband would have "lived," as De Beauvoir put it (478). Indeed, a man would hang the bloody sheets from the bedroom window to confirm both that the marriage had been consummated and that his bride had been as pure as her white wedding dress claimed.

Maurice Merleau-Ponty wrote that a "red dress a fortiori holds with all its fibers onto the fabric of the visible, and thereby onto a fabric of invisible being. A punctuation in the field of red things ... it is also a punctuation in the field of red garments" (*The Visible* 250). In saying this, he didn't mean to pass a general comment about red dresses per se but to indicate that there is no singular "red dress." Rather, an experience of a particular red dress in a specific visual spectacle "makes diverse regions of the colored or visible world resound at the distances." Such a dress becomes "less a color [red] or a thing [dress] ... than a difference between things and colors, a momentary crystallization of colored being or of visibility" (250). It becomes an example of what phenomenologists like him call *qualia*, which refers to one's personal experience of a color or feeling. For Julie it is an unqualified experience of pain: not in making the wrong choice, but in her choosing to embrace womanhood on her own terms.

Stella Bruzzi writes that the "critical issue" when reading sartorial choices in film "is whether to look at or through the clothes." Looking through a period costume, for example, tends to invite analysis of its accuracy and authenticity, its place in the broader historical framework. Looking *at* clothes, however, offers an alternative discourse, Bruzzi writes, "one that usually counters or complicates the ostensible strategy of the overriding narrative," one that prioritizes "eroticism"

(36). In the latter case, women's clothing is often the sign of shame reaching all the way back, wrote Kenneth Burke, to Eve and the Fall. But "creation," he added, "implies authority in the sense of originator. The possibility of a 'Fall' is implied in a Covenant insofar as the idea of a Covenant implies the possibility of its being violated" ("On the First" 38). Doesn't Southern etiquette present itself likewise in *Jezebel?* "Not in New Orleans" is a Covenant that raises the very possibility of its being violated—just as those starched whites practically scream for a little color. It is ironic that, because this film was shot in black-and-white, we never actually *see* the red of Julie's red dress.[12] It adds to our sympathy for Julie, whose only crime was that she experienced herself as ready for womanhood in New Orleans, that is ready and new to the world, but could not express this maturity in the "faded wardrobe" of its stuffy traditions.

"Why grope among the dry bones of the past?" wrote Ralph Waldo Emerson, which Adam Phillips interprets as a kind of cultural necrophilia. "If you put living generations into a masquerade by dressing them in old, second-hand clothes," writes Phillips, "they are all dressed up with nowhere to go" ("Against Biography" 45). Here is a woman with somewhere to go and a feeling (qualia) about how to get there. This red dress is her portal. Hence, when Pres forces Julie to dance, he repudiates the sentiment expressed by Jane Austen in *Pride and Prejudice* that "to be fond of dancing was a certain step towards falling in love." As they dance, they fall out of love. Perhaps it is even worse than that. The subtitle of Frances Burney's *Evelina* (1778), "A Young Lady's Entrance into the World," encapsulates the notion that a young woman's "coming out" in high society meant more to her than merely entering a social scene. This was her entrance into the *world* itself, and her social "stock" could rise or fall on the strength (or folly) of the impression she made there. What Burney's naive heroine, Evelina, wanted most of all was "a book of the laws and customs a-la-mode, presented to all young people upon their first introduction into public company." But Julie does not long for such a guide. Like the narrator of Scorsese's *Age*, such guides are for the "hieroglyphic world" in which "the real thing was never said or done or even thought, but only represented by a set of arbitrary signs." Such signs are about "more than a simple snubbing: they were . . . an eradication." It is the strength of Davis's performance, writes Molly Haskell, that rouses her from her depression. "When coolness is called for," Haskell writes, "Davis gives us a cold chill: when warmth, a barely suppressed passion. Her charm, like her beauty, is something willed into being . . . through sheer, driving guts she turns herself into a flower of the Old South" (626). Julie's red dress does more than strike a glancing blow at the stuffy old customs of the South; it issues a demand for new customs on behalf of a new generation of women excluded from so much of society. Julie's red dress does not just burst from the white background, it repudiates it—along with the stale values and dry customs still being dragged into the modern era.

8

Tabular Outrages

Dinner

Taste is the refusal of other tastes.

—Pierre Bourdieu, *Distinction*

~

Torture and table manners go hand in glove. The ability of the parvenu to pass in polite society often stands or falls at dinner, noted Charles William Day, who remarked that "nothing indicates a well-bred man more than a proper mode of eating his dinner. A man may pass muster by *dressing well*, and may sustain himself tolerably in conversation; but if he be not perfectly 'au fait,' *dinner* will betray him" (33). Likewise, Ralph Waldo Emerson quipped of the English that their capital institution is not the "Trial by Jury, but the dinner," and that "guests are expected to arrive within half an hour of the time fixed by the card of invitation, and nothing but death or mutilation is permitted to detain them" ("English Traits" 522). The formal occasion of eating begins to resemble a torture chamber, Emerson seems to imply, when stiff social form constricts the freedom of the appetite.

Governed Appetites: Norbert Elias's Civilizing Process

Every meal is a lesson learned.

—Victorian proverb

"Food loathing," writes Julia Kristeva, "is perhaps the most elementary and most archaic form of abjection" (*Powers* 2). Tony Richardson's *Tom Jones* (1963) contains one of the most unforgettable dining scenes in film history. Having rescued Mrs. Waters (Joyce Redman) from being raped by a British officer, the film's hero, Tom (Albert Finney), offers his coat to preserve her modesty (as well as to resist the fires of his own temptation). Tom is attempting to substantiate (to himself as well as to society) his moral decency and gentlemanliness having had his name impugned. The scene is thus a curious one, as Judith Bailey Slagle and Robert Holtzclaw point out, for it demonstrates "Tom's weaknesses of the flesh (and other flaws) while still building a case for his essential humanity—in spite, or because, of his essential humanness" (195). Tom's human (all too human) nature is subsequently tested by Mrs. Waters, who rewards him with a lavish dinner at a local inn. As they tuck heartily into a meal of whole crab, oysters, and game, the pair soon begin to arouse one another with the voracity of their appetites (see Figures 8.1 and 8.2).

In a scene lasting three minutes and consisting entirely of intercut point-of-view shots, the diners eye one another seductively over the candlelit table as they rip and gnaw, smash and suck, pull and lick at the sumptuous meal. The scene ends with Tom and Mrs. Waters retiring to their bedroom, gazing lustfully at one another by the light of a single candle. With fast-fading restraint, the pair lightly kiss as Tom reaches out to extinguish the flame.

I have always found this scene an uncomfortable watch and considered Tom's coy gesture of extinguishing the candle—to gain some privacy for their lovemaking—somewhat ironic: after such a graphic carnal meal, what is meant as a pre-coital signal in fact reads like a postcoital repose.

The film was adapted by John Osborne from Henry Fielding's 1749 novel, set at a time of some importance to what Norbert Elias called "The Civilizing Process." In his book of the same name, Elias charts the progress of manners throughout the ages, noting that as

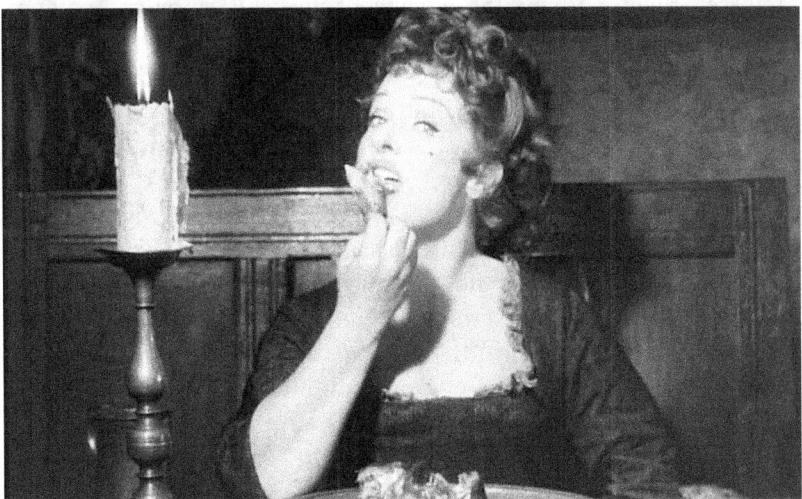

Figures 8.1. and 8.2. Scoffing in *Tom Jones*. Tony Richardson, United Artists, 1963. Digital frame enlargement.

time has passed, civilization has become increasingly restrained and polite from a history of roughness and crudity. In the medieval books on manners addressed to young nobleman to teach them how to behave at court, many of the instructions attended to table manners, particularly on controlling the body (prohibitions against snorting, gobbling, slurping, and belching, and so on). From the sixteenth century, rules on table manners become more refined, and for Elias this coincided with the rise of the fork (there are certainly no forks on display in the *Tom Jones* scene—Tom smashes his crab with his bare hands). Despite being introduced to Western Europe in the eleventh century, forks were considered an awkward and strange luxury. As Johan Goudsblom and Stephen Mennell point out, the rise of the fork and increase in restrictions around knives at the table were not isolated but formed part of the general trend toward mannered self-control (see Elias, "Rise of the Fork" 52). The idea is raised in *The Lion in Winter* (1968), set in 1183, during a scene in which three adult royal siblings demonstrate their confusion over forks (which they casually throw at one another). Later, they quarrel over which of them will succeed their father on the throne. Suddenly, Richard (Anthony Hopkins) pulls a knife, at which the other two brothers back off in alarm. However, their mother—the estranged queen, Eleanor of Aquitaine (Katharine Hepburn)—despairs at her uncouth sons: "Of course he has a knife, he always has a knife, we all have knives. It's 1183 and we're barbarians!" to which she dolefully adds, "How clear we make it."[1]

Conduct changes are not linear, Elias argued, and take time. But the behavior of others exerts an immense pressure, propelling us into mannered comportment. The rise of the fork signified this pressure. After all, what is its use, Elias asked—beyond simply lifting food to one's mouth? Why not use one's fingers, as do Tom and Mrs. Waters? Because, as one etiquette guide from 1859 put it, to eat with one's fingers is "cannibal." To ask why this is cannibal is moot, Elias pointed out: "It is self-evidently cannibal, barbaric, uncivilized, or whatever else it is called" ("Fork" 52). To probe the rationale for this logic risks collapsing the principle. "On account of hygiene," one might say (that is, fear of contamination). A reasonable claim, Elias wrote, but one that begins to wear thin in societies that don't share plates of food. Well, because it is "dirtier," then! This is certainly true, but why would cleanliness drive behavior in this way? (Tom and Mrs. Waters are already sharing more than a simple repast.)

Once our "rational" explanations get exhausted, Elias wrote, one must conclude that "distaste" at bad table manners is simply irrational.

Let us compare the scene from Tom Jones with another, this one set in the twentieth century. In Elia Kazan's *A Streetcar Named Desire* (1951), Stanley Kowalski (Marlon Brando) chews, open-mouthed, on chicken legs as his wife, Stella (Kim Hunter), glowers at him across the table. Stanley's sister-in-law, Blanche (Vivien Leigh), attempts to tell an amusing story, but Stanley ignores her, concentrating instead on noisily sucking his fingers, which are slick with grease, one by one. Unable to restrain herself, Stella bursts, accusing her husband of "making a pig of himself." She berates him by saying, "Your face and your fingers are disgustingly greasy," before adding, "Go wash up and then help me clear the table!"

In response, Stanley brings his fist down onto his plate and swipes it across the room. The women cower as he stands over them (see Figure 8.3). With his mouth still full of chicken meat, he scolds them for hen-pecking before declaring himself the king. To punctuate his point, Stanley smashes more crockery before announcing that he has now cleared his place as asked, mockingly offering to clear theirs. The terrified women shake their heads, prompting him to (finally) swallow his mouthful before broodingly walking away.

Figure 8.3. Marlon Brando making a pig of himself in *A Streetcar Named Desire*. Elia Kazan, Warner Bros., 1951. Digital frame enlargement.

"The fork is nothing other than the embodiment of a specific standard of emotions and a specific level of revulsion," wrote Elias (52). Feelings of displeasure, disgust, fear, or shame become ritualized or institutionalized, embedded in forms of conduct.[2] Stanley is some three hundred years out of date. Already in Courtin's guide to manners in 1672 (and well before Fielding's novel) it was written that "to touch anything greasy, a sauce or syrup, etc., with your fingers" is "very impolite." And worse, it "obliges you to commit two or three more improper acts"—to wipe your hands on a serviette and soil it, or on a piece of bread, or else to lick them, "which is the height of impropriety" (qtd. in Elias, "Fork" 53). Not "dirty" but "improper," Elias stresses. But improper *because* dirty; dirty because anyone witnessing you wipe your mouth this way feels "nauseated" at the sight (see also Emily Post on greasy fingers [584–85]). Along with his fingers, such incivilities besmear a man's character. Stanley is not merely acting like an animal; he *is* an animal—an offensive pig, not just in his action but his very being. According to Stella, he is too busy "making himself a pig" to contribute to their discussion (that is, his mouth is not only too full of flesh to speak, but to think). As with one who breaks the law, we move very quickly from the act of transgression to the labeling of the transgressor as "criminal," as "pig," and so on.

Class and masculinity are also at play in Stanley's violation of table manners. Pierre Bourdieu noted that working-class men eat "with whole-hearted gulps and mouthfuls" and eat robust meats that can be torn from the bone with the teeth. Fish, for example, is both too insubstantial for a working man (hungry after a hard day's graft) and requires too much finesse to debone. It is a "fiddly" food that a man's hands cannot cope with, rendering him childlike (or womanlike). "Taste, a class culture turned into nature, that is, *embodied*, helps to shape the class body," wrote Bourdieu (188). What interested Elias, however, was the way such feelings of disgust arise in communities where previously they would have been absent. Such feelings begin with a small circle and gradually spread out to larger social circles by "numerous authorities and institutions," especially through etiquette guides. Likewise, while children are not born with such disgust mechanisms, they quickly learn them. A child caught reaching across the dinner table for something greasy, saucy, or syrupy with their fingers is soon told to use a serving spoon, along with the reminder that "You must not do that, 'people' do not do things like that." Which people, Elias wonders? The anonymous "one" who "does not do," and in not doing promptly becomes the measure of propriety. The "one" whose example sets a course of behavior which, through habit, repetition, and reinforcement (often including punishment), the child will gradually inculcate. Finally, they become the "one" who "does not do," and who thereafter feels the same nausea when confronted by those who "do."

In *Tom Jones*, the meal "degenerates." At first, Tom and Mrs. Waters simply eat with their fingers. It is with their eyes and ears that they begin to transgress. As Tom slurps his soup, Mrs. Waters notices and slurps back. When he tries (and fails) to release the stubborn crab meat from its shell, she responds by skillfully teasing hers out with her probing tongue. By contrast, in *Streetcar* Stanley makes "like a pig" with his bad table manners because he is simply enjoying his food and ignoring his guest. When he smashes the crockery, however, he makes a statement of mannered violation. This is how a beast really behaves, he seems to say—forsaking what little etiquette he had hitherto been observing.

The *Streetcar* scene was given a middle-class twist by Sam Mendes in *American Beauty* (1999), in which a bored advertising executive, Lester (Kevin Spacey), dramatically quits his job following a mid-life crisis to take up a position (with zero responsibility) at a local burger bar. His wife, Carolyn (Annette Bening) is furious, browbeating him over dinner as he quietly asks to be passed the asparagus. They quarrel as their teenage daughter, Jane (Thora Birch), embarrassedly attempts to keep the peace—but neither will be stilled. Carolyn accuses her husband of sabotaging their lives by giving up a lucrative job, while Lester accuses his wife of histrionics. Again, he asks to be passed the asparagus. The dinner table is oversized and pretentiously set with candles while American swing music plays in the background (the song is, appropriately, Bobby Darin's "Call Me Irresponsible"). As Lester and Carolyn ramp up their argument (pointedly gesticulating with their forks), Jane gets up to leave, at which Lester screams for her to remain. She sits, meekly, as her father gets up from the table to fetch the asparagus for himself and Carolyn expresses incredulity at her husband's outrageous behavior. She continues to blaze him for his inconsiderateness, and as she does so, Lester quietly stands, a smirk forming at the corners of his mouth, while balancing a plate of asparagus on his upturned hand. Lester suddenly turns and hurls the plate against the opposite wall, causing Carolyn to fall silent. Imitating Brando, Lester lords over his wife and daughter and grins before ironically saying, "Don't interrupt me, honey." He returns to his seat to continue eating as Carolyn and Jane sit in silence, aghast (see Figure 8.4).

The argument is, we suspect, a kind of performance rehearsed many times over the years of their marriage. Carolyn berates her husband in a mocking singsong tone, referring to herself in the third person and asking multiple rhetorical questions. He responds in kind, with flippant disregard and a sneering air of disdain. But when he smashes the plate, Lester has clearly transcended the usual bickering—which, as Stanley Cavell pointed out, is what a happy marriage sounds like (*Pursuits* 86). It is in the moment of Lester's (uncharacteristic) violence, and the stunned silence that follows, that their marriage really appears on the rocks. It also reminds us just how fragile and insecure the dinner table really is.

But it is this that gets to the heart of Elias's point about the "rise of the fork": the increase of manners in table etiquette not only does the job of circumscribing the conduct and emotional life of a child, it erases the process by which these conducts and emotions came to be for the adult, too. "Since the pressure or coercion of individual adults is allied to the pressure and example of the whole

Figure 8.4. Lording it in *American Beauty*. Sam Mendes, DreamWorks Pictures, 1999. Digital frame enlargement.

surrounding world," Elias wrote, "most children, as they grow up, forget or repress relatively early the fact that their feelings of shame and embarrassment, of pleasure and displeasure, are moulded into conformity with a certain standard by external pressure and compulsion" ("Fork" 54). From the early manuals on manners by writers like Courtin, who hoped to dissuade adults from eating with their fingers to spare others the distasteful spectacle and shame of eating with soiled fingers, we arrive at an inner automatism, "the imprint of society on the inner self, the superego,"—one forbidding us from eating any other way: whence, "The done thing." If the provenance of various rules of etiquette often seems so difficult to substantiate, perhaps it is because "politeness" originates not from within but from without. Not instinct but injunction.

The disgust subsequently felt in the presence of men like Stanley as he licks his greasy fingers is *experienced* as something personal, something "inward," implanted from nature—not something cultural or social. Yet it is his violence against the women that disturbs in a more instinctive way; the way he sneers at them after terrifying them into silence arouses a more fundamental disgust. It is the same with Lester.

Pushed to the extreme, disgust can manifest itself as an eating disorder, where all thought of food comes to be seen as potentially polluting. Contrastingly, Adam Phillips points out that children's refusal to eat can be another way of challenging the apparent arbitrariness of table manners, as what he calls "experiments in living":

> What kind of mother or father will I have, or create, if I say I'm not going to bed, or say I love my teacher more than my mother, or indeed, if I refuse to eat, or eat too much? . . . One straightforward answer is, you will be faced with people you would prefer not to talk to, people who are frantic, bossy, manipulative, defeated, enraged, concerned and so on. People, in other words, obsessed by food. ("On Eating" 288)

Reason fails when children refuse to eat. Isn't this what Stanley and Lester represent when they smash their plates: the failure of reason, a refusal to "stomach" the rules they have until now accepted as the "done thing," but will accept no longer? They appear to indulge their appetites (for chicken and asparagus) and seem resentful of the wives who will deny this satisfaction, but what we really witness in these scenes are two men whose carnal desires have become strangulated, and who resort to lashing out at the wives they blame for their own lack of appetite. By refusing to eat, children insist on keeping their appetite intact, on not spoiling it by eating.[3] It is as if the insatiable "appetite-desire" had become confused with the (temporarily) satiable "hunger-need"—as though one's appetite to live, to be agreeable, was itself already full.

On reflection, then, my "gut" reaction to that carnal dinner in *Tom Jones* is mostly social, and probably also a bit personal. It is social in the sense that in a society (including theirs), one should clearly not "make a pig of oneself" while eating out of consideration of others. It is personal because I am possibly more squeamish about bad table manners than most. It is also unfair, one might argue, because Tom and Mrs. Waters are eating a private meal—they are not offending one another, and have no idea that I exist, that I am watching them eat. Perhaps it is me who is behaving badly? But of course, films invite us to spy on their subjects, being windows into their private worlds. And in any case, Tom does seem to know we are watching him, as he proves when, in a different scene (his mouth again full of food), he refers to a fellow with "big hungry daughters to feed," at which a comedic musical note plays and Tom grins. Turning to face the camera, he breaks the fourth wall to joke, "*Most* hungry, I can vouch for it."

Having suppressed his desire to ravish Mrs. Waters at the sight of her torn clothing and exposed upper body, Tom has conducted himself rather well. In the other two examples, however, we glimpse something cruel amid the candelabra and silverware. Phillips concludes his essay by wondering if eating disorders are belated attempts to restore the viability of an appetite that has become pathologized, attached to instances of trauma or frustrations of the will not easily overcome or repaired. In such cases, Phillips writes, the patient's will has itself become "appetized," "translated into a question about eating and being eaten, about digesting and being digested" ("On Eating" 294). For such people (all of us, to an extent), fussiness about what we put into our bodies represents an attempt to reestablish control over our appetite for life itself.

Tabular Desecration: *Hannibal*

> No cruelty, no feast.
>
> —Nietzsche, *On the Genealogy of Morality*

"Put on the joint!" demands the Red Queen in Lewis Carroll's *Through the Looking Glass* (1871)—an effort to break a long uncomfortable silence at the feast celebrating Alice's "promotion," in chess terms, to the status of queen. The waiters promptly arrive with a leg of mutton and the assembled diners look to Alice to carve. Having never carved a joint before, however, Alice squirms and, to relieve her anxiety, the Red Queen proposes to introduce her to the meat, "Alice—Mutton: Mutton—Alice" (199). At this, the mutton gets up and gives a polite bow to which Alice responds in kind. Not knowing whether to be frightened or amused, Alice takes up her knife and fork and offers to carve a slice for the queen, but the latter balks: "Certainly not . . . it isn't etiquette to cut anyone you've been introduced to. Remove the joint!"[4]

As demonstrated by Erasmus in 1530, the carving of meat was once proudly performed at the table in front of one's guests, and a well-bred man was expected and required to be good at carving a roast. However, over time this process fell out of fashion, probably due to the distancing of the household from the act of slaughtering, and hence an increasing distaste toward the butchery of animals. Elias noted that processing meat gradually became so distasteful that its living origins had to be disguised (*Civilizing Process* 101–2). In an amusing scene from George Stevens's *Giant* (1956), a group of children delight in a turkey running around in his coop. As they throw feed, they coo at him, "You eat your dinner like a good boy, Pedro" (adorably, they pronounce his name, "Pey-dro"). Stevens cuts from this scene to Thanksgiving dinner. A servant enters the dining room carrying a tray with a sumptuously cooked turkey. The family gather around the table and gasp with delight as the roast is ceremonially placed at the head of the table ("Auld Lang Syne" plays patriotically in the soundtrack). However, as grace is intoned, Stevens cuts to the children looking quizzically at the meat until one of them tentatively ventures to ask, "That Pey-dro?" When one of the adults confirms it, the children begin to cry. Their sobbing becomes distraught when a carving fork is plunged into the meat (one of them wails "no," as if Pedro's corpse is being disgraced). Inconsolable, they are eventually ushered from the room by Elizabeth Taylor, who comforts them in the hallway. "The increasingly strong tendency to remove the distasteful from the sight of society clearly applies, with few exceptions" wrote Elias, "to the carving of the whole animal" (*Civilizing* 103). A minimum of carving, limited to the carved portions on one's plate, became the norm. What had been a spectacle had now become distasteful and had to be *"removed behind the scenes of social life"* (*Civilizing* 103). In some societies, even the carving knife has been banished from the table.

What the children experience in the scene from *Giant* is what most meat-eating adults disavow when they sit down to eat dinner. As Margaret Visser points out in *The Rituals of Dinner*, eating is intrinsically violent: "Animals are murdered to produce meat; vegetables are torn up, peeled, and chopped; most of what we eat is treated with fire; and chewing is designed remorselessly to finish what killing and cooking began. People naturally prefer that none of this should happen to them" (3). The risk of slipping from diner to dish goes to the heart of table manners, which were originally social agreements intended to ensure that the process of eating ran smoothly, especially when dining with strangers. Hence the limits on knife usage at the table (with carving increasingly taking place in the kitchen), and prohibitions against eating off the knife. This latter aims not just to protect the licker from harming the soft parts of the mouth but to avoid giving even the impression that blood (even by one's own hand) might be spilled at the table. Recall the moment Klaus Kinski's eyes light up when his guest (Bruno Ganz) cuts his finger slicing bread in *Nosferatu the Vampyre* (1979)—a clear case in point for the French rule prohibiting the cutting of bread with a table knife (instead, they tear it with their fingers).

Cannibalism presents a problem, however. Under special circumstances, one is permitted to kill one's enemies (war, for example), but it is never permissible to eat them. People can be classed as enemies but not as food. It is such an effective taboo, Visser writes, that it "has always been one of the major 'effects' a writer can rely on when he or she reaches for some fully fledged enormity, an atrocity to make our skins crawl" (6). Cannibalism is everything civilization is not (hence Shakespeare giving to his "savage" in *The Tempest* the name Caliban, a near-anagram of "Cannibal"). It is the ultimate *crimen exceptum* (a crime so exceptionable that established rules of justice need not apply).

But an amusing thought quickly occurs to Visser. Anthropologists have long confirmed that cannibalism existed, and that it existed in relatively advanced civilizations. Moreover, it was itself practiced in an orderly and societal way. "As social beings," Visser deliciously concludes, "cannibals must have manners" (6). Visser does not just mean cannibalism from necessity (for example, the infamous Donner Party in the mid-nineteenth century); she means societies for whom eating human flesh was a considered, publicly approved, repeated, and ritualized act (8). In such societies (the Aztecs, for example), the eating of humans held a sacrificial significance. To fail to eat according to the proprieties and rituals laid down was to invite the wrath of the gods to whom such sacrifices were being made in the first place—it risked provoking the gods to "become violent and brutish themselves, descend to earth, and eat people just as indiscriminately and with as little regard for protocol and etiquette as people had shown earlier" (11). Cannibalism involved all the ceremony and care of the Sunday feast in the Christian tradition ("neatness and propriety governed every gesture"). Even when violent aggression reigned, concludes Visser, "there were social preferences, tastes, and traditions; something almost amounting to a cuisine" (16).

Of the introduction of Anthony Hopkins's Hannibal Lecter to the world in *The Silence of the Lambs* (1991), Murray Pomerance writes that he "might have crumbled into shards of moral deformity, but instead we are treated to Anthony Hopkins's sonorous voice as he enunciates in mocking wisdom, a fountainhead of forensics knowledge, a sense of right and wrong that shame the heroine's, and a poetic sensibility that comes through in his soft, even musical speech" ("Villain" 120). His crimes ought to put him beyond the pale, but despite the acts of savage and remorseless brutality for which he is being held in a maximum security prison, the courtesy he shows Special Agent Clarice Starling (Jodie Foster), and the bond they forge playing mind games ("quid pro quo") to catch a serial killer, render him a kind of diabolical antihero. We are also compulsively drawn to Lecter, adds Pomerance, "because his exceptional charm and social grace, not to say his astounding erudition, make him something of an object of wonder for us" ("Villain" 123). And finally, Lecter is a man who makes a point of "eating the rude"—that is, he selects as his victims only those vulgarians who offend against moral or aesthetic decency.

In the sequel, *Hannibal* (2001), Lecter is on the loose in Florence. He had escaped at the end of *Silence*, and now the film picks him up older, more sedate—but no less cruel or vicious. For example, in one scene he bleeds to death a street thief attempting to obtain his fingerprints, while in another he eviscerates the Italian detective attempting to sell him to bounty hunters. However, such acts, notes Pomerance, "fail to mobilize our moral indignation because they are committed against . . . characters deserving of vengeance." But in the climactic scene of the film, Lecter does something that finally goes too far. As Pomerance puts it, he does something so offensive that "he becomes *degraded*" ("Villain" 123).

Woozy from morphine, having sustained a wound rescuing Lecter from mercenaries, Clarice (now played by Julianne Moore) enters a dining room to find Special Agent Paul Krendler (Ray Liotta)—her nemesis at the Bureau—strapped to a wheelchair and drugged. Krendler incongruously wears casual clothes and a baseball hat (back to front) while Lecter has dressed Clarice in a lavish black gown with a plunging neckline, and he is himself dressed in an expensive (Italian) suit. As Lecter heats a skillet next to Paul's chair, Clarice suspects something awful is going to happen. Before they start their first course, Lecter invites Paul to say grace. He starts out well but slips into making lewd and scornful remarks about Clarice, at which Lecter smiles and compares him to the Apostle Paul, "who also hated women." However, when Paul continues to make rude comments about Clarice, Lecter accuses him of being rude (". . . that word 'grace' / In an ungracious mouth is but profane," *Richard II* [2.3.88–89]). Krendler criticizes the flavor of the broth his host periodically squeezes into his mouth. Lecter remonstrates that his has had a little something "added." "But I assure you," he soothes, "the next course is divine."

After stopping Clarice from attacking him with a table knife, Lecter gently (but firmly) sits her down and removes Krendler's cap. The hat had been covering a line of stitches around the circumference of Krendler's head, stitches Lecter now carefully removes with a surgeon's scalpel. The surgical tools mixed with the cooking utensils already suggest that Elias's civilizing process is about to rapidly fall apart, and so it proves as Lecter gently removes the last stitch from Krendler's head and lifts the scalp clean off to expose his brain. Clarice gasps in terror and is reduced to the kind of silence John O'Neill describes as one that descends on us when we experience violence so awful that it "tests in us the sense of our own humanity" (57). "*Dr. Lecter*," Clarice (barely audibly) gasps, to which Lecter responds, "You see the brain itself feels no pain, Clarice, if that's what concerns you. For example, Paul won't miss this little piece, here [he gestures with the surgical knife], which is the part of the prefrontal lobe, which they say is the seat of good manners." This gives a material twist to the adage that "it doesn't hurt to be polite." Pain and manners are entwined, although ironically Paul has neither. Finding her voice, Clarice tremulously begins to reason with Lecter, offering him a "trade" if only he'll stop (like their "quid pro quo" from the earlier film). But Lecter responds with disgust in his voice. "Trade? How does that word *taste* to you, Clarice? Cheap and metallic, like sucking on a greasy coin?" Finally, he gently teases away the thin, translucent protective membrane to reveal the pink meat of the brain (the kind of pink Roland Barthes noted as popular in "ornamental cookery" [*Mythologies*, 78]), cuts a slice of Krendler's cerebrum, and sautés it in garlic and butter ("in the distanced and professional manner of a three-star chef," notes Pomerance ["Villain" 124]). As his own brain sizzles in the pan, Krendler (who is completely ignorant about what is going on) genuinely exclaims, "That smells great!" To cap off this

Figure 8.5. Tabular desecration in *Hannibal*. Ridley Scott, MGM, 2001. Digital frame enlargement.

awful moment, Lecter feeds the cooked meat to Krendler (see Figure 8.5), causing Clarice to gag.

For Pomerance, the scene is about ending our fascination with Lecter, by having him descend lower than a mere killer or even a cannibal. From Clarice's perspective, what we witness here is the "turning of Krendler into conscious meat (yet meat that is not conscious of *itself* as meat); the conversion of Krendler into a cannibal of the self; and all merely for Starling's—which is to say, our—momentary edification, nay, instruction" ("Villain" 124). We aren't released from the horror of being put in this place (which Pomerance says requires a "public execution, even more brutal"), and the film ends with Hannibal escaping once again. On a flight to who knows where, he meets a young boy who, dissatisfied with the in-flight meal, has refused to eat it. Lecter congratulates him on being so discerning and opens a lunchbox with a little cheese, some fruit, and part of Krendler's cooked brain. The final moment of the film has Lecter feeding this boy, who delights in this exotic taste.

In an interview, Derrida argued that western society is dominated by a "sacrificial structure," since we believe in a need for what he called a "noncriminal putting to death," adding that "such are the executions of ingestion, incorporation, or introjection of the corpse." We cannot bring ourselves, he said, to sacrifice the sacrifice ("Eating Well" 112–13). Hence, the commandment "Thou shalt not kill" (man, thy neighbor) presupposes a recognition of "subjecthood" not extended to other living beings (like turkeys, but also, for Hannibal, misogynists like Krendler). But eating flesh is both real and symbolic, as the children's reaction in *Giant* demonstrates clearly enough. And if cannibalism is mainly symbolic (unless you are dining with Dr. Lecter), then it raises ethical questions not only about the opposition man-animal (eater-eaten), but of how we are to negotiate "several infinitely different modes of the conception-appropriation-assimilation of the other," until "the question will come back to determining the best, most respectful, most grateful, and also most giving way of relating to the other and of relating the other to the self." In other words, Derrida writes that we live in a time in which "one must eat well," by learning to eat and giving to eat ("Eating Well" 114). There can be no grace at Hannibal's table, for to feast with him is to be disgraced.

An Improper Attack: *American History X*

> One might say that confronting another morally risks one's identity.
>
> —Stanley Cavell, "The Good of Film"

One of the more absurd scenarios in Salman Rushdie's magical realist novel *Two Years Eight Months and Twenty-Eight Nights* (2015) comes when rival philosophers from the twelfth century—resurrected in the present day by evil spirits—resume a fierce disagreement on matters of theology and morality. Still entombed in the ground, hence with mouths full of dirt, the first philosopher tells the other that even in death they must continue to "discuss matters in the proper way, courteously as to the person, ferociously as to the thought." The second philosopher, however, disagrees. On the contrary, he demurs, the "application of a degree of ferocity to the person usually brings his thinking into line with my own." This comical disagreement over the etiquette of arguing puts me in mind of Montaigne, who in "On the Art of Conversation" wrote that he relished a particular form of debate above all others; one in which strong-minded opponents would joust with him on difficult subjects, pressing "on his flanks" and pricking him to provide a robust response, or else concede defeat. "Nothing so sharpens our delicate sensibilities," wrote he, "as the feeling of our adversary's superiority and of his scorn for us." However, he concluded that "I accept and admit any kind of attack that is directed in the proper way, however feeble it may be, but I am far too intolerant of those that are not made in due order" (289).

Erving Goffman remarked that the dinner table is a prime example of what he called an "open region" in which, because of the necessity of "focused interaction," the face-to-face encounter with others establishes the feeling of shared bonds through the sharing of food resources. Hence, with bellies full, the open region of the table provides the perfect framework for artful conversation (*Behavior in Public Places* 132).

In Tony Kaye's *American History X* (1998), however, a postprandial debate following a family meal quickly turns ugly and violent. The film is about an impressionable teenager, Danny Vinyard (Edward Furlong), who—on the very day that his brother, Derek (Edward

Norton), is to be released from jail for a vicious, racist murder—is tasked by his African American teacher to reflect on his own hateful ideology; having turned in an inflammatory paper at school on *Mein Kampf*, he must now write a new paper, titled "American History X" (the subject of his brother's corruption by race hate), or else be excluded from school. As Danny thinks of his brother, he recollects an after-dinner debate following Sunday lunch some years before (told here in black-and-white flashback). The scene has been well analyzed for the violence of Derek's final outburst, which exposes to his family the full extent of his fascist ideology. In a perspicacious analysis, Leighton Grist reads the violence that erupts during the meal as suggesting more widely that "the USA has something of an innate affinity with fascism" (Grist, *Fascism* 58). But what is less commented on is the conversation that precedes the violence—a conversation, I want to argue, that already constitutes a racist violation via a series of rhetorical and expressive shifts in Derek's postprandial discourse.

The scene begins at the conclusion of a traditional protestant Sunday roast to which Doris Vinyard (Beverly D'Angelo)—Danny and Derek's mother—has invited her Jewish friend (and would-be romantic partner), Murray (Elliot Gould). Murray knows he must tread with care. Not only is he an outsider, but he is wary of seeming like he wants to install himself in the place of the siblings' father—a police officer murdered on duty a couple of years earlier. Murray politely engages Derek in a conversation about the L.A. riots that recently followed in the wake of the acquittal of the police officers who beat Rodney King.[5] Also at the dinner table is Derek's ideologically liberal sister, Davina (Jennifer Lien), and his right-wing girlfriend, Stacey (Fairuza Balk).

The conversation starts out civil enough, with Murray commenting that the riots were "an expression of rage by people who feel neglected and turned away by the system." Derek casts a dark and unsettling look at Murray talking politics. His skinhead haircut and goatee beard render Edward Norton's boyish face hard, although his clean white shirt demonstrates that he has dressed for dinner. Derek listens patiently as Murray speaks, but with Gould out of focus and with Norton at the center of the shot, Kaye makes it clear that Derek listens only because he is waiting to speak and that, moreover, he regards their guest warily. However, his portentous expression vanishes when he speaks, which he does intelligently and cordially.

To Murray's liberal views, Derek offers a counter logic that is right wing if not (yet) explicitly racist, undertaking a series of subtle and considered rhetorical shifts—such as referring to the rioters as "these people" (meaning blacks), a phrase that becomes more overtly racially charged when he wonders if "these people" have a "racial commitment to crime." Murray falls silent as Derek begins to dominate the conversation, which soon becomes an oratory. Doris begins to feel embarrassed, and at one point she lays a reassuring hand on Murray's arm, urging him to speak up. But his feeble response only emboldens Derek, who continues unabated. Shortly after, Derek's use of the generalizing "these people" slips (possibly intentionally) when he uses the racial slur "these monkeys," as he fantasizes a violent hypothetical involving his younger brother to turn the screw. Doris interjects and suggests they have dessert. With a big smile she begs them to just "drop this Rodney King thing."

Doris's plea marks the perfect opportunity to change the subject for everyone at the table. However, and somewhat surprisingly, it is Murray who breaks the awkward silence, insisting that they are "having a discussion." For him, the conversation cannot end there, for two reasons. First, because he must get Derek on his side if he is to be accepted by him (and Doris's injunction has killed the conversation dead). He knows that by giving his consent to Derek to continue, he demonstrates that he is not an outsider "taking sides" with mom against him. And second, because he feels compelled to challenge Derek's views and still believes he can. However, he is in for a nasty surprise. Doris gives up and leaves the room to prepare the dessert, and it is at this point that Derek shifts his entire manner and demeanor. Rather than raise his voice, he lowers it. Rather than gesticulate and exhort he leans in and confides. Derek is no longer oppositional but conspiratorial.

His views become markedly more racist against African Americans, and while he knows full well that Murray does not share his toxic views, he co-opts the other diners as though "preaching to the choristers." Murray becomes visibly distressed by the language Derek uses, in which he more deliberately redeploys the racist slur ("monkeys"). Murray can either stay silent or speak up. He risks the latter, gently challenging Derek on his last rant that the "struggling black man" has had a hundred and fifty years to "overcome his 'historical injustices,'" to which Murray responds that "Jews have been persecuted for over five thousand years; are you saying that it's wrong to feel sensitive about antisemitism?" In response, Derek does nothing more than raise an eyebrow and smirk (see Figure 8.6). By equating Jewish and African American suffering, Murray has not only personalized the argument but put his very *being* as a Jew "on the table," so to speak. Far from seeing this as a sign that he should back off, that the conversation has gotten too personal, Derek likewise "unconceals" himself, as it were.[6] He exposes the true object and target of his contemptuous speech: their Jewish guest.

To return to Montaigne, Derek has effectively launched the conversational equivalent of an "improper attack," one that takes aim not at Murray's liberal views but at the man himself. It is an *ad hominem* attack against the man, a Jewish man, who would replace his father. The moment echoes Woody Allen's dinner table confrontation with the "classic Jew-hating" grandmother in *Annie Hall* (1977), in which Allen imagines himself under her stern glare (as he is served ham!) reduced to a religious stereotype (dressed as a Hasidic Jew).[7] Like this moment in *Annie Hall*, the scene in *American History X* is about the double-bind table etiquette induces in us when, having "broken bread" with a stranger we lower our guard.

After Derek's smirk, a precipitous decline in decorum follows as Murray is plunged into silent despair. Davina takes up the argument, provoking her brother to snap, whereupon he viciously assaults her by stuffing slices of leftover roast beef into her mouth (to shut her up), before unleashing an obscene racist tirade against Murray, who tries to intervene. Doris returns, bewildered, to witness Derek unbutton his smart white shirt to reveal a starched white vest under which we can just about make out that his muscular body is heavily tattooed. "You see this?" he snarls at Murray as he pulls the vest top down to reveal a giant tattooed swastika over his heart. "That means, '*Not Welcome*'" (see Figure 8.7).

In one sense, Derek's revelation of the tattoo and vicious tirade of racist insults (along with his assault on his sister) constitute the worst of the violence in the scene. He threatens to cut off Murray's "Shylock nose" and makes a pointed reference to his mother ("You think I'm gonna sit here and smile while some fucking kike tries to fuck my mother?"—a statement Grist reads as being as much Oedipal as antisemitic [*Fascism* 37]). But that smirk does violence, too. It closes the table as an "open region," just as Derek shuts Murray down after

Figures 8.6. and 8.7. Edward Norton smirks and snarls in *American History X*. Tony Kaye, New Line Cinema, 1998. Digital frame enlargement.

he exposes his Jewishness to their "discussion."⁸ Murray is served up (that is, betrayed), "cut" by Derek who refuses to see him as his equal, as a man of equivalent worth.

The key to this dining scene, as Grist points out (*Fascism* 39), is found in another of Danny's flashbacks from much later in the film. This memory is chronologically earlier than the Sunday lunch scene, and at this point in the film Danny has begun to renounce his hateful ideology and truly, deeply reflect on the source of his brother's corruption to neo-Nazism. In this second, deeper memory, the siblings are gathered around the breakfast table with their father, Dennis (William Russ), who asks Derek about how he is getting on at school. Derek now cuts a very different figure. With longer hair and a pubescent, pimply smiling face, we now see the boyish Norton—a picture of angelic goodness. Derek is enthusing about a fantastic course on African American literature and expresses his wonder and delight at reading Richard Wright's *Native Son*. Dennis, however, raises a patronizing eyebrow and warns Derek that such literature is a part of what he calls "affirmative action crap," which is the very reason, he says, that he has black officers watching his back at work rather than (more competent) white ones. Derek falters. With a weakly reassuring smile, he merely nods at his father's instruction and falls silent.

The implication is clear. Having brought to the table the subject of race, his father has shut it down—weakening Derek's appetite by diluting, if not polluting, his budding taste for African American literature, for African American history (which is, of course, American history). A wider implication is also clear. When his father is killed, Derek's anger is not just fueled by his loss; he rages against an entire system that (as his father explained it to him here) is weakened by the affirmation of the African American "Other."[9] Here is one more instance of an "improper attack." With an eagerness practically bursting from the young Derek's impassioned face, we glimpse something of the voracious appetite being awakened in his reading of books like *Native Son*. However, with his bigoted and dismissive remark, Derek's father (clearly not a reader) hardens that expression in his son's face. Derek is smart enough to catch his father's warning in full: not only is it impolitic (in this house) to bring a topic of conversation like this to the dinner table, but Derek's (literary) appetites are, themselves, unacceptable. In his discussion of eating disorders, Adam Phillips wonders if anxieties over parental controls lead to the profound and paradoxical question of what it would mean to keep one's appetite "pure." "What interferes with hunger is eating," writes he, and "the refusal of appetite is a belated attempt to restore the viability of appetite" ("On Eating" 294). To paraphrase Phillips, what Derek discovered in this scene with his father was that his appetite for literature—for African American literature—got him in trouble. It is that same trouble we see erupting in the later scene with Murray. This youthful appetite is the "X" of the title, an "X" that must be reclaimed, renamed, and returned to the dinner table.

Dine with Me:
Edward Scissorhands, *Greystoke*, and *Babette's Feast*

> He who makes a beast of himself gets rid of the pain of being a man.
>
> —Samuel Johnson

I want to end on a short observation based on Virginia Woolf's claim that "one cannot think well, love well, sleep well, if one has not dined well" ("A Room of One's Own" 20). In an essay all about the importance of having a "room" in which to think and create, Woolf's remark is about appetite in the widest possible sense. In Herman Koch's *The Dinner*, the narrator observes that "you sometimes hear about people who have lost their sense of smell and taste: for those people, a plate of the most delicious food means nothing at all. That was how I looked at life sometimes, as a warm meal that was growing cold. I knew I had to eat, otherwise I would die, but I had lost my appetite" (205). Let me end with three films that, along with the example of *Tom Jones*, offer counterpoints to the torturous table etiquettes examined in this chapter.

The first is *Edward Scissorhands* (1990), which introduces Edward (Johnny Depp)—a monstrous humanoid creation of an elderly inventor (Vincent Price) who suffers a heart attack before he can finish him. As such, Edward has scissors for hands and shuns the world for fear of rejection. When he is rescued from this state by a curious saleswoman, Peg (Dianne Wiest), Edward is invited to live with her and her family. At first Edward is shy and awkward, and inspires fear in Peg's children, Kim (Winona Ryder) and Kevin (Robert Oliveri), and mistrust in her husband, Bill (Alan Arkin). During an awkward dinner, Edward attempts to use the shears he has for hands to pick up the cutlery, but he keeps sending them crashing to the table. He tries again and again, but with no luck. Director Tim Burton cuts to the family sitting at the other end of the table, who sit in awkward silence (Edward's shears keep poking into the bottom of the frame as he hopelessly fumbles the cutlery). As Edward continues to drop the knife and fork, Peg chides her son, Kevin, for staring. Then, Bill brightly exclaims, "Well, this must be quite a change for you, Ed?" Again, Peg corrects her family ("'Edward,' dear, I think he prefers Edward"). Eventually, Edward relaxes enough to begin using his shears themselves to cut his food and lift it (mostly unsuccessfully) to his face. But now the atmosphere has softened. Bill continues to make small talk with "Ed" (again, unsuccessfully) and Kevin keeps staring, and remarks on how "cool" and "sharp" Edward's shear-like fingers are (before wondering—as twelve-year-old boys will—how easily Edward could cut a man's head off). But when Peg offers Edward some butter for his bread he smiles, thanks her, and manages to dab his lips with a napkin. He has eaten no food, but in the smile on his face, Edward is clearly finding an appetite for sociality with this warm and welcoming family. Murray Pomerance says Edward's "pure subjectivity and his material poverty render him incessantly subject to human kindness, human deceit, human violence, and human definition, since without hands he cannot even spell himself." In this lovely scene, Peg uses table manners to overcome Edward's "material poverty" (*Johnny Depp* 209). That this happens ought not surprise us, Pomerance writes, since the film is about our falling in love with this monster and accepting him as we accept that which is "monstrous" in us (as one definition has it, *mōnstrāre* means "to point out, to show").

The second example is from Hugh Hudson's *Greystoke: The Legend of Tarzan, Lord of the Apes* (1984), in which the problem of how to convey food to one's mouth is solved by a very different breach of manners and covered by the host via a no less gracious response. During a dinner at the ancestral home, the guests look on in horror as Tarzan (Christopher Lambert)—fresh from the jungle and dressed in a tuxedo—immediately lifts his soup bowl to his mouth and begins slurping (ignoring the spoon). It is the ultimate faux pas and betrays his incivility. Yet at the head of the table, the Earl (Ralph Richardson) quickly exclaims, "Oh!" before chucking his spoon down and declaring, "Quite right, quite right. I *hate* spoons." He picks his own bowl up and proceeds to slurp likewise (Pomerance evocatively describes the gesture as "stentorious slurping" [*Virtuoso* 189]). The response of the host legitimizes Tarzan's method of eating, drawing appreciative smiles from the assorted guests.

Both moments remind me of the lesson Pen Vogler offers in the conclusion to her history of dining etiquette, in which she states that most people are quite content with "good manners," which "doesn't have the fussy and fusty connotations of 'etiquette' but suggests adaptability and putting the ease of another person first." Good manners,

Vogler writes, "consisted not in *not spilling* the gravy boat, but in *not noticing* that the gravy boat had been spilt." The earl's gesture is one of generous acceptance that might well have been outrage at the affront to decency. He extends to Tarzan the true power of the honored guest as one who ought not to conform to the table, but for whom it is the table that will conform. After all, a "companion" is not simply defined, writes Margaret Visser, as "a person with whom we share bread"—they are also one with whom the *manner* of our sharing will be negotiated and agreed (6).

In this sense, *Babette's Feast* (1987) offers the antidote to the horror of diners like Lecter and Derek, who de-serve their guests. In this film, a group of Puritanical Danish Lutherans eat meals of stale bread porridge provided by sisters Martine (Birgitte Federspiel) and Filippa (Bodil Kjer). The food hardly arouses the taste buds, and that is exactly the point. According to them, the tongue is the "strange little muscle" that "unleashed evil and deadly poison." To feast is to be tempted to sin, so they eat "as if we never had the sense of taste." Hence, when an acclaimed chef, Babette (Stéphane Audran), of the classy Café Anglais takes on the role of the sisters' housekeeper and cook after the fall of the Paris commune in 1871, she initially resists letting on about her epicurean prowess. Gradually, however, Babette begins to improve both the nutritional and tasting quality of the meals she provides, bringing increasing pleasure to those who sup from her offerings. For her final feast, Babette elevates her cooking into an art, serving turtle soup, blinis, and quail in puff pastry.

Babette is a gourmand, but she is not a gastronome (one well versed in gastronomy). The difference is crucial, wrote Pierre Bourdieu, for while the gourmand has a natural gift for recognizing and perfecting *taste*, the gastronome obsesses over the "set of *rules* which govern the cultivation and *education* of taste" (61). Babette leads the Lutherans by the senses, as it were, stimulating their appetites. She is a delicate connoisseur—unlike the gastronome, who is "a pedant" with food as the grammarian is with language. So, Bourdieu wrote, just as a great writer is her own grammarian (whether she knows the rules or not), a "gourmet is his own gastronome." The latter are required, then, for those without taste, for there is such a thing as bad taste. People with refinement know this instinctively. "For those who do not, rules are needed" (61). What the Lutherans learn from Babette is that food is not decadent. It is about sharing and communality, and taste and celebration. Far from being sinful, to feast with Babette is to show one's *good grace* and upstanding virtue among one's fellows.

Manners matter in this world, words matter. An "improper attack" like Derek's raises once again the specter of violence at the dinner table, whereby a carving knife no longer carries the symbolic potential of a shared and sharing community (*Tom Jones*), but of the desecration of the other (*Hannibal*). Formalities can be suspended to welcome and invite (*Greystoke*) or to antagonize and torment (*American Beauty*), just as the art of conversation can be abused (*American History X*) to deny an invited guest his humanity. Let me end with a powerful statement by Lester D. Friedman, who wrote that "the ability to act like a human being in a world in which people are treated like animals is, in and of itself, an act of humanity, an ethical form of resistance which mocks a world of obscene cruelty" (197).

9

Tresses and Distresses

Intimacy

> Remembering all the hugs, and handshakes, and the intimate moments.
>
> —Denzel Washington, *Philadelphia* (1993)

∼

"WILL YOU JUST WATCH THE HAIR!" So responds Tony Manero (John Travolta) to being clipped around the head by his father at the dinner table in *Saturday Night Fever* (1977). He moans to his mother that "He hits my hair." The ache in Tony's head pales next to the potential embarrassment on the disco dancefloor as his reputation rests as much on his bouffant hairstyle (lovingly coiffed in front of the mirror) as his famous moves. The threat posed by tousled hair is due to what Anthony Synnott calls the "fluid *process*" of fashioning (and refashioning) the adolescent ego to fix gender and ideology when maturing into adulthood. Hair, in this sense, masks (the feeling of) incompleteness. In the context of *American Hustle* (2013), "fixing" hair works similarly to establish and protect an identity vulnerable to attack. Having painstakingly concealed his bald crown with a glued toupee and comb-over, conman Irving Rosenfeld (Christian Bale) is doubly exposed as a hustler when a rival, Richie DiMaso (Bradley Cooper), publicly reveals his baldness. Irving is exposed as a hustler, both professionally and personally. A certain type of (working-class) masculinity is in both films concealed by "fixing" a "do," which, when "unfixed," risks exposing the façade and undermining the constructed identity. Looking at hair styling and un-styling, both onscreen and off, shows the performance of masculine identity and its manipulation. It is extremely bad etiquette to mess someone's hair. It is, in Tony's words, a form of hitting.

There are numerous anecdotes of industry "concealment" in the work of legendary Hollywood hair stylist Sydney Guilaroff, as well as moments of "exposure." Consider the moment Sean Connery purposefully distanced himself from playing James Bond in *Diamonds Are Forever* (for which he wore a hairpiece) with his balding appearance in *The Anderson Tapes* (both 1971). As with the moment Richie "unfixes" Irving's hair—which is also an attempt to make a claim on Irving's girlfriend, Sydney Prosser (Amy Adams)—the masking or unmasking of the hair "cheat" builds or bursts the performative act ("Do you think I'm losing my hair?" Tony worries throughout *Saturday Night Fever*). With female hair the matter is, I think, a little more complex.

"One of the great joys in life is having one's hair brushed." So remarks Vanessa Redgrave as she gently brushes Amanda Seyfried's hair in *Letters to Juliet* (2010). This tender moment between the two women confirms their relationship as the "joy" of hair brushing ushers in Redgrave as a surrogate mother to the lovelorn Seyfried, who finds comfort and reassurance in the safe embrace of a remembered maternal caress. Indeed, it is a tender scene that makes more violating a moment in Michael Haneke's *Amour* (2012) when Anne (Emmanuelle Riva), an elderly woman incapacitated followed a devastating stroke, has her hair roughly combed by the nurse (Dinara Drukarova) hired by her beleaguered husband, Georges (Jean-Louis Trintignant), to help him cope. While it might appear that the nurse's act seeks to replicate Redgrave's nurturing gesture in *Letters to Juliet*, Haneke makes it quite clear that in this moment it constitutes a violation. "There you go," soothes the nurse as she roughly brushes Anne's hair—so roughly the brush keeps catching, jerking Anne's head to the side. "You want to look your very best, so everybody can admire you." One wonders for whom Anne must look her "very best" as she struggles to cope with the painful indignity of her impending death. Anne is, in this scene, exposed and objectified by the nurse's treatment, and yet, we might ask what it is that separates the revivifying act of hair brushing in *Letters* from the humiliating act of hair brushing in *Amour*. Despite the discomfort inflicted on Anne, it seems difficult to articulate just why the nurse's actions appear so cruel, so torturous. When Georges shortly sacks the nurse, she seems surprised and annoyed. After pressing him as to the reason, he finally calls her "incompetent," and when she asks what he means, Georges responds, "I won't discuss it with you, and you wouldn't understand anyway." Haneke also leaves it at that.

This scene from *Amour* stayed with me for a very long time, and I just couldn't figure out why. By looking at a series of examples from elsewhere in cinema that offer a preliminary sketch of how the intimacy of hair has been used to illustrate a profound connection between women, however, I think I found an answer. This chapter will explore how hair brushing, styling, and cutting involve a kind of intimacy that bypasses etiquette, transcends it even, but also involves a different set of considerations for the other. We might find some of these considerations in other intimacies not covered in etiquette manuals but that are no less often (and perhaps more) subject to violation.

Tresses: Fixing

Hair brushing is used as an expression of tenderness between women in several indelible moments in cinema, moments that tend to fall into one of two categories: maternal and/or erotic. In James Cameron's *Aliens* (1986), Ripley (Sigourney Weaver) brushes the hair and cleans the face of an orphaned girl, Newt (Carrie Henn), cementing their bond. In Amma Asante's *Belle* (2013), a servant, Mabel (Bethan Mary-James), passes on her own mother's advice about "brushing the ends" to Dido (Gugu Mbatha-Raw), whose struggle with her hair reminds her of the maternal absence in her life. Moments like these confirm a strong filial bond between mothers and daughters, whether long standing or, as in these examples, newly established. There are important ethnographic distinctions between black and white hair, as observed by bell hooks, who wrote that to "fix" (that is, straighten) one's hair with others formed an intimate ritual in which black women would meet and take the time "to talk with one another, to listen to the talk." She writes that "it was a world where the images constructed as barriers between one's self and the world were briefly let go, before they were made again. It was a moment of creativity," she wrote, "a moment of change" (111).

Such creative moments with hair also work to establish sexuality and suggest erotic encounters. The sensual power of hair is expressed in Jonathan Dayton and Valerie Faris's *Battle of the Sexes* (2017). In the scene, Andrea Riseborough gives Emma Stone (playing Billie Jean King) a haircut, and, as the pair lock eyes in the mirror, their mutual attraction is communicated through touch as Riseborough's character playfully draws her fingers through Stone's hair. It is a moment that echoes Robert Redgrave shampooing Meryl Streep's hair in *Out of Africa* (1985), the shampoo running suggestively into the stream behind them. "What do you want?" Riseborough asks Stone, whose face is a mixture of confusion and enchantment as she replies, "What do you mean?" "With your *hair*," the hairdresser clarifies, giggling at the innuendo. "What do you want me to *do* with it?" What kind of "do" should be done is her question, but Stone is right to read it as double entendre. "Will you let me just give you a little trim?" suggests Riseborough. "It'll make you feel like a whole new person!" The mirror is here offered up as a "third space" in which any etiquette restricting the extent to which one might touch and indeed play with a stranger's hair is suspended.

The transformative power of cutting hair also recalls films in which women on the run change their appearance to evade capture: Madeleine Stowe in *12 Monkeys* (1995) recreates the moment in *Vertigo* of Judy's transformation into Scottie's "Madeleine," and likewise Naomi Watts cuts Laura Harring's hair in *Mulholland Dr.* (2001) to escape murderous thugs (a moment initiating sex). Another sensual moment is Matt Damon cutting Franka Potente's hair in a Paris hotel room in *The Bourne Identity* (2002). The reenergizing potential of getting a radical haircut, as Murray Pomerance suggested to me, finds its fullest expression in William Wyler's *Roman Holiday* (1953), when Ann (played by Audrey Hepburn) goes into a salon and demands to have her hair cut very short, shorter than the poor stylist can bear, who initially finds the act of shearing Ann's long luscious locks unconscionable. Of course, the power of the moment is its establishment of an iconic look—once the "do" is "done," Ann effectively becomes "Audrey Hepburn" (see Figure 9.1).

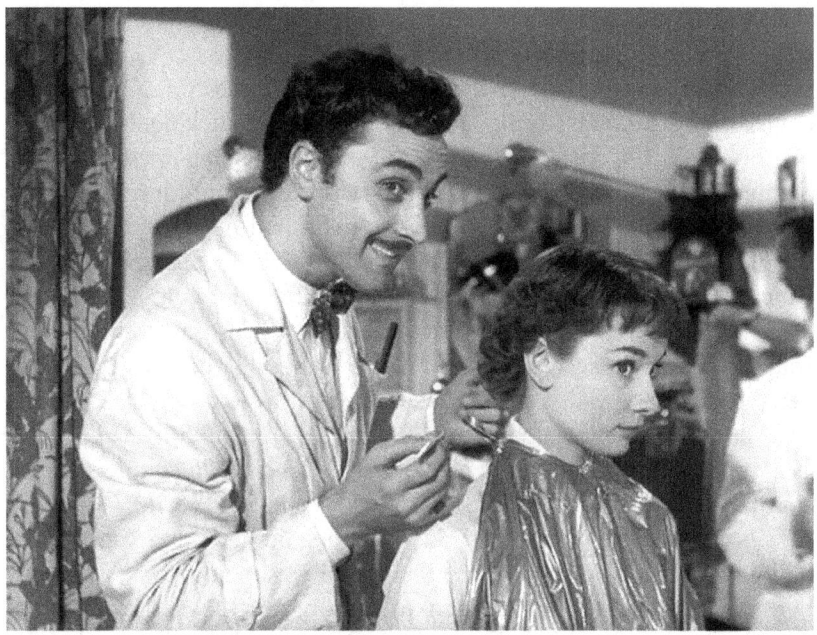

Figure 9.1. Audrey Hepburn in *Roman Holiday*. William Wyler, Paramount Pictures, 1953. Digital frame enlargement.

In a reversal of the usual transformation process, the princess becomes the film star. Such moments—even empowered ones, as in *Roman Holiday*—require trust, a certain "letting go" of control. She must consent to her hair being brushed, cut, or shampooed as an act of submission inviting soothing nostalgia or initiating seductive play. In either case, the "great joy" described by Redgrave in *Letters to Juliet* is one of intimacy and trust, of surrendering to a touch—maternal, sexual—sometimes narcissistic (but without conceit), and one that is singularly revivifying.

Of course, transforming Audrey Hepburn into "Audrey Hepburn" was the subject of so many of her most indelible roles. The introduction of her iconic Little Black Dress in *Sabrina* (1954), for example, or her resistance to being made over by Kay Thompson (as the brilliant Maggie Prescott) in *Funny Face* (1957)—which comes to a head when Thompson comes at Hepburn with "big scissors." And of course, her "Pygmalion," in which her Cockney flower girl complies with the styling wishes of Rex Harrison in *My Fair Lady*

(1964), culminating in her collapse and resurrection as a lady. This idea is more complex in other "makeover" scenes, especially when the woman being made over either cedes, or never really has any control: one perhaps thinks of Anne Hathaway flicking her hair in slo-mo in *The Devil Wears Prada* (2006) after being made over by Stanley Tucci in a sequence that ends with her gliding into the office in front of her disbelieving colleagues (who had been bitching about her lack of style). Or the moment in *The Princess Diaries* (2001) in which Hathaway is made over by Larry Miller, who complains of her "frizzy, frizzy, frizzy" hair. When he breaks his brush attempting to roughly comb those frizzy locks, Miller snaps Hathaway's glasses in petty retaliation. (See also Michael Caine's reaction to seeing Sandra Bullock for the first time in *Miss Congeniality* [2000].) With Judy Garland (as Esther Blodgett) in *A Star is Born* (1954), one can see echoes of her uncomfortable makeover scene in *The Wizard of Oz* (1939). By contrast, with Mia Farrow the moment that "shocked a nation" was the revelation—onscreen in an episode of *Peyton Place*—of her new "drastically" bobbed haircut, a haircut with which the actress would later be identified (Farrow called it her "little girl hair"). The producers of the show had to hurriedly write the haircut into the storyline. Such makeovers run the risk of "unmaking."[1]

These tonsorial examples of "fixing" and "unfixing" hair can be matched by equally sensuous moments when hair is literally "let down." One could point to some obvious examples in such transformative moments as Olivia Newton-John's ironic appearance at the end of *Grease* (1978), but equally to subtler gestures. In Ridley Scott's *Blade Runner* (2007 [1982]), an intimate scene occurs when Sean Young (playing Rachael) is rocked by the knowledge that she is a "replicant." She lets her hair down to experience a moment of private existential confirmation. Cradling photographs of someone else's mother, Rachel reflects on the memories of her own family—implanted by her creator—as the hard lines and shiny textures of her femme fatale identity give way to the soft textures of a linen shirt over which cascading brunette curls unfurl to reveal her new relation to the world.[2]

In Dua Lipa's hit video for her song, "New Rules" (2017), a group of girls figuring out ways to help their friend forget and get over a bad relationship sit combing one another's hair (like grooming monkeys). It is as if they are literally combing the man out of their lives, an idea that seems borrowed from Mitzi Gaynor singing, "I'm gonna wash that man right out of my hair" in Joshua Logan's film adaptation of Rodgers and Hammerstein's *South Pacific* (1958). As Gaynor sings, her girlfriends join in too (as in the Lipa video). One learns the "new rules," then, in order to form a community—a group of women singing in harmony, helping one another get through hard times. It is difficult to miss the connotations of baptism and new beginnings in the act of washing men away. Of course, this is not always so successful, as Julie Andrews discovers in Blake Edwards's *Victor/Victoria* (1982), when she literally washes the "man" she's been pretending to be out of her hair (unknown to her, James Garner is watching, concealed in the closet), revealing she is a woman. Sometimes, a woman might not want to wash a man out of her hair. In *Swing Time* (1936), Fred Astaire sings "The Way You Look Tonight" as Ginger Rogers lathers up her hair at the sink in the next room. Distracted by his performance, she neglects to wash the shampoo out and instead dreamily wanders over to join him at the piano. They lock eyes as he finishes the song, and the scene ends with Rogers scampering off to rinse after embarrassedly clocking her reflection in the mirror.

Unlike these women, while men figuratively "let their hair down" they tend not to do so quite so literally. It seems equally evident that while a man might (and should!) wash his hair, he would be unlikely to wash anything "out" of it. (There are, of course, several exceptions to this—from *Easy Rider* [1969] to *American Hustle* [2013]—but they are far fewer in number.)[3]

What these examples illustrate is that "fixing" hair can be a means to expand and deepen relationships, a point of rebirth or transition in which oneself and the world is reborn. It is not just through styling, but in the connections forged through the intimacy (whether explicitly sexual or not) that such gestures invite exploration of the body that is sensual, nonpenetrative (notwithstanding the act of running one's fingers, or a comb—or indeed scissors—through another person's hair). Playing with hair constitutes a nonverbal means of revealing oneself to another—as in *Letters to Juliet* and *Battle of the Sexes*—or, by way of a decisive cut, marks a transformation of the self—as in *Roman Holiday*, or with Rita Hayworth, whose red locks (made famous in *Gilda* [1946]) were cut short and dyed blonde for *The Lady from Shanghai* (1947). That this is so often an experience for women marks this out as fertile ground for exploring the twentieth century's rethinking of the way the senses relate to thinking. Does this shift repudiate the Enlightenment emphasis on reason and rationalism as male and masculine modes of experience associated with the disembodied mind (the Cartesian "ghost in the machine")? The sensuous experience of touch, in this way, becomes a phenomenological, not to say philosophical, act.

It is against this context, then, that Haneke's *Amour* is not only unsettling as a cinematic experience, but intellectually; as an example of how this gesture of trust can be so profoundly violated, it undermines the very value such gestures afford.

Distresses: Scalping

In F. Scott Fitzgerald's short story "Bernice Bobs Her Hair" (1920),[4] a wealthy but socially awkward adolescent is tutored by her socialite cousin on how to be fashionable and popular. Cousin Marjorie's lessons in etiquette—which include giving advice on how to tell amusing anecdotes, tips on how to dress, and of course tutorials on flirting etiquette—become so successful, however, that when Bernice starts to command the limelight, even attracting the attention of one of Marjorie's beaus, the teacher betrays her student by duping her into cutting her hair into a bob. The result is total humiliation, and, realizing she has been hoodwinked, Bernice decides to leave town to avoid the scandal of attending an upcoming party at which she had been hoping to be confirmed as a high society girl. In a final act of malicious revenge, however, Bernice cuts her cousin's braids as she sleeps, leaving the detached locks on the porch of the boy who came between them before leaving town for good. The violating experience of the "bobbing" of Bernice's hair is recalled in the torture-interrogation scene in *V for Vendetta* (2005), in which Natalie Portman—and really, undeniably Natalie Portman—similarly beguiled by someone she trusted, has her head shaved. It is a scene that, unlike the shaving of the head as a right of initiation/rebirth (in examples like Sigourney Weaver in *Alien 3* [1992], Demi Moore in *G.I. Jane* [1997], and more recently Cate Blanchett in Tom Tykwer's *Heaven* [2002]), is intended to degrade and humiliate, to reduce and denude her.

The very image of a woman being shaved in this way carries echoes of the victims of religious hate crimes, particularly the cutting of religious beards, or the de-lousing of prisoners of war in concentration camps, as well as the "ugly carnival," as Antony Beevor put it, of the women whose heads were shaved after being denounced for engaging in sexual relations with occupying Nazi soldiers in occupied France ("*collaboration horizontale*"), as depicted in Alain Resnais's *Hiroshima mon amour* (1959) and Martin Ritt's *Five Branded Women* (1960).[5] The practice was historically used as a form of correction for a prostitute, whose cropped hair supposedly removed her sexuality such that as it grew back, she might gradually "win her way to piety," as Eric Trudgill put it (qtd. in Ofek 66). Such forms of haircutting do incalculable damage to a person's psyche, a point made clear in Fitzgerald's story by the language Bernice uses to describe the effect of sitting in the hairdressers waiting to be "guillotined," as she puts it. Consider the pain on Anne Hathaway's face as she tearfully has her hair cut to sell during the "Lovely Ladies" number in Tom Hooper's *Les Misérables* (2012). Her pained expression is in part due to her hair being roughly hacked off, but also at the shock of finding her body subject to such crude valuation (indeed, marketing her hair constitutes a gateway to pawning her teeth, and, eventually selling her body). Her sense of self-worth, along with her physical worth as a tradable commodity, is diminished. Hathaway's Fantine is at least nominally consenting. Bernice, however, cuts Marjorie's hair while she sleeps, the violence of her act located in the humiliation it will cause, much less (in fact not at all) in the physical pain it will inflict. What Bernice describes as an "amputation"—a "scalping," even—will not even cause a stir in her slumbering victim, who will go on dreaming of the moment she will arrive as the belle of the ball. Likewise, when Robert Jordan meets and becomes transfixed at the sight of Maria in Ernest Hemingway's *For Whom the Bell Tolls* (1940), he cannot stop himself from thinking that "she'd be beautiful if they hadn't cropped her hair" (24). Maria, a victim of Falangist fascists whose brutal treatment of her included the ritual shaving of her hair, was also beaten and raped and witnessed the execution of her parents. But it is the shaving of her head that seems to mark her. While she tries to move past it, Robert persists. "'You have a very beautiful face,' says he, 'I wish I would have had the luck to see you before your hair was cut'" (26).

A woman's hair is, in these examples, a site of manipulation for men. In Hitchcock, we might point to a number of memorable examples in which hair seems to inflict punishment (mostly, but not always, for a man). In *Vertigo* (1958), Kim Novak unsuccessfully resists James Stewart's attempt to style her hair, while in *Rebecca* (1940), Mrs. Danvers (Judith Anderson) ominously lectures the new Mrs. De Winter (Joan Fontaine) on how Rebecca had styled hers. In *Suspicion* (1941), Joan Fontaine suspects Cary Grant's motivations when he "fixes her hair." Elsewhere, one might also think of Natalie Wood's hair as a marker of contestation in John Ford's *The Searchers* (1956). Her pigtails with bird feathers come to represent (at least as John Wayne's Ethan comes to see it) a "spoiled identity."

Unlike the trust experienced by women getting their hair fixed by a "do," these examples constitute a betrayal leading to her "undoing." It is this betrayal that marks the hair brushing scene in Haneke's *Amour* as a moment in which Anne is effectively "scalped" in her bed—although unlike Bernice remains fully conscious. As the nurse blithely comments on Anne's appearance while roughly brushing her hair, Haneke's camera remains fixed as Anne's face writhes and contorts (see Figure 9.2).

In a film in which the incommunicability of Anne's pain, as well as the challenges her care pose for her husband, are at the center of the drama, one gets a sense of what Elaine Scarry meant when she made the distinction between physical pain as either "making" or "unmaking" the world. In one scene, as Anne and Georges sing a song

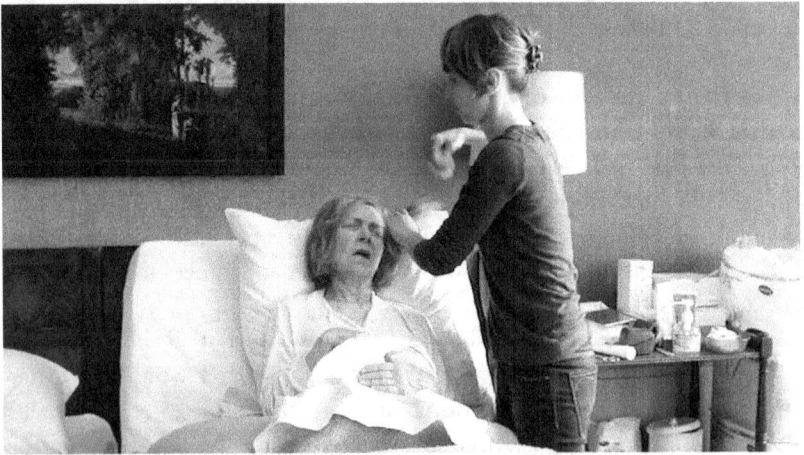

Figure 9.2. Emmanuelle Riva hurts in *Amour*. Michael Haneke, Les Films du Losange, 2012. Digital frame enlargement.

together (he sings while she hums along), her pain is "upbuilding." In the hair brushing scene, however, it works oppositely. Perhaps the greatest humiliation comes when, toward the end of the hair brushing scene, the nurse thrusts a vanity mirror up to Anne's face, asking her if she wants to look. Anne desperately wrenches her face around to avoid seeing her reflection as the nurse comments on her in the third person. "Well, isn't she beautiful?"

Elsie Walker points out that the nurse's privileging of Anne's appearance over her voice is contrasted with George's patient efforts to listen to Anne and help her communicate. The nurse denies Anne's subjectivity (196), a somewhat grim example of Emily Post's statement that "everybody knows the nurse is either the comfort or the torment of the house" (152).

It is the ultimate moment of humiliation and is "violating" in two senses, suggested by the ambiguity of "violating intimacy." On the one hand, it is the intimate gesture of hair brushing generally that is being used to violate. But, at the same time, the moment violates the intimacy of the gesture itself. In this sense, it is not unlike other acts of torture that take the form of and pervert recuperative gestures, such as reliving tooth pain in *Marathon Man* (1976), or feeding someone in *Hannibal* (2001). Beyond even these examples, the scene in *Amour* is the violation of hair brushing as "one of the great joys in life," a joy that constitutes nothing less than the means to discover or recall passion and intimacy. The moment marks the violation of an intimate gesture, a betrayal of trust. In this scene, Haneke illustrates the infantilizing and humiliating treatment of a woman whose dignity at the end of her life is a precious and fragile thing. As for the nurse—who has her own hair tellingly tied back as she mechanically goes about her business with Anne: she will not, cannot, as Georges damningly puts it, be made to understand the feminine joy that she so torturously violates.

Conclusion

As Time Goes By

All works which describe manners, require notes in sixty or seventy years, or less.

—Samuel Johnson

~

How to summarize all this? In his defense of manners, which he argued to be intrinsic to underpinning morals, Henry Hazlitt wrote that manners essentially "consist in consideration for others. They consist in deferring to others." In this book we have looked at a range of examples. In some, torture proceeds from etiquette because a person has blundered or committed a well-intentioned faux pas. In other examples, torture arises because manners have been jettisoned by the rude, or because the correct etiquette was simply not known. In yet other examples, however, manners have been the instruments of torture, wielded knowingly and with the intention of demeaning and causing pain to others. But Hazlitt urged us to embrace mannered behavior as an intrinsic and essential good. "One tries to deal with others with unfailing courtesy. One tries constantly to spare the feelings of others" (Hazlitt n.p.). Who could argue with the well intentioned? However, I hope this book has also shown there are examples in which etiquette itself is systemically torturous. I want to end with an example of how etiquette as a system intended to lubricate social interaction can become, over time, an impediment to smooth relations. Among the examples Hazlitt gave was the "traffic rule" that symbolized the decision concerning who goes first through a doorway. "The gentleman yields to the lady," wrote Hazlitt, "the younger yields to the older; the able-bodied yield to the ill . . . the host yields to the guest," and so on. Such rules, argued he, "take the minor jolts and irritations out of life" (n.p.).

Now, Hazlitt admitted that there are instances—let us call them "exceptions"—where such rules become unclear or confused. They are exceptions, however, that prove the (general benefit of the) rule. What interests me is the way the number of exceptions seems to have increased over time. In his essay on "Gay Etiquette," Jeff Weinstein points out that from the teapots of London to the fountains of Fontainebleau, etiquette has always really existed "to promote the survival of the status quo" rather than "trickle down" to raise the standards of behavior (and thus standards of living) among the masses (34). The problem, writes he, is that while late Victorian and early twentieth-century social mobility required the codification of etiquette in the handbooks of Post and Vanderbilt, et al., such tomes no longer function today. Given the social upheavals of the late twentieth and early twenty-first centuries (from civil and equal rights in the 1960s and 1970s to Black Lives Matter and Me Too in the 2010s), social reform raises significant problems for etiquette. On the one hand, it could be argued we are "post-Post" etiquette, as Weinstein puts it. However well intentioned the erstwhile authors of etiquette guides in their desire to universalize mannered behavior, it is surely incongruous to speak today of *the* (singular) "proper" mode of expression, dress, and comportment given the rapid evolutions and devolutions in how we speak to, touch, and engage with others (from political correctness to social distancing, for example), not to mention how we conduct ourselves online in our increasingly digital lives (so called "netiquette"). Post-Post etiquette is becoming, Weinstein is tempted to think, simply post-etiquette: "Once social etiquette fractions and particulates it begins to lose its raison d'être, which is a way for every diner at civilization's table to be higher or lower than someone else. . . . The old corset of etiquette is simply too inelastic to conceal the limps and edges of any crucial social change—the full acknowledgement, for example, of same-sex love" (35, 38). However, rather than cast aside etiquette in favor of a brave new world unencumbered by imaginary (sometimes arbitrary, sometimes prejudiced) walls separating the "civilized" (us) from the "savages" (them), Weinstein suggests a way to use "the old dame" before she "disintegrates completely" (35).

In a brilliant twist on the "traffic rules" mentioned by Hazlitt, Weinstein recalls the "gratifying instant" he experienced this rule of etiquette being undermined. Not by violating it but by following it *to the letter*. The rule in question gave priority to couples over groups along a footpath too narrow for more than two persons to pass. The rule, however, clearly privileged heterosexual couples, Weinstein complained, since gay couples tended not to be considered "couples." On one occasion, Weinstein and his (male) partner refused to budge for a heterosexual couple coming from the opposite direction. After a brief (and somewhat awkward) exchange of confused looks, the other couple parted for Weinstein and his partner to be given right of way. In Weinstein's thinking, the hypocrisy of etiquette is better exposed by holding it up to the model of behavior it is designed to sustain (but which in practice it fails to measure up to), than to oppose it. In this case, the etiquette giving priority to "couples" discriminated against same-sex couples—but only in practice (de facto). Weinstein concluded that "laminating older rules of etiquette onto situations that will rot their foundation can yield priceless results" (37). Interpretation is all.

Commenting on the paradox of agreeing a universal set of principles governing etiquette, Mark Caldwell writes that "manners are trivial, profound, and amorphous beyond compassing. Manners are what is left when serious issues of human relations are removed from consideration; yet without manners serious human relations are impossible" (2). Throughout this book I have tried to argue both for and against etiquette; to demonstrate that etiquette can be liberating and welcoming just as it can be stifling and exclusionary. I have suggested its rules can work as a set of easily learned principles to aid in the civilizing education of those not born to privilege, but it can also be wielded as a set of capricious, arbitrary, ambiguous, and corruptible edicts designed to reinforce social hierarchies. Etiquette can be all these things. It can be torture. But can it be discarded? And will the looser, rather more general sense of "manners"—that is, simply "doing what is right"—keep our communities together, given good conduct in public discourse appears increasingly less assured?

This question is raised in Virginia Woolf's novel *To the Lighthouse* (1927) when the Ramsay family finally get to dine with their friends and guests after several unforeseen delays. As they finish their plates of "perfect" *Bœuf en Daube*, Lily Briscoe seethes at the bad form of the men who discuss politics and issues of propriety while ignoring the women. As Lily works herself up, she spies the misanthropic student, Charles Tansley, whose social awkwardness has left him incapable of breaking into the men's conversation. However, instead of engaging Tansley in conversation herself, as good etiquette dictates, Lily reflects on his earlier rudeness about her painting and derogatory sexist comments regarding her intellect. Hence, Lily reasons for and against doing the "done thing":

> There is a code of behaviour, she knew, whose seventh article (it may be) says that on occasions of this sort it behoves the woman, whatever her own occupation may be, to go to the help of the young man opposite so that he may expose and relieve the thigh bones, the ribs, of his vanity, of his urgent desire to assert himself; as indeed it is their duty, she reflected, in her old maidenly fairness, to help us, suppose the Tube were to burst into flames. Then, she thought, I should certainly expect Mr. Tansley to get me out. But how would it be, she thought, if neither of us did either of these things? So she sat there smiling. (137)

Is it for the better that the "code of behavior" might just as easily be ignored in favor of more progressive relations? Or will we be left, as Lily and Mr. Tansley are, in self-righteous isolation?

Either way, the medium of cinema delights in torturous etiquettes, which give expression to the pressure we are all under to conform and perform in social life. Such "tortures" going on beneath the surface of the skin tend to go unnoticed by others (which is the point), but are betrayed by the all-seeing camera (and conveyed to us, the attentive audience). Our civilized world is one "balanced so precariously," as the narrator of *The Age of Innocence* puts it, "that its harmony could be shattered by a whisper." Film is a medium in which a whisper can go off like an explosion. Of the intensity of the closeup—which he called the "soul of the cinema" (9)—Jean Epstein wrote that it "modifies the drama by the impact of proximity. Pain is within reach. If I stretch out my arm I touch you, and that is intimacy. I can count the eyelashes of this suffering. I would be able to taste the tears" (13). Here is the cinematic "language" of torturous etiquettes: it is a language that, in the whispers and glances, the gestures and modulations, we "speak" with our bodies more than our manners would like us to "tell," about the joys and pains of sharing this world with others.

Notes

Introduction

1. Frantz Fanon discussed the psychology of torturers apropos of colonial violence in *The Wretched of the Earth* (1961), but it has more recently been tackled in a provocative book by Rachel M. MacNair, *Perpetration-Induced Traumatic Stress: The Psychological Consequences of Killing* (New York: Author's Choice Press, 2005).

2. They include Michael Flynn and Fabiola F. Salek's edited collection on torture and politics, *Screening Torture: Media Representations of State Terror and Political Domination* (New York: Columbia University Press, 2012), and Hilary Neroni's book, *The Subject of Torture: Psychoanalysis & Biopolitics in Television & Film* (New York: Columbia University Press, 2015), as well as Steve Jones's book on the "torture-porn" genre, *Torture Porn: Popular Horror After Saw* (Basingstoke: Palgrave Macmillan, 2013), Steven Allen's book on torture in relation to pleasure, *Cinema, Pain and Pleasure: Consent and the Controlled Body* (Basingstoke: Palgrave Macmillan, 2013), and Mark de Valk's edited collection on the tortured body, *Screening the Tortured Body: The Cinema as Scaffold* (London: Palgrave Macmillan, 2016).

Chapter 1

1. The most famous examples include manuals by the philosopher and theologian Desiderius Erasmus (1466–1536), the Italian diplomat Baldassare Castiglione (1478–1529), the Florentine poet Giovanni della Casa (1503–1556), and the French diplomat Antoine de Courtin (1622–1685). But also important to the renaissance, notes Colin MacCabe, was the spread of the "vulgar" tongue—especially following Dante's decision to write his *Divine Comedy* in Italian rather than Latin, the "official" language of Europe since the Roman Empire. To fully appreciate this, it is worth remembering that Thomas Cromwell had his countrymen executed for daring to read the bible in the English language. That said, it is

worth noting that Dante's decision to write in Italian was not to make his poetry available to the common people, notes MacCabe, but "to write for those who are *volgari e non litterati*, those who are increasingly able to read Italian though unlettered [including women]. . . . It is the audience of his own class and their social superiors whom he wishes to seduce from the sordid pork-barrelling of papal politics in favour of an impossible imperial ideal in which the political order would fuse with the moral in a society which encouraged instead of frustrated the development of the individual." See Colin MacCabe, *The Eloquence of the Vulgar: Language, Cinema and the Politics of Culture* (London: BFI, 1999), 148.

2. This rule began with Hitchcock's injunction to audiences in 1960 that "it is <u>required</u> that you see *Psycho* from the very beginning," after which (to preserve the integrity of the plot) audiences would be refused admission.

3. For a more extensive treatment of these headings, see Goffman, *Relations* 29–40.

4. "When man howls with laughter, he surpasses all animals by his coarseness." Nietzsche, *Human, All Too Human* (243).

5. Watergate refers to the major political scandal following the arrests of five men attempting to break into the Democratic National Committee headquarters in the run up to the 1972 presidential election. It was discovered that the Nixon campaign had not only been involved in orchestrating the burglary (which aimed to disrupt the Democratic candidates' election campaign), but that it attempted to thwart the subsequent criminal investigation and had been taping private conversations in the Oval Office. Ironically, Nixon needn't have bothered: he easily won the election by a historic landslide.

6. This scene is not unlike the famous courtroom climax to *A Few Good Men* (1992), in which a hotshot lawyer (Tom Cruise) baits a decorated colonel (Jack Nicholson) into losing his temper so that he will admit to breaking the law because he believes himself to be above it (the scene features Nicholson's famous line "You can't handle the truth!").

7. In *Cape Fear*, Max Cady responds to being called a "white trash piece of shit" (by Sam Bowden's private detective): "It's not necessary to lay a foul tongue on me"—as though rude speech itself were equivalent to laying hands on a person. In more affirmatory terms, the "multilingualism" of the hands is explored in the photography of Steve McCurry, collected in Bonnie McCurry, *A Life in Pictures* (2018).

8. The point is rather ironically treated in a scene from *The Dark Knight Rises* (2012), in which the villainous Bane (Tom Hardy) enters the Gotham Stock Exchange with a motorcycle helmet covering his face. When security personnel ask for it to be removed to check his identity, Bane politely complies and removes the helmet to reveal his disturbing mask, after which he proceeds to use said helmet to beat the terrified security guards.

9. A familiar technique in Demme's work, used to the same purpose—albeit with different meanings (!)—in *The Silence of the Lambs* (1991).

Chapter 2

1. In fact, the lines appear in the troubadour's song "What Is a Youth?" (composed by Nino Rota).

2. "I love you, but, because inexplicably I love in you something more than you—the *objet petit a*—I mutilate you." Jacques Lacan, *The Four Fundamental Concepts of Psychoanalysis*, translated by A. Sheridan (London: The Hogarth Press and the Institute of Psychoanalysis, 1998).

3. As we watch the film, Alex Gerbaz (2011) writes, Haneke wants us to feel shame and embarrassment at the pleasure we derive from the family's suffering, as when "someone catches us watching," as in Sartre's example from *Being and Nothingness* (168).

4. Following on from the last discussion, incidentally, Michael Haneke declares that "an emotional director is worthless!" See Carrière.

Chapter 3

1. "In educating the young we steer them by the rudders of pleasure and pain." Aristotle, *The Nicomachean Ethics* (qtd. in Freeland 57).

2. For more on Austen's style, see David Davies, "Misreading Emma," in *Jane Austen's Emma: Philosophical Perspectives*, ed. E. M. Dadlez (Oxford: Oxford University Press, 2018), 184–215.

3. Incidentally, Diarmuid Lawrence's 1996 television movie (adapted by Andrew Davies) follows this same sequence in the Box Hill scene.

4. See Freeland 58.

5. More in line with Austen's famous intention to use *Emma* to write "a heroine whom no one but myself will much like" (qtd. in M. Butler 394).

6. In 1870 (some seventy years before Harding wrote this), Juliet Pollock suggested that what induced Austen's readers to commiserate with her characters "is not the image of sorrow, of suffering, or want . . . but the exhibition of petty aims, vain strivings, low intellects, and mean jealousies, which excites pain, as it augments our appreciation of the weakness of human nature and the narrowness of life and thoughts when contracted to certain conditions" (369). See Pollock 369–70.

Chapter 4

1. When asked by a reader as to the correct way to eat saltwater taffy, Judith Martin (aka "Miss Manners") replied, "With the mouth closed. Actually, that is the way to eat all food, but taffy is the only food capable of enforcing the rule" (202).

2. In joking relationships between males, observed John Dollard, "[one] does not touch upon actual weaknesses" (qtd. in Locke 37).

3. This is truer in some cultures than others. Kate Fox notes how a visiting Canadian businessman fell afoul of the British "polite procrastination rule"—that all business meetings should begin with several minutes of light banter. The Canadian's mistake? He suggesting they get on with their meeting. "They all looked at me like I'd farted or something," the Canadian remarked, "like, how could I be so crass?" (287). Polite procrastination is important to the British, Fox notes, because we (a) tend to find formality awkward or embarrassing, and (b) disdain the earnestness such formalities tend to occasion.

4. If I repeat a joke, remarked Freud, "I must, if I am not to spoil its effect, *behave* in telling it exactly like the person who made it" (145, emphasis mine).

5. In Freud's examples the subjects in smutty exchanges are almost always male, their objects female. While this must surely vary, the present example upholds this gendered view.

6. "A person who laughs at smut that he hears is laughing as though he were the spectator of an act of sexual aggression" (97). By contrast, were the target of smut to take the solicitation seriously this imaginary dimension would dissolve—the smut-talker would, as it were, be "called out" (see Freud 99).

7. The word "obscene," from *obscēnus*, means a bad augury (hence ugly), but also potentially "ob-" against + *scaena*, a stage (scene).

8. On the comic potential of a character's physical traits, see Freud 104, 231n.

9. The basic setup and structure was lifted from *Goodfellas* and redeployed in *Black Mass* starring Johnny Depp.

10. With thanks to Murray Pomerance, who gave invaluable suggestions on an early draft of this chapter.

Chapter 5

1. Scarlett's presumption that Prissy ought to possess such instincts regarding childbirth originates in the "idea," noted Richard Dyer, "that non-whites are more natural than whites . . . that they have more 'life,'" that is, an intuitive understanding of the body, emotions, sensuality and spirituality, "a logically meaningless but commonsensically powerful notion" (152). For a discussion of this in the Francophone theory of *"négritude"* from the 1950s, see Fanon 102–14.

2. For a journalistic overview of the decision by HBO Max to pull *Gone With the Wind* in 2020 for its "blatant demonization of race," see Andrew Pulver's article from *The Guardian Online* (June 10, 2020), https://www.theguardian.com/film/2020/jun/10/gone-with-the-wind-dropped-from-hbo-max-over-depiction-of-slavery.

3. On the film's central depiction of torturous etiquettes in relation to Julie's fatal faux pas, see Chapter 7, "Garments of the Mind," in this book.

4. Contributions to the screenplay were made by Clements Ripley, Abem Finkel, and John Huston, so it is difficult to know who was responsible for Pres's words.

5. My thanks to Carol Smith for pointing this reference out to me.

6. The *Get Out* example clearly echoes the "malfunctioning" wife at the party in *The Stepford Wives* (1975).

7. Indeed, while Mr. Stevens considers the thought of intruding on the private conversation of his employer unspeakably unprofessional, he does admit to overhearing his employer's views on the looming war with Hitler's Germany, and clearly struggles to reconcile Lord Darlington's Nazi sympathies, perhaps even collaborationist views, with the detached "dignity" his butler's duties demand. Contrast Judith Martin's advice on the inappropriateness of eavesdropping in the workplace (*Miss Manners* 233).

8. A similar instruction is offered by Hugh Glass (Leonardo DiCaprio) to his mixed-race son, Hawk (Forrest Goodluck), in *The Revenant*: "I told you to be invisible," Glass remonstrates when the boy speaks up against a racist comment by one of the other frontiersmen. "They don't hear your voice. They only see the color of your face."

9. The film Charlie refers to is, of course, *Guess Who's Coming to Dinner* (1967).

10. In his appearance before the House Select Subcommittee in 1969 to discuss the establishment of a national commission on "Negro History and Culture," James Baldwin praised Poitier's "beautiful and modest role" in *Guess Who's Coming to Dinner*, but he also criticized the movie as a "cop out" for presenting Dr. Prentice as no "ordinary citizen." He concluded by saying that "it obviously would be a different movie if he were able to play a real man." See Baldwin, "N——r" 117–18.

11. Arthur Knight lucidly explores the "dichotomous readings" of Sidney Poitier in his essay "Sidney Poitier: It Is No Great Joy to Be a Symbol"; see esp. 160–61.

12. The moment inverts the classic view of the butler, espoused by Lumière in the "Be Our Guest" number from *Beauty and the Beast* (1991), that "life is so unnerving for a servant who's not serving / he's not whole without a soul to wait upon."

13. In "Africa Is People" (1998), Chinua Achebe claimed Descartes's formulation as expressive of the European individualistic ideal, the African version of which represents a more "communal aspiration": "A human is human because of other humans." See Chinua Achebe, *Africa's Tarnished Name* (London: Penguin Books, 2018).

Chapter 6

1. Baldwin did not mention the date, but Poitier starred in the original production, which premiered in 1959 and attracted unprecedented numbers from the black community to the theaters in its fifteen-month run, which culminated in Daniel Petrie's film adaptation (1961), also starring Poitier.

2. The butler's rebuke recalls the scene in *Guess Who's Coming to Dinner* when the Drayton's black housekeeper, Tillie (Isabel Sanford), gives Dr. Prentice

a complete dressing-down, punctuating her scold with the (somewhat dubious) line, "You ain't even that *good lookin'*!" In both scenes the point is clear: Poitier is rocking the boat.

3. This entire scene is exaggeratedly recapitulated in Quentin Tarantino's *Django Unchained* (2012). When a newly freed slave, Django (Jamie Foxx), accompanies his white liberator, Dr. Schultz (Christoph Waltz), to help him apprehend a wanted man working at a plantation house, he, too, rides alongside cotton pickers suffering in the searing midday heat. Tarantino's film is set in the antebellum South, though it clearly recalls *In the Heat of the Night*. But as Django rides his horse, proudly dressed in an all-blue suit with a white ruffle (styled after the son of a wealthy merchant in Thomas Gainsborough's painting *The Blue Boy* [1779]), he demonstrates none of Tibbs's guilt or shame. Instead, Django looks deeply into the eyes of the confused, bewildered slaves, presenting himself—peacock-like—as a symbol of liberation. The scene ends with the same kind of flamboyance and phantasmatic unreality that has become typical of Tarantino's late work: apprehending his quarry in the fields, Django brings the slaver's whip down onto the slaver, beating him to death (Poitier's slap, à la Tarantino).

4. In this moment, Ma is the weighty embodiment of Langston Hughes's poetic response to the question, "What happens to a dream deferred?" Does it dry up or fester, he asked? Stink or crust over? "Maybe it just sags / Like a heavy load" ("Harlem" [1951]).

5. In Oscar Wilde's *An Ideal Husband* (1895), it is said that "vulgarity is the conduct of other people."

6. We are responsible for the "new being" aroused by looking, Sartre claimed, "as is shown very well by the education system, which consists in making children ashamed of what they are" (*Being and Nothingness* 246).

7. On the importance of appreciating "lived experience" in discourse on race, see also Frantz Fanon, "The Lived Experience of the Black Man," in *Black Skin, White Masks*, 89–119, in which he wrote that "ontology does not allow us to understand the being of the black man, since it ignores the lived experience" (90).

Chapter 7

1. The Shepherd's son in Shakespeare's *The Winter's Tale* agreed with Post: "See you these clothes? Say you see them not and think me still no gentleman born; you were best say these robes are not gentlemen born" (5.2.135–141).

2. The line was adapted by Graham Greene from his own novel of the same name (1958).

3. Another detail. When Clarice is injured in the rescue attempt, Hannibal carries her out of the chamber as the ravenous pigs break through their holding pen. They do not attack Lecter, however, but (after sniffing at his bare feet) move on to devour his would-be torturers—all lower-class mercenaries.

4. Thanks to Pomerance for pointing me to this quote.

5. In John Guare's play from which the film was adapted (by Guare himself), the characters address the audience directly. Here, Honess transubstantiates the direct address by cross-cutting between the Kittredge's self-indulgent retelling of the story and the evening leading up to the burglary itself.

6. The AIDS epidemic reached its peak in the mid-nineties and disproportionately affected black men. In Susan Sontag's essay "Aids and Its Metaphors" (1988), she argues that AIDS was described as an "invader," just as Paul has invaded the Kittredge's apartment. See *Illness* 103–4, 151.

7. The word "thing," observed Offred in Margaret Atwood's *The Handmaid's Tale*, was a "word she used when whatever it stood for was too distasteful or filthy or horrible to pass her lips. A successful life for her was one that avoided *things*, excluded *things*. Such *things* do not happen to nice women" (65).

8. The hero of George Bernard Shaw's play *Pygmalion* (1912). A renowned professor of phonetics, Higgins makes a bet with a pal that he can teach a common flower girl, Eliza Doolittle, to speak and act well enough like a lady that she can "pass" in high society (in the 1938 film adaptation, Higgins was played by Leslie Howard, Eliza by Wendy Hiller; in the 1964 film adaptation of the musical *My Fair Lady*, Higgins was played by Rex Harrison, Eliza by Audrey Hepburn).

9. John Guare based *Six Degrees* on a story he heard from pals who had been conned by a young man, David Hampton, also posing as the son of Sidney Poitier. As in Guare's play, the friends discovered Hampton in bed with a hustler and threw him out, learning later that "David Poitier" had been conning his way around New York's elite. Hampton was eventually charged and later died of an AIDs-related illness. The full story, as well as an interview with David Hampton, can be found in Janie Kasindorf's "Six Degrees of Impersonation," *New York Magazine*, March 25, 1991. https://books.google.co.uk/books?id=9ugCAAAAM-BAJ&pg=PA40&redir_esc=y#v=onepage&q&f=false, retrieved January 19, 2022.

10. Since its invention in the nineteenth century, the two-piece suit signified a demand for men to see themselves as part of an establishment dedicated to securing profits and falling into step with production lines engaged in mass manufacture. But the suit also "acquired social and cultural significance in that it became an indication of a man's removal from manual labor and his position as the owner of property and thus his status and power" (Tolliver 264). Hence, the wearing of a suit in the early twentieth century by black intellectuals like W. E. B. Du Bois and Cornel West had and "has a special significance for the definition and assertion of black identity," an identity harnessed especially by Poitier in his roles in *Guess Who* and *In the Heat of the Night* (both 1967).

11. But of course, a white dress can be just as scandalizing if worn in the wrong context, as the new Mrs. De Winter (Joan Fontaine) discovers when she unwittingly descends the stairs to a grand ball wearing the old Mrs. De Winter's dress in Alfred Hitchcock's *Rebecca* (1940).

12. I'm reminded of Jean-Luc Godard's famous response when questioned about the amount of blood and violence in his films, to which he simply quipped, "Not blood, red."

Chapter 8

1. Thanks to Eric Schramm for pointing me to this reference.

2. Indeed, a neurotic overreaction to a simple dirty fork can be found in Steve Coogan's performance in *The Dinner* (2017), which threatens to ruin the decorum of a fancy restaurant. The idea was taken to the extreme, however, in the "Dirty Fork" sketch from the surreal British comedy *And Now for Something Completely Different* (1971). The sketch opens with a diner (Graham Chapman) at a five-star restaurant bringing to the attention of their waiter (Terry Jones) a dirty fork, who immediately apologizes and informs the head waiter (Michael Palin), who sacks the entire washing staff before escalating the complaint to the manager (Eric Idle), who despairs at this failure of basic standards and futilely attempts to commit hara-kiri with the offensive fork. As the manager wails in despair, the head chef (John Cleese) arrives armed with a meat cleaver, fuming at the diners whom he brands "vicious, heartless, bastards!" for causing so much upset with their trivial grousing (!)

3. They are in good company with this attitude, for the Romans believed in not spoiling their appetite. "I shall bring to dinner," Cicero said, "an appetite untampered with" (quoted in De Quincey, *Miscellaneous Essays*).

4. The word "cut" is a play on words. It implies carving, but also the Victorian notion that failing to acknowledge a greeting or invitation made by another guest at dinner constitutes a "cut."

5. Rodney King was an African American construction worker who, on March 3, 1991, was violently beaten by LAPD officers during arrest. The incident, which was filmed and released to the media, sparked a six-day riot in 1992 after four officers tried on charges of police brutality were acquitted.

6. The moment recapitulates Norton's final reveal as a cold-blooded killer in *Primal Fear* (1996), when he drops the poor, suffering schizoid act and breaks into a wide grin, all innocence wiped.

7. My thanks to Murray Pomerance, who pointed this connection out to me.

8. I don't want to push this point too much, but it is worth noting that Kaye, who is Jewish, was ejected from the film when the studio disagreed with his first cut. He later (acrimoniously) disowned the movie.

9. It is notable that the children all have alliterative Christian names—Derek, Danny, and Davina—to echo their parents' names—Dennis and Doris—*except the baby*, who is called Ally, the implication being that to name the children thus was the father's choice (he was presumably killed before Ally was named).

Chapter 9

1. See *Peyton Place*, Mia Farrow haircut (first broadcast February 15, 1966) http://greghowelldesign.com/iconservation/the-haircut-episode-peyton-place-february-11-1966/.

2. See Caroline Wintersgill and Savithri Bartlett, "Empowering the Replicant: Visual and Haptic Narratives in *Blade Runner*," in *The Erotic Cloth* (2018). Also, consider the irony of Deckard's "soft" interrogation of Zhora (Joanna Cassidy) at the club, as he stands in her dressing room claiming to be from the union against workplace harassment. He inappropriately glances at her as she undresses and as she blow-dries her hair, revealing her "natural" look. Paradoxically, Deckard seems not to be entirely sure of her replicant status *until* she drops her performance.

3. A more masculine story about torture and hair features in Vladimir Nabokov's short story "Razor," in which a barber who was tortured during the war is astonished one day to find his torturer in his barbershop, and completely at his mercy.

4. The story was adapted into a short film (1976) directed by Joan Micklin Silver and starring Shelley Duvall as Bernice, with Veronica Cartwright playing Marjorie.

5. Also seen in Robert Capa's haunting photographs.

Bibliography

Améry, Jean. *At the Mind's Limits: Contemplations by a Survivor on Auschwitz and Its Realities* (1966). Trans. Sidney Rosenfeld and Stella P. Rosenfeld. London: Granta, 1999.
Appiah, Kwame Anthony. *The Honor Code: How Moral Revolutions Happen.* New York: W. W. Norton, 2011.
Austen, Jane. *Emma.* Ed. with an introduction by George Justice. New York: W. W. Norton, 2012.
Bakhtin, M. M. "Forms of Time and of the Chronotope in the Novel: Notes toward a Historical Poetics." In *The Dialogic Imagination: Four Essays*, 84–258. Trans. Caryl Emerson and Michael Holquist. Austin: University of Texas Press, 2014.
Baldwin, James. "The N——r We Invent." In *The Cross of Redemption: Uncollected Writings*, 117–18. New York: Vintage International, 2011.
Baldwin, James. "Sidney Poitier." In *The Cross of Redemption: Uncollected Writings*, 222–29. New York: Vintage International, 2011.
Baldwin, James. "Theater: The Negro In and Out." In *The Cross of Redemption: Uncollected Writings*, 19–28. New York: Vintage International, 2011.
Barnes, Hazel E. "Take Clothes, For Example." In *Etiquette: Reflections on Contemporary Comportment*, ed. Ron Scapp and Brian Seitz, 239–48. Albany: State University of New York Press, 2007.
Barthes, Roland. *Mythologies.* Trans. Annette Lavers. London: Jonathan Cape, 1972.
Barthes, Roland. *The Pleasure of the Text* (1973). Trans. Richard Miller. New York: Hill and Wang, 1975.
Batchelor, David. *Chromophobia.* London: Reaktion Books, 2000.
Bates, J. A. V. "The Communicative Hand." In *The Body as a Medium of Expression*, ed. Jonathan Benthall and Ted Polhemus, 175–94. London: Allen Lane, 1975.
Bazin, André. "Theatre and Cinema." In *Film Theory and Criticism: Introductory Readings*, 6th ed., ed. Leo Braudy and Marshall Cohen, 418–28. Oxford: Oxford University Press, 2004.
Benjamin, Walter. *Charles Baudelaire: A Lyric Poet in the Era of High Capitalism.* London: Verso, 1997.

Bothwell, J. S. *Falling from Grace: Reversal of Fortune and the English Nobility 1075–1455*. Manchester: Manchester University Press, 2008.

Bourdieu, Pierre. *Distinction: A Social Critique of the Judgement of Taste*. Trans. Richard Nice. London: Routledge, 2010.

Brown, William. "Against Brainlessness." In *La Furia Umana* (37), 2019. http://www.lafuriaumana.it/index.php/70-lfu-37/898-william-brown-against-brainlessness, retrieved July 12, 2021.

Bruzzi, Stella. *Undressing Cinema: Clothing and Identity in the Movies*. London: Routledge, 1997.

Burke, Kenneth. "On the First Three Chapters of Genesis." *Daedalus* 87, no. 3 (Summer 1958), 37–64.

Burke, Kenneth. *On Symbols and Society*. Ed. Joseph R. Gusfield. Chicago: University of Chicago Press, 1989.

Butler, Judith. *Excitable Speech: A Politics of the Performative*. New York: Routledge, 1997.

Butler, Marilyn. "Emma." In *Emma* by Jane Austen, ed. George Justice, 385–96. New York: W. W. Norton, 2012.

Byrne, Katherine. "New Developments in Heritage: The Recent Dark Side of *Downton* 'Downer' *Abbey*." In *Upstairs and Downstairs: British Costume Drama Television from* The Forsythe Saga *to* Downton Abbey," ed. James Leggott and Julie Anne Taddeo, 177–89. New York: Rowman and Littlefield, 2015.

Caldwell, Mark. *A Short History of Rudeness: Manners, Morals, and Misbehavior in Modern America*. New York: Picador, 1999.

Carrière, Christophe. "An Emotional Director Is Worthless." In *Michael Haneke Interviews*, ed. Roy Grundmann, Fatima Naqvi, and Colin Root, 107–9. Jackson: University Press of Mississippi, 2020.

Carroll, Lewis. "Hints for Etiquette: Or, Dining Out Made Easy." 1849. In *Hints on Etiquette: A Shield against the Vulgar*, 87–92. London: Pushkin Press, 2016.

Cavell, Stanley. "The Good of Film." In *Cavell on Film*, ed. William Rothman, 333–48. Albany: State University of New York Press, 2005.

Cavell, Stanley. *Must We Mean What We Say? A Book of Essays*. Updated ed. Cambridge: Cambridge University Press, 2019.

Cavell, Stanley. *Pursuits of Happiness: The Hollywood Comedy of Remarriage*. Cambridge, MA: Harvard University Press, 2003.

Cavell, Stanley. *The World Viewed: Reflections on the Ontology of Film*. 1971. Enlarged ed. Cambridge, MA: Harvard University Press, 1979.

Dadlez, E. M. "Introduction." In *Jane Austen's Emma: Philosophical Perspectives*, ed. E. M. Dadlez, 1–21. Oxford: Oxford University Press, 2018.

Day, Charles William. "Hints on Etiquette and the Usages of Society." 1842. In *Hints on Etiquette: A Shield against the Vulgar*, 6–85. London: Pushkin Press, 2016.

De Beauvoir, Simone. *The Second Sex*. 1949. Trans. and ed. H. M. Parshley. London: Vintage Books, 1997.

Deleuze, Gilles. *Masochism: Coldness and Cruelty*. New York: Zone Books, 1991.
Derrida, Jacques. "'Eating Well,' or the Calculation of the Subject: An Interview with Jacques Derrida." In *Who Comes after the Subject?* ed. Eduardo Cadava, Peter Connor, and Jean-Luc Nancy, 96–119. New York: Routledge, 1991.
Derrida, Jacques. *Of Hospitality*. Trans. Rachel Bowlby. Stanford, CA: Stanford University Press, 2000.
Doane, Mary Ann. *Femme Fatales: Feminism, Film Theory, Psychoanalysis*. New York: Routledge, 1991.
Du Bois, W. E. B. *The Souls of Black Folk*. 1903. Milton Keynes: Lightning Source, 2021.
Duffy, Richard. "Introduction: Manners and Morals." In *Etiquette: The Original Guide to Conduct in Society, Business, Home, and More* by Emily Post, xv–xxiii. 1922. New York: Skyhorse Publishing, 2017.
Dyer, Richard. *The Matter of Images: Essays on Representations*. London: Routledge, 1993.
Elias, Norbert. *The Civilizing Process: Sociogenetic and Psychogenetic Investigations*. Trans. Edmund Jephcott. Rev. ed. Malden, MA: Blackwell Publishing, 2000.
Elias, Norbert. "The Rise of the Fork." In *The Norbert Elias Reader*. Ed. Johan Goudsblom and Stephen Mennell, 51–55. Oxford: Blackwell Publishers, 1998.
Ellison, Ralph. *Invisible Man*. London: Penguin Books, 2001.
Emerson, Ralph Waldo. "English Traits." In *The Essential Writings of Ralph Waldo Emerson*, ed. Brooks Atkinson, 467–617. New York: Modern Library, 2000.
Epstein, Jean. "Magnification and Other Writings." Trans. Stuart Liebman. *October* 3 (Spring 1977): 9–25.
Evans, Dylan. *An Introductory Dictionary of Lacanian Psychoanalysis*. London: Routledge, 2007.
Fanon, Frantz. *Black Skin, White Masks*. 1952. Trans. Richard Philcox. London: Penguin Classics, 2021.
Foucault, Michel. *Discipline and Punish: The Birth of the Prison*. 1975. Trans. Alan Sheridan. London: Penguin Books, 1991.
Fox, Kate. *Watching the English: The Hidden Rules of English Behaviour*. London: Hodder, 2014.
Fox-Genovese, Elizabeth, and Eugene D. Genovese. *The Mind of the Master Class: History and Faith in the Southern Slaveholder's Worldview*. Cambridge: Cambridge University Press, 2005.
Freeland, Cynthia. "Emma's Pensive Meditations." In *Emma* by Jane Austen, ed. George Justice, 55–83. New York: W. W. Norton, 2012.
Freud, Sigmund. *Jokes and Their Relation to the Unconscious*. Standard Edition. Trans. and ed. James Strachey. London: Vintage Books, 2001.
Friedman, Lester D. *Hollywood's Image of the Jew*. New York: Frederick Ungar Publishing, 1982.
Garcia, Desirée J. *The Migration of Musical Film: From Ethnic Margins to American Mainstream*. New Brunswick, NJ: Rutgers University Press, 2014.

Gateward, Francis. "Sidney Poitier in *In the Heat of the Night*." In *Close-Up: Great Cinematic Performances Volume 1: America*, ed. Murray Pomerance and Kyle Stevens, 169–77. Edinburgh: Edinburgh University Press, 2018.

Gerbaz, Alex. "The Ethical Screen: *Funny Games* and the Spectacle of Pain." In *The Cinema of Michael Haneke: Europe Utopia*, ed. Ben McCann and David Sorfa, 163–71. London: Wallflower Press, 2011.

Gleiberman, Owen. "The Beguiled." *Variety* vol. 336, issue 4 (May 30, 2017), 110. www.proquest.com/docview/1906805873/7233A322A19B48D2PQ/2?account id=27803, retrieved September 14, 2020.

Goffman, Erving. *Behavior in Public Places: Notes on the Social Organization of Gatherings*. 1963. New York: Free Press, 1966.

Goffman, Erving. *Forms of Talk*. Philadelphia: University of Pennsylvania Press, 1981.

Goffman, Erving. *Interaction Ritual: Essays on Face-to-Face Behavior*. London: Allen Lane, 1972.

Goffman, Erving. *The Presentation of Self in Everyday Life*. London: Penguin, 1990.

Goffman, Erving. *Relations in Public: Microstudies of the Public Order*. New Brunswick, NJ: Transaction Publishers, 2010.

Grissemann, Stefan. "To Make a Film That Is Funny and Horrible at the Same Time." In *Michael Haneke Interviews*, ed. Roy Grundmann, Fatima Naqvi, and Colin Root, 47–60. Jackson: University Press of Mississippi, 2020.

Grist, Leighton. *Fascism and Millennial American Cinema*. London: Palgrave Macmillan, 2018.

Grist, Leighton. *The Films of Martin Scorsese, 1978–99: Authorship and Context II*. Basingstoke: Palgrave Macmillan, 2013.

Hamann, Trent H. "Impolitics: Toward a Resistant Comportment." In *Etiquette: Reflections on Contemporary Comportment*, ed. Ron Scapp and Brian Seitz, 59–68. Albany: State University of New York Press, 2007.

Hanich, Julian. *Cinematic Emotion in Horror Films and Thrillers: The Aesthetic Paradox of Pleasurable Fear*. New York: Routledge, 2010.

Harding, D. W. "Regulated Hatred: An Aspect of the Work of Jane Austen." In *Emma* by Jane Austen, ed. George Justice, 378–81. New York: W. W. Norton, 2012.

Haskell, Molly. "Female Stars of the 1940s." In *Film Theory and Criticism: Introductory Readings*, 6th ed., ed. Leo Braudy and Marshall Cohen, 620–33. Oxford: Oxford University Press, 2004.

Hazlitt, Henry. "The Social Value of Manners" (October 17, 2016). fee.org/articles/the-social-value-of-manners/, retrieved January 15, 2022.

Hemphill, C. Dallett. *Bowing to Necessities: A History of Manners in America, 1620–1860*. Oxford: Oxford University Press, 2002.

Hoeller, Hildegard. "Branded from the Start: The Paradox of (the) American (Novel of) Manners." In *Etiquette: Reflections on Contemporary Comportment*, ed. Ron Scapp and Brian Seitz, 135–50. Albany: State University of New York Press, 2007.

hooks, bell. *Black Looks: Race and Representation*. London: Routledge, 2015.
hooks, bell. *Reel to Real: Race, Sex, and Class at the Movies*. New York: Routledge, 1996.
hooks, bell. *Talking Back: Thinking Feminist, Thinking Black*. Boston, MA: South End Press, 1989.
Hughes, Geoffrey. *Swearing: A Social History of Foul Language, Oaths and Profanity in English*. Cambridge, MA: Blackwell, 1991.
Knight, Arthur. "Sidney Poitier: It Is No Great Joy to Be a Symbol." In *New Constellations: Movie Stars of the 1960s*, ed. Pamela Robertson Wojcik, 160–82. New Brunswick: Rutgers University Press, 2012.
Knights, Pamela. "The Social Subject in *The Age of Innocence*." *The Cambridge Companion to Edith Wharton*, ed. Millicent Bell, 20–46. Cambridge: Cambridge University Press, 1999.
Krämer, Peter. "The Good German? Oskar Schindler and the Movies, 1951–1993." In *Hollywood's Chosen People: The Jewish Experience in American Cinema*, ed. Daniel Bernardi, Murray Pomerance, and Hava Tirosh-Samuelson, 125–40. Detroit: Wayne University Press, 2013.
Kristeva, Julia. *The Powers of Horror: An Essay on Abjection*. New York: Columbia University Press, 1982.
Kristeva, Julia. *Strangers to Ourselves*. Trans. Leon S. Roudiez. New York: Columbia University Press, 1991.
Kristeva, Julia. "Word, Dialogue and Novel." In *The Kristeva Reader*, ed. Toril Moi, 34–61. Oxford: Blackwell Publishing, 2002.
Lacan, Jacques. "The Function and Field of Speech and Language in Psychoanalysis." In *Écrits: A Selection* (1966), trans. Alan Sheridan, 33–125. London: Routledge Classics, 2003.
Langbein, John H. "The Legal History of Torture." In *Torture: A Collection*, ed. Sanford Levinson, 93–103. Oxford: Oxford University Press, 2004.
Locke, John L. *Duels and Duets: Why Men and Women Talk So Differently*. Cambridge: Cambridge University Press, 2011.
Lorde, Audre. *The Master's Tools Will Never Dismantle the Master's House*. London: Penguin Books, 2018.
MacDonald, Kevin. "The American Guest." In *Etiquette: Reflections on Contemporary Comportment*, ed. Ron Scapp and Brian Seitz, 163–71. Albany: State University of New York Press, 2007.
MacKendrick, Karmen. "Make It Look Easy: Thoughts on Social Grace." In *Etiquette: Reflections on Contemporary Comportment*, ed. Ron Scapp and Brian Seitz, 199–206. Albany: State University of New York Press, 2007.
MacPherson, Charles. *The Butler Speaks: A Return to Proper Etiquette, Stylish Entertaining and the Art of Good Housekeeping*. Toronto: Random House, 2013.
Martin, Judith. *Guide to Excruciatingly Correct Behavior*. New York: W. W. Norton, 2005.
Merleau-Ponty, Maurice. "The Visible and the Invisible." In *Basic Writings*, ed. Thomas Baldwin, 247–71. New York: Routledge, 2004.

Monaghan, David. "*Emma* and the Art of Adaptation." In *Emma* by Jane Austen, ed. George Justice, 449–56. New York: W. W. Norton, 2012.

Montaigne, Michel de. "On the Art of Conversation." In *Essays*, trans. J. M. Cohen, 285–310. London: Penguin Books, 1993.

Morgan, John. *Debrett's New Guide to Etiquette and Modern Manners*. London: Headline Publishing, 1996.

Morreal, John. "Verbal Humor without Switching Scripts and without Non-Bona Fide Communication." *International Journal of Humor Research* (January 2004): 393–400. www.researchgate.net/, retrieved September 14, 2021.

Nietzsche, Friedrich. *Human, All Too Human*. Trans. Marion Faber and Stephen Lehmann. London: Penguin Books, 1994.

Nietzsche, Friedrich. *On the Genealogy of Morality*. Ed. Keith Ansell-Pearson. Trans. Carol Diethe. Cambridge: Cambridge University Press, 2010.

Nietzsche, Friedrich. "On the Uses and Disadvantages of History for Life." In *Untimely Meditations* (1910), 57–123. Cambridge: Cambridge University Press, 2014.

Ofek, Galia. *Representations of Hair in Victorian Literature and Culture*. Farnham: Ashgate, 2009.

O'Neill, John. *Sociology as a Skin Trade: Essays Towards a Reflexive Sociology*. London: Heinemann, 1972.

Pappas, Nickolas. "Aristotle's Aesthetiquette." In *Etiquette: Reflections on Contemporary Comportment*, ed. Ron Scapp and Brian Seitz, 7–16. Albany: State University of New York Press, 2007.

Pastoureau, Michel. *Red: The History of a Color*. Trans. Jodie Gladding. Princeton, NJ: Princeton University Press, 2017.

Perkins, V. F. *Film as Film: Understanding and Judging Movies*. New York: Da Capo Press, 1993.

Phillips, Adam. "Against Biography." In *Writing: Essays on Literature*, 43–63. London: Penguin Books, 2019.

Phillips, Adam. "On Eating, and Preferring Not To." *Promises, Promises: Essays on Literature and Psychoanalysis*, 282–95. London: Faber and Faber, 2002.

Pinkerton, Nick. "Mother! Review: Darren Aronofsky's Symphony of Domestic Disquiet." *BFI* (November 8, 2018). www2.bfi.org.uk., retrieved January 30, 2022.

Pollock, Juliet. "Jane Austen." In *Emma* by Jane Austen, ed. George Justice, 369–70. New York: W. W. Norton, 2012.

Pomerance, Murray. *Johnny Depp Starts Here*. New Brunswick, NJ: Rutgers University Press, 2006.

Pomerance, Murray. "Three Small Gestures." *Screening the Past* issue 45 (December 2020). www.screeningthepast.com/issue-45-first-release/three-small-gestures/, retrieved October 27, 2021.

Pomerance, Murray. "Tom Ripley's Talent." In *Bad: Infamy, Darkness, Evil, and Slime on Screen*, ed. Murray Pomerance, 315–29. Albany: State University of New York Press, 2004.

Pomerance, Murray. "The Villain We Love: Notes on the Dramaturgy of Evil." In *B Is for Bad Cinema: Aesthetics, Politics, and Cultural Value*, ed. Claire Perkins and Constantine Verevis, 105–27. Albany: State University of New York Press.

Pomerance, Murray. *Virtuoso: Film Performance and the Actor's Magic*. London: Bloomsbury Academic, 2019.

Poovey, Mary. "The True English Style." In *Emma* by Jane Austen., ed. George Justice, 401–6. New York: W. W. Norton, 2012.

Post, Emily. *Etiquette: The Original Guide to Conduct in Society, Business, Home, and More*. 1922. New York: Skyhorse Publishing, 2017.

Rees, Nigel. *Good Manners: The Complete Guide to Manners and Etiquette in the 1990s*. London: Bloomsbury, 1994.

Rogers, Anna Backman. "And That I See a Darkness: The Stardom of Kirsten Dunst in Collaboration with Sofia Coppola in Three Images." In *Film-Philosophy* 23, no. 2. https://www.euppublishing.com/doi/full/10.3366/film.2019.0105, retrieved July 19, 2022.

Roodenburg, Herman. "The 'hand of friendship': Shaking Hands and Other Gestures in the Dutch Republic." In *A Cultural History of Gesture: From Antiquity to the Present Day*, ed. Jan Bremmer and Herman Roodenburg, 152–89. Cambridge: Polity Press, 1994.

Ross, Thomas. "White Innocence, Black Abstraction." In *Critical White Studies: Looking Behind the Mirror*, ed. Richard Delgado and Jean Stefancic, 263–66. Philadelphia: Temple University Press, 1997.

Saltman, Kenneth J. "The Breathing Breach of Etiquette." In *Etiquette: Reflections on Contemporary Comportment*, 41–47, ed. Ron Scapp and Brian Seitz. Albany: State University of New York Press, 2007.

Sartre, Jean-Paul. *Being and Nothingness: An Essay on Phenomenological Ontology*. 1943. London: Routledge Classics, 2003.

Scapp, Ron, and Brian Seitz. "On Being Becoming." In *Etiquette: Reflections on Contemporary Comportment*, ed. Ron Scapp and Brian Seitz, 1–6. Albany: State University of New York Press, 2007.

Scarry, Elaine. *The Body in Pain: The Making and Unmaking of the World*. New York: Oxford University Press, 1985.

Shingler, Martin. "Making an Entrance: Bette Davis's First Appearance in *Jezebel* (1938)." In *Film Moments: Criticism, History, Theory*, ed. Tom Brown and James Walters, 34–37. London: Palgrave, 2010.

Slagle, Judith Bailey, and Robert Holtzclaw. "Narrative Voice and 'Chorus on the Stage' in *Tom Jones* (1963)." In *The Cinema of Tony Richardson: Essays and Interviews*, ed. James M. Welsh and John C. Tibbetts, 189–205. Albany: State University of New York Press, 1999.

Sorfa, David. "Superegos and Eggs: Repetition in Funny Games (1997, 2007)." In *The Cinema of Michael Haneke: Europe Utopia*, ed. Ben McCann and David Sorfa, 172–78. London: Wallflower Press, 2011.

Sontag, Susan. *Illness as Metaphor & AIDS and Its Metaphors*. London: Penguin Books, 2002.

Sontag, Susan. *Regarding the Pain of Others*. 2003. London: Penguin, 2019.
Southward, David. "Jane Austen and the Riches of Embarrassment." In *Studies in English Literature, 1500–1900* 36, no. 4 (Autumn 1996): 763–84.
Spencer, Herbert. "The Physiology of Laughter." *Macmillan's Magazine* (March 1860): 395–402. https://wellcomecollection.org/works/agb23fva, retrieved January 1, 2023.
St. Clair, Kassia. *The Secret Lives of Colour*. London: John Murray, 2016.
Stam, Robert, and Louise Spence. "Colonialism, Racism, and Representation: An Introduction." In *Film Theory and Criticism: Introductory Readings*, 6th ed., ed. Leo Braudy and Marshall Cohen, 877–91. Oxford: Oxford University Press, 2004.
Still, Judith. *Derrida and Hospitality: Theory and Practice*. Edinburgh: Edinburgh University Press, 2013.
Swift, Jonathan. "A Treatise on Good Manners and Good Breeding." www.bartleby.com/27/9.html, retrieved May 20, 2017.
Toles, George E. *A House Made of Light: Essays on the Art of Film*. Detroit: Wayne State University Press, 2001.
Tolliver, Willie Jr. "Transcending Paul Poitier: *Six Degrees of Separation* and the Construction of Will Smith." In *Poitier Revisited: Reconsidering a Black Icon in the Obama Age*, ed. Ian Gregory Strachan and Mia Mask, 253–70. London: Bloomsbury Academic, 2016.
Visser, Margaret. *The Rituals of Dinner: The Origins, Evolution, Eccentricities and Meaning of Table Manners*. 1991. London: Penguin Books, 2017.
Vogler, Pen. *Scoff: A History of Food and Class in Britain*. London: Atlantic Books, 2020.
Wagner, Karin. "The Guest and the Intruder." *Film International* 15, no. 4 (2017): 25–36.
Walker, Elsie. *Hearing Haneke: The Sound Tracks of a Radical Auteur*. Oxford: Oxford University Press, 2018.
Weinstein, Jeff. "Gay Etiquette: A Brief Consideration." In *Etiquette: Reflections on Contemporary Comportment*, ed. Ron Scapp and Brian Seitz, 33–40. Albany: State University of New York Press, 2007.
Wheatley, Catherine. *Michael Haneke's Cinema: The Ethic of the Image*. New York: Berghahn Books, 2009.
Woolf, Virginia. *A Room of One's Own*. London: Penguin Books, 2000.
Žižek, Slavoj. *How to Read Lacan*. London: Granta Books, 2006.
Žižek, Slavoj. *The Plague of Fantasies*. London: Verso, 2008.

Index

Achebe, Chinua, 229n13
Age of Innocence, The (Martin Scorsese, 1993), 7, 171–72, 222
AIDS, 33–36, 166, 231n6
Aliens (James Cameron, 1986), 209
American Beauty (Sam Mendes, 1999), 187–88, 206
American History X (Tony Kaye, 1998), 197–202
American Hustle (David O. Russell, 2013), 207, 213
Améry, Jean, 1, 8
Amour (Michael Haneke, 2012), 208–209, 214, 216–17
Anderson Tapes, The (Sidney Lumet, 1971), 208
And Now for Something Completely Different (Ian MacNaughton, 1971), 232n2
Annie Hall (Woody Allen, 1977), 200
apology, 25, 53, 58–59, 77, 134, 147, 167, 232n2; to cover embarrassment, 26, 93; demanding an, 39–40; as sarcasm, 129; as torture, 6, 58
appetite, 232n3; frustration of, 181, 190, 202; to live, 190, 204–205; loss of, 19, 203; voracity of, 182, 202
Aristotle: on the comic, 102; on educating the young, 227n1; on manners, 76

Audran, Stéphane, 205
Austin, J. L.: on rudeness, 108
Babette's Feast ([*Babettes Gæstebud*] Gabrielle Axel, 1987), 205–206
Babette's Feast (Isak Dinesen [Karen Blixen]), 164
bad taste, 63, 205. *See also* distaste
Bainter, Fay, 174
Bakhtin, Mikhail: on "the third person," 126, 129
Baldwin, James: on black performers, 117, 130–31, 137, 147; on Henry Fonda, 116–17, 121; on "lived experience," 151; on Sidney Poitier, 130–31, 137–38, 143–45, 229n10
ballrooms, 6, 173–77 passim
Barthes, Roland: on class, 170; on "ornamental cookery," 195
Bates, Kathy, 162
Batman Begins (Christopher Nolan, 2005), 3
Battle of the Sexes (Jonathan Dayton and Valerie Faris, 2017), 210
Beard, Stymie, 118, 174
Beauty and the Beast (Gary Trousdale and Kirk Wise, 1991), 229n12
Beguiled, The (Don Siegel, 1971), 52
Beguiled, The (Sofia Coppola, 2017), 48–54
Belle (Amma Asante, 2013), 209

bell hooks: on black hair, 209–10; on cultural appropriation, 148; on looking, 145, 150–51
Bening, Annette, 187
Benjamin, Walter: on Baudelaire, 164
"Bernice Bobs Her Hair" (F. Scott Fitzgerald), 214–15, 216
Bigger Splash, A (Luca Guadagnino, 2015), 63–68
Blade Runner (Ridley Scott, [1982] 2007), 212, 233n2
blues, the, 146, 148, 151
Bogart, Humphrey, 7, 111, 112, 113, 159
Bond, James, 7, 159, 160, 208
bonding, 31, 50, 97, 193; over dinner, 197; following embarrassment, 94; over hair, 209–10; with a handshake, 31–32; over a joke, 94–99
Boseman, Chadwick, 147–48
Bourdieu, Pierre: on class, 186; on taste, 181, 186, 205
Bourne Identity, The (Doug Liman, 2002), 210
Brando, Marlon, 184–86, 188
Brent, George, 119–20
Burke, Edmund: on manners, 1
Burke, Kenneth: on breaking covenants, 178; on "comic correctives," 109
Butler, The (Lee Daniels, 2013), 127–35, 137, 138

cannibals: barbarism of, 184, 192–93, 196; manners of, 193
Cape Fear (Martin Scorsese, 1991), 15, 21–24, 226n7
Carrey, Jim, 95–99
Carroll, Lewis: on etiquette, 89–90, 94, 191
Casablanca (Michael Curtiz, 1942), 111–12

Casino Royale (Martin Campbell, 2006), 7, 159
Catch Me If You Can (Steven Spielberg, 2002), 161, 162, 164
Cavell, Stanley: on acknowledging pain, 63; on Bette Davis, 173–74; on confrontation, 197; on *Gone With the Wind*, 117–18; on manners, 164; on marriage, 188
Channing, Stockard, 165
Chinatown (Roman Polanski, 1974), 100–103, 106
chivalry, 3, 13
Civilizing Process, The (Nobert Elias), 13–14, 156, 182–84, 186–87, 188, 191–92, 194. See also fork, rise of the
codeswitching, 15, 24–30, 98, 101, 104, 107
Connery, Sean, 7, 208
courtesy, 17–18, 50, 155, 159, 193, 219
Courtin, Antoine de, 155, 186, 189, 225n1

Damon, Matt, 163, 210
Dark Knight Rises, The (Christopher Nolan, 2012), 226n8
Davis, Bette, 118, 120, 173–75, 176, 178–79
Davis, Viola, 146, 148
Day, Charles William: on etiquette, 2, 89–90, 181
Defiant Ones, The (Stanley Kramer, 1958), 138, 144
Deleuze, Gilles: on sadism, 59
De Niro, Robert, 21–22, 39
Depp, Johnny, 203–204, 228n9
Derrida, Jacques: on "eating well," 196; on hospitality, 44, 54–55, 58, 60–61, 63, 65; on sacrifice, 196
Descartes, René, 135, 229n13

Devil Wears Prada, The (David Frankel, 2006), 212
Diamonds Are Forever (Guy Hamilton, 1971), 208
DiCaprio, Leonardo, 31, 124, 160–64, 169, 229n8
Dickinson, Angie, 171
Dinner, The (Herman Koch), 203
discomfort, 5, 58, 60, 133, 171, 209
discomposure, 48
discourtesy, 18
disgrace, 5, 25, 30, 76, 192, 196
disgust, 22, 23, 31, 34, 59, 96, 100, 102, 141, 155, 185–86, 189, 195
distaste, 79, 184, 189, 231n7; at butchery, 191–92. See also bad taste
Django Unchained (Quentin Tarantino, 2012), 31, 124, 230n3
Downton Abbey (Julian Fellowes, 2010–15), 145, 150
Drukarova, Dinara, 208
Du Bois, W. E. B., 131, 134, 231n10
Dunaway, Faye, 100, 102
Dunst, Kirsten, 9, 49

Eastwood, Clint, 52, 73
Edward Scissorhands (Tim Burton, 1990), 203–204
Elias, Norbert: on butchery, 191–92; on "the civilizing process," 13–14, 182, 194; on communal manners, 184, 186–89; on disgust, 186; on the fear of giving offense, 62; on table manners, 184. See also fork, rise of the
Emerson, Ralph Waldo: on clothes, 178; on English manners, 63, 157, 181; on good manners, 5, 164; on insults, 70
Emma (Autumn De Wilde, 2020), 79, 81–85
Emma (Douglas McGrath, 1996), 79–83

Emma (Jane Austen), 75–82
Emma (Jim O'Hanlon, 2009), 79–83
English manners, 19, 26, 29, 62–63, 156–57, 181, 228n3
Epstein, Jean: on closeups, 222
Erasmus, Desiderius, 155, 191, 225n1
Evelina (Frances Burney), 178

Fanning, Elle, 49
Fanon, Frantz, 112–16, 122, 225n1, 228n1, 230n7
Fargo (Joel and Ethan Coen, 1996), 9
Farrell, Colin, 49, 53
Farrow, Mia, 212, 232n1
Festen ([*The Celebration*] Thomas Vinterberg, 1998), 3
Few Good Men, A (Rob Reiner, 1992), 226n6
Fiennes, Ralph, 63, 66
Finney, Albert, 182
Five Branded Women (Martin Ritt, 1960), 215
Fonda, Henry, 116–17, 119–23, 174, 176
footing, 24–26, 29, 108
fork, 69, 90, 163, 187, 191–92, 203; dirty, 232n2; rise of the, 184–86, 188–89
For Whom the Bell Tolls (Ernest Hemingway), 215
Foucault, Michel, 15, 41, 170; on "the politics of discomfort," 60; on torture as entertainment, 7
Foxx, Jamie, 124, 230n3
Freeman, Morgan, 91–93
Freud, Sigmund, 53, 125; on joking, 91, 102, 228n4; on smut, 99–100, 102, 228n5, 228n6; on "tendentious" joking, 95–97, 228n8
Frisch, Arno, 55
Frost/Nixon (Ron Howard, 2008), 15, 25–30
Funny Face (Stanley Donen, 1957), 211

Funny Games (Michael Haneke, 1997), 55–60, 67
Furlong, Edward, 197

Ganz, Bruno, 192
Garai, Romola, 79–83
Gates, Larry, 140
gay etiquette, 220
Get Out (Jordan Peele, 2017), 124–25, 229n6
Giant (George Stevens, 1956), 113, 191–92, 196
Giering, Frank, 55
Gilda (Charles Vidor, 1946), 112, 213
Girl with the Dragon Tattoo (David Fincher, 2011), 61–63
Glengarry Glen Ross (James Foley, 1992), 9
Goffman, Erving, 14, 226n3; on class, 170; on "codeswitching," 24–25; on "face," 29; on "footing," 24–25; on interruptions, 29; on profanity, 29; on "spoiled identities," 34, 216; on the table as "open region," 123–24, 197, 200; on territorial violations, 19–20, 23, 113; on "territories of the self," 19, 33, 102
Goldfinger (Guy Hamilton, 1964), 7
Gone With the Wind (Victor Fleming, 1939), 117, 119, 172
Gonzalez, Pedro Gonzalez, 171
Goodfellas (Martin Scorsese, 1990), 103–108, 109, 228n9
Gosford Park (Robert Altman, 2001), 3, 124, 145
Gould, Elliot, 198
Graham, Stephen, 38
Grant, Lee, 139, 143
Gran Torino (Clint Eastwood, 2008), 73–75
Green Book (Peter Farrelly, 2018), 34–35, 115–16
Greenstreet, Sidney, 7, 159

Greystoke: The Legend of Tarzan, Lord of the Apes (Hugh Hudson, 1984), 204, 206
Guess Who's Coming to Dinner (Stanley Kramer, 1967), 137–38, 169, 229n9, 229n10, 229n2, 231n10
Guilaroff, Sydney, 208
Guinness, Alec, 157–58, 160

Handshaking. *See* bonding
Hanks, Tom, 33
Hannibal (Ridley Scott, 2001), 3, 159, 194–96, 206, 217, 230n3
Harding, D. W., 81–82, 227n6
Hardwick, Paul, 46, 48
Harris, Ed, 45
Hathaway, Anne, 3, 212, 215
Hayworth, Rita, 112, 213
Hazlitt, Henry, 1, 219–21
Hepburn, Audrey, 210–11, 231n8
Hepburn, Katharine, 130, 184
Hiroshima mon amour (Alain Resnais, 1959), 215
Hobbes, Thomas, 30
Hoffman, Dustin, 6, 20, 62
Hoffman, Philip Seymour, 163
Hopkins, Anthony, 126, 159, 184, 193
Hunter, Kim, 185

Ideal Husband, An (Oscar Wilde), 230n5
I Love You Phillip Morris (John Requa and Glenn Ficarra, 2009), 95–99
impolitics, 108, 114–16, 123, 144, 202
impropriety, 2, 29, 115, 121–22, 186; an "improper attack," 197, 200, 202, 206
Interiors (Woody Allen, 1978), 172
interpellation, 40
In the Heat of the Night (Norman Jewison, 1967), 129, 137–45, 230n3, 231n10
Invisible Man (Ellison, Ralph), 111–12

Index

Irishman, The (Martin Scorsese, 2019), 15, 38–41

Jane Eyre (Charlotte Brontë), 32
Jezebel (William Wyler, 1938), 118–23, 124, 125, 156, 173–79
Johnson, Dakota, 64
Johnson, Samuel, 203, 219

Kidman, Nicole, 49
Kierkegaard, Søren, 125
Killing, The (Stanley Kubrick, 1956), 36–38
Kingsley, Ben, 15
Kinski, Klaus, 192
Kovacs, Ernie, 158
Kristeva, Julia: on abjection, 68, 182; on strangers, 53, 54

Lacan, Jacques: on desire, 52, 54, 227n2; on "punctuation," 122–23
Lady from Shanghai, The (Orson Welles, 1947), 213
Lambert, Christopher, 204
Langella, Frank, 25, 28
language: bad, 5, 73, 114–15, 122; injurious, 40–41, 215; mannered, 6, 108, 205; racist, 37–38, 96–98, 139, 141, 199–200, 229n8; torturous, 5–7; vulgar, 225–26n1
Laurence, Oona, 49
Lawrence, Jennifer, 9, 45
Leigh, Vivian, 117, 172, 185
Letters to Juliet (Gary Winick, 2010), 208, 211, 213
Lion in Winter, The (Anthony Harvey, 1968), 184
Liotta, Ray, 104–105, 194
Lives of a Bengal Lancer, The (Henry Hathaway, 1935), 6
Lorde, Audre, 135
Lothar, Susan, 55
Lynch, John Carroll, 73

Maltese Falcon, The (John Huston, 1941), 7, 159
Mansfield Park (Jane Austen), 176
Ma Rainey's Black Bottom (George C. Wolfe, 2020), 146–51
Marathon Man (John Schlesinger, 1976), 6, 7, 62, 217
Martin, Judith (Miss Manners), 6; on eating, 227n1; on eavesdropping, 126, 229n7; on "etiquette orders," 40; on joking, 89, 90; on wearing white, 176
McKellen, Ian, 165
McQueen, Butterfly, 117
medieval manners, 13, 183–84
Melancholia (Lars von Trier, 2011), 9
Merleau-Ponty, Maurice, 35, 177
Michael Hall, Anthony, 168
Midnight Cowboy (John Schlesinger, 1969), 20
Misérables, Les (Tom Hooper, 2012), 215
Mississippi Burning (Alan Parker, 1988), 113–14, 115
Montaigne, Michel de: on conversation, 197, 200; on hands, 30
Moore, Julianne, 159, 194
Mother! (Darren Aronofsky, 2017), 9, 45–46
Mühe, Ulrich, 55
Mulholland Dr. (David Lynch, 2001), 210
My Fair Lady (George Cukor, 1964), 211–12, 231n8

Native Son (Richard Wright), 202
Neeson, Liam, 15, 19
Nicholson, Jack, 100–101, 226n6
Nietzsche, Friedrich, 7, 8, 14, 191, 226n4
1984 (George Orwell), 4
Nolte, Nick, 21

Norton, Edward, 197–98, 201–202, 232n6
Nosferatu the Vampyre (Werner Herzog, 1979), 192
Nymphomaniac (Lars von Trier, 2013), 20

Oates, Warren, 138
O'Hara, Maureen, 158
Olivier, Lawrence, 6–7, 62
Our Man in Havana (Carol Reed, 1959), 156–60
Out of Africa (Sydney Pollack, 1985), 210
Oyelowo, David, 127

Pacino, Al, 3, 38, 159
Palm Beach Story, The (Preston Sturges, 1942), 3
Paltrow, Gwyneth, 79–83, 91
Parks, Rosa, 115
Parry, Natasha, 47–48
Payton, Lew, 120, 122–23
Perkins, V. F.: on public privacy, 59
Pesci, Joe, 103, 105, 107
Pfeiffer, Michelle, 45, 171–72
Philadelphia (Jonathan Demme, 1993), 15, 32–36, 207
Pitt, Brad, 91
Poitier, Sidney, 137–38, 166, 231n10; as trailblazer, 134–35, 143–45, 229n1; as well-mannered, 139–40, 142; as "white man's fantasy," 129–31, 168–69, 229n10
Portman, Natalie, 214
Post, Emily: on appreciation, 103; on ballrooms, 6, 173, 176; contemporary relevance of, 220; on dignity, 134; on the gentleman, 163; on good breeding, 4, 47, 156, 163; on handshaking, 32; on hospitality, 43, 45, 217; on joking, 90; on outsiders, 44; on table manners, 186

Pretty Woman (Garry Marshall, 1990), 3
Pride and Prejudice (Jane Austen), 178
Primal Fear (Gregory Hoblitt, 1996), 232n6
Princess Diaries, The (Garry Marshall, 2001), 3, 212
Psycho (Alfred Hitchcock, 1960), 226n2
Public Enemy, The (William A. Wellman, 1931), 31

Raisin in the Sun, A (Lorraine Hansberry), 138
Rebecca (Alfred Hitchcock, 1940), 216, 231n11
Redgrave, Vanessa, 208, 211
Redman, Joyce, 182
Remains of the Day, The (Kazuo Ishiguro), 125–26
Revenant, The (Alejandro González Iñárritu, 2015), 229n8
Richardson, Ralph, 204
Rio Bravo (Howard Hawks, 1959), 170–71
Riva, Emmanuelle, 208, 216
Roman Holiday (William Wyler, 1953), 210–11, 213
Romeo and Juliet ([*Romeo e Guilietta*] Franco Zeffirelli, 1968), 7, 46–48
Romeo and Juliet (William Shakespeare), 4, 47
Russ, William, 202
Russell, Bertrand, 155–56

sacrifice, 5, 45, 67, 164, 193, 196
Sartre, Jean-Paul: on "bad faith," 125; on performing, 111, 160; on shame, 149, 227n3, 230n6
Saturday Night Fever (John Badham, 1977), 207, 208
Scarface (Brian De Palma, 1983), 159
Scent of a Woman (Martin Brest, 1992), 3

Index

Schindler's List (Steven Spielberg, 1993), 15–19
Schoenaerts, Matthias, 64
Searchers, The (John Ford, 1956), 216
Second Sex, The (Simone De Beauvoir), 176–77
Seven (David Fincher, 1995), 91–95
Seyfried, Amanda, 208
Shakespeare (plays): *Love's Labour's Lost*, 97; *A Midsummer Night's Dream*, 130; *Richard II*, 194; *Romeo and Juliet* (see main entry); *The Tempest*, 192–93; *The Winter's Tale*, 230n1
Sheen, Michael, 25, 28
Silence of the Lambs, The (Jonathan Demme, 1991), 193–94, 226n9
Singin' in the Rain (Gene Kelly and Stanley Donen, 1952), 176
Six Degrees of Separation (Fred Schepisi, 1993), 165–70, 231n9
Smith, Will, 165, 167–69
Southern manners, 31, 50, 114, 116, 117, 118–20, 140, 143, 174, 177, 178–79
South Pacific (Joshua Logan, 1958), 213
Spacey, Kevin, 187
Spencer, Herbert, 89
Star is Born, A (George Cukor, 1954), 212
Steiger, Rod, 138, 140
Streetcar Named Desire, A (Elia Kazan, 1951), 184–87
Suspicion (Alfred Hitchcock, 1941), 216
Sutherland, Donald, 165, 168
Swift, Jonathan, 45
Swing Time (George Stevens, 1936), 213
Swinton, Tilda, 63
Syriana (Stephen Gaghan, 2005), 7

table manners, 3, 10, 129, 131, 169, 181, 183–90 passim, 192, 204

Talented Mr. Ripley, The (Anthony Minghella, 1999), 163
Taylor, Elizabeth, 113, 192
Taylor-Joy, Anya, 79, 81–85
Tempest, A (Aimé Césaire), 127, 133
Third Man, The (Carol Reed, 1949), 111–12, 139
Through the Looking Glass (Lewis Carroll), 191
Titanic (James Cameron, 1997), 7, 161–63, 164, 169–70
Tom Jones (Henry Fielding), 182, 186
Tom Jones (Tony Richardson, 1963), 182–84, 187, 190, 203, 206
To the Lighthouse (Virginia Woolf), 85, 222
Travolta, John, 207
Trintignant, Jean-Louis, 208
True Romance (Tony Scott, 1993), 37–38
Turman, Glynn, 147
Twain, Mark, 95
12 Monkeys (Terry Gilliam, 1995), 210
Two Years Eight Months and Twenty-Eight Nights (Salman Rushdie), 197

undecidable, 44, 60–61, 63. *See also* Derrida, Jacques

Vang, Bee, 73
Vertigo (Alfred Hitchcock, 1958), 210, 216
V for Vendetta (James McTeigue, 2005), 214
Victorian etiquette, 89, 182, 220, 232n4
Victor/Victoria (Blake Edwards, 1982), 213
Virginian, The (Owen Wister), 36, 71–73, 75
Visser, Margaret: on cannibalism, 192–93; on the dinner table, 123, 205; on eating as violence, 6, 192

Waiting for the Barbarians (J. M. Coetzee), 6
Waltz, Christoph, 31, 124, 230n3
Washington, Denzel, 33, 207
Washington, Kerry, 124
Watergate scandal, the, 25, 30, 226n5
Wayne, John, 170–71, 216
We Have Always Lived in the Castle (Shirley Jackson), 51
Welles, Orson, 111, 112, 139
Wharton, Edith, 156
Whitaker, Forest, 127, 131–32
White Ribbon, The ([*Das weiße Band*] Michael Haneke, 2009), 6
Wilson, Dooley, 112
Winfrey, Oprah, 129
Winslet, Kate, 162
Woolf, Virginia: on dining, 203; on "the done thing," 222; on human decency, 85

xenia (guest-friendship), 68

York, Michael, 46–47
Young, Sean, 212

Zane, Billy, 161

www.ingramcontent.com/pod-product-compliance
Lightning Source LLC
Chambersburg PA
CBHW060947230426
43665CB00015B/2099